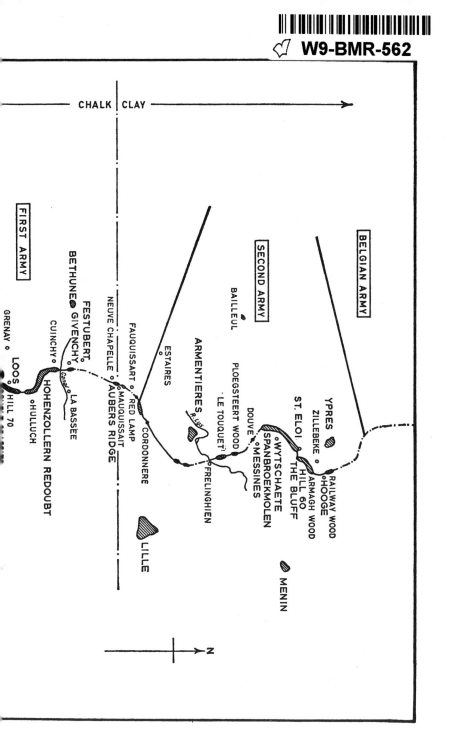

WAR UNDERGROUND

WAR UNDERGROUND

The Tunnellers of the Great War

by

ALEXANDER BARRIE

TOM DONOVAN
LONDON

ISBN: 1-871085-00-4

Published by: Tom Donovan Publishing Ltd
52 Willow Road
Hampstead
London NW3 1TP

First published in Great Britain 1962
This edition first published 1988
Reprinted 1990, 1993

PREFACE

IT has not been easy to write this book, 45 years after the events described. Tunnellers were hardy, uncomplicated men of action, not much given to paper work. Records of exactly what they did and where they did it are scarce, incomplete and—it must be admitted—sometimes inexact. This account, though aided by earlier writings touching on the subject, has been mainly compiled from eyewitness accounts. The names of the many people who have helped me (in some cases with extreme generosity), appear elsewhere.

Former tunnellers and others with intimate knowledge of the subject will notice that some events descibed here contradict earlier versions. There is disagreement even with such authoritative statements as the *Official History of the War*, by Brigadier-General Sir James Edmonds, and the *Work of the R.E. in the European War*, published by the Institution of Royal Engineers. It was only with slow reluctance that I was persuaded to the view that these important histories were occasionally in error on minor points.

For instance, how many mines were laid beneath the Messines Ridge? The Official Historian says (effectively) 23, of which 19 were fired. Almost certainly this information came from the Inspector of Mines, Brigadier-General R. N. Harvey, a man who, though an able and hard driving commander, was quite often inaccurate on points of detail. I am sure it is not true that 23 were made ready; it was 21. That left two unfired underground after the action—two that Harvey's office staff came to know as the "terrible twins". The Belgians were worried about them at first and, as it turned out, with good cause when one exploded suddenly in 1955 (see text). Of course, there must still be one left. There may at least be comfort to the Belgians to know that there *is* only one and not three as earlier figures have suggested.

Then there is the matter of who dug the shaft known as M3 at Hill 60 in early March, 1915. The *Work of the R.E. in the European War* states that it was the French. But Garfield Morgan, a Welsh miner with slow, meticulous speech and an astounding memory for long-ago detail, has convinced me that that is wrong. M3 was dug by Morgan and others of the then newly-formed 171 Tunnelling Company.

I shall pick out no further examples of disagreements although there are others to be found.

The reader may wonder whether memory can be trusted after so many years. I am sure the answer is Yes, if it is aided and checked. It is amazing what powers of recall most people have when stimulated. And in two years of painstaking probing and prodding, of comparing the recollections of one man with those of another, of checking remembered incidents with established data, of raking over and over points of doubt with the men who were there, I am satisfied that this account comes close to the truth.

And it is perhaps fair to say that for the first time the man in the street will learn here about the fighting tunnellers; about their bravery, endurance and ability and about their contribution to the Great War of 1914—a contribution that was somehow most unjustly overlooked by all but a few.

They deserve recognition, however late.

CONTENTS

ILLUSTRATIONS

MAPS AND DIAGRAMS

ACKNOWLEDGEMENTS

THIS book has been written with the help of more than 200 people who gave information and whose kindness I acknowledge with much gratitude. Sixty-eight were former tunnellers, of whom 26 were interviewed face to face; letters (often lengthy ones) were exchanged with 37 of the remainder and information from five more came via intermediaries. It was upon these men who actually fought the underground war that the brunt of my inquiries fell.

Looking back at the many detailed interviews and the multitude of letters that have been received and written in my quest for accurate, "hard fact" information, I am amazed at the trouble many tunneller veterans have allowed me to put them to. It is hardly practicable to mention all the names I would like to and I must ask the indulgence of those who helped and are now anonymously (but sincerely) thanked.

However, I feel particular mention must be made of my indebtedness to the following ex-officers and men (ranks and decorations are omitted except in the cases of regular or very senior officers): First, to Geoffrey Cassels for much detailed information about Hooge and other matters, and John Westacott for his great patience in the reconstruction of 2nd Canadian Tunnelling Company actions; also to W. P. Abbott; C. H. Cropper; J. A. Douglas; A. E. Eaton; P. W. Ellis; B. C. Hall; W. C. Hepburn; H. M. Hudspeth; Major-General F. G. Hyland, C.B., M.C.; H. R. Kerr; H. Leather; R. Leonard; C. W. Lowman; W. J. McBride; R. S. Mackilligin; M. W. Maxwell; C. N. Mitchell, V.C.; G. Morgan; F. J. Mulqueen; L. A. Mylius; B. D. Plummer; E. J.

Pryor; J. MacD. Royle; T. H. Smith; Brigadier R. S. G. Stokes, D.S.O, O.B.E., M.C.; H. Tatham; O. H. Woodward; and A. S. W. Wood. All went to much trouble on my behalf.

I also owe thanks to the many people, not tunnellers, who were able to pass me information and unstintingly did so. Among them I take the opportunity to name: Colonel A. D. Bingmann, of the German Pioneers; Sir Harry Brittain, K.B.E.; Dr. A. Caenepeel, who spent so much time showing me round the Messines Ridge; Major C. H. Cowan, R.E., for access to his father's most informative diary; Dr. W. E. David; E. Dyson; J. Ebgringhoff, for his energetic pursuit of German information; Viscount Elibank, C.M.G.; B. Excell; Mrs. L. C. Hill for her husband's notes; Lt.-Col. F. C. Hitchcock, M.C.; W. G. Jones; John Milne; A. G. Moore; Gwladys Lady Norton-Griffiths, for the loan of her unpublished autobiography and other generously-given help; Sir Peter Norton-Griffiths, Bart.; A. Ried; C. A. Tizard; Brigadier-General E. G. Wace, C.B., D.S.O.; and A. F. Waley. My thanks are also due to General Windisch and S. Lewington for rare photographs reproduced in this book, and to D. J. Mankiewitz for painstaking translations.

Much help has also been freely given by various institutions and I am specially indebted to: The Bavarian Haupstaatsarchiv, Munich; the Bibliothek f. Zeitgeschichte Weltkriegsbücherei, Stuttgart; the Belgian Government and its Military Attaché in London; the librarians of the Imperial War Museum, for seemingly inexhaustible patience; the Secretary and Librarian of the Institution of Mining and Metallurgy; the Institution of Royal Engineers, and in particular Brigadier J. H. S. Lacey, C.B.E., for many kindnesses; the Department of National Defence, Ottawa; and D. J. Branton of the National Union of Mineworkers. Regulations do not permit certain other sources to be named and so my indebtedness to them must pass without acknowledgement.

A number of people provided me with information that was not used. To them I would like to send thanks coupled with an apology. Some, I know went to much trouble, usually in response to requests from me that they should do so. The information they provided was often full of interest and they are bound to wonder why it was omitted. I can only say that as a book shapes up into a unity, some information is found not to fit and must, regrettably, be put aside. I must rely upon their good nature to understand.

Lastly, my thanks to Dorothea Benson for seeing a potential in this book and for urging me to complete it.

PROLOGUE

B Y midnight, August 4th, 1914, the British and German peoples knew: it was to be war after all—and the mobs in the streets were glad. Tension had tugged at the two empires for years and was eased by this sudden promise of action.

A heady patriotism swept through Britain and her Empire. Old men promised the Kaiser a lesson he would long remember and younger ones luxuriated in the knowledge that it was to them the country now looked. Everywhere there was an ebullient optimism. The war was just and God's help could be counted on. It would be swift. And of course it would be won.

Few people even glimpsed the colossal misery that lay ahead— and most of those who did kept their forebodings to themselves. One brave exception was Horatio Kitchener, Field-Marshal, Earl of Khartoum, a national idol and brilliant though ageing soldier of 64. Kitchener was at once appointed Secretary of State for War. With heroic gloom he predicted a three-year flat-out struggle. "I am put here to conduct a great war," he complained. "And I have no army."

It was almost true. For a while, the Government even hoped it could declare war and still somehow avoid sending soldiers away to fight. To it and the people, the war stood half-way between a military tattoo and an angry diplomatic note. It was a gesture, a proud act, the best way to stop Germany being rude to her betters. The death and pain of the thing would be wept about later.

European States in pre-Great-War days were well used to playing a non-stop grown-up version of catch-as-catch-can. As soon as one nation fell weak, a neighbour would annex a strip of its borderland.

Germany had only recently converted herself from a rabble of
squabbling States into a nation to reckon with. But she had de-
feated Denmark, with Austria's help, and taken a half share in the
little Danish border state of Schleswig-Holstein as reward. She
had beaten Austria next—and grabbed the other half. She had
thrashed France—and taken Alsace and Lorraine. She had made
important friendships, too—with the humbled but still strong
Austria, with Russia and with Italy.

Yet for all this, she was a discontented nation. Those were days
when an empire was an asset—and Germany's was too small and
too unprofitable for her liking. The cause was simply that she had
arrived at nationhood too late and all the colonies were taken. It
meant there was nowhere of her own for her population overspill
to go. She found it galling to see her young, fit, often well-trained
men go off to help the colonies of other nations prosper. Her re-
sentment grew and grew.

To the British she seemed highly, and specially, provocative.
When trouble flared in Britain's empire, German immigrants were
often found to be involved. During Britain's long and ignominious
struggle in South Africa, Germany backed the Boers. The German
Press was rudely critical of almost every British move. And as
Germany's temper shortened, her shooting power increased.

Britain moved into alliance with France and Russia—a step
which she saw as purely self-defensive. To Germany it looked like a
threat. She claimed she had been encircled, and year by year the
stress and tension grew.

In 1908, Austria annexed 20,000 square miles of Serbia (Jugo-
slavia today). She was already administering the area by inter-
national agreement—and now she claimed it as hers. On June 28th,
1914, Austria's unloved Archduke Francis Ferdinand went to look
at his country's new possession. The world gasped to hear that,
while there, he and his wife were shot by two youths in Sarajevo
town. With numbing speed, Europe fell apart.

On July 28th, Austria declared war on Serbia, and looked to
Germany for help. Germany gave it—by declaring war on Russia,

friend of the Slav nations. Two more days and Germany included France in the declaration. Britain teetered uncertainly on the brink for another two days, and then, when she learned that German armies had attacked and entered Belgium, joined in.

The pace of the war at first was fast. The Germans swept through Luxembourg, crashed over stoutly held Belgian defences and sped south towards Paris. They were making a full 30 miles a day on foot.

With frantic haste, the French army grouped itself for a return offensive aimed at about the centre of the marching Germans. On August 14th this assault began and for eleven fantastically bloody days was maintained. It failed. More than three hundred thousand men were lost—in what proved to be the fastest wastage rate of the war. The French were forced into hurried retreat.

The main British force crossed to France on the nights of August 12th and 13th and headed for the westmost part of the line. By the 23rd, a Sunday, 86,000 Britons commanded by Field-Marshal Sir John French were waiting on a 20-mile front near the Belgian mining town of Mons. The Germans were known to be close—and still coming. Nothing at all was known of the French.

It was a living tableau of war—thrilling, theatrical, Napoleonic. The officers perched on slaghumps and in trees scanning the north horizon with their glasses. The men sang and joked. Some hardy citizens of Mons emerged in their Sunday clothes to go to church. The sun shone warmly. And at ten o'clock that morning the Germans came.

Old-fashioned, open-country, close-up fighting now began. The sides saw each other's wounds and heard the screams. At five o'clock a messenger arrived with startling news: the French army had left the scene in retreat. So the little British force discovered it had been standing alone against the massive German army without knowing it. At once the British joined the French in disciplined but headlong flight.

The retreat went on for more than 100 miles until in early September the Allies suddenly stood their ground for the width of

France a few miles north of Paris. The German armies had split and spread as they advanced, had outrun much of their food supply, and lost some troops taken for use on the Russian front. Tired, hungry and aware of weakness, they stopped; and then retired about 30 miles to the banks of the east-west River Aisne.

There the two sides settled down. Winter was on its way. The quick war, the war of movement, was over. The long, hideous slog that Kitchener almost alone among public figures predicted, began.

Conditions were good for mining—an old-established siege-war technique. When they found themselves baulked on the surface, both sides began to burrow beneath each other's lines to lay and fire heavy explosive charges.

A separate, almost private war between the rival sappers started. It was a three-year, bloody, claustrophobic, uncomfortable, primitive, exhausting war-within-a-war. Military experts predict that nothing like it will ever again be seen.

1

THE IDEA

JOHN NORTON GRIFFITHS, 42-year-old Conservative Member of Parliament for Wednesbury, watched the flurried antics of European diplomats impatiently. He was a man of large physique and gigantic personality, a swashbuckling, trail-blazing, loyalist demagogue of the old school. Sooner than most, he had seen what was bound to happen—that there must be a great war and that Britain must be in it. And while the tired and anxious men whose responsibility it was to take their countries into or away from thec onflict procrastinated and talked, Norton Griffiths called loudly for action.

Throughout July, 1914, German, Austrian, French, Russian and other troops were moving and mobilizing quickly. But Britain was preoccupied with domestic affairs. There, life went on unchanged. Talk was of summer holidays and the Irish Question, motor-cars and suffragettes. To the restless, fearless mind of Norton Griffiths, it seemed that priceless time was being lost. He discussed his view with a well-connected friend, the Hon. Gideon Murray, then on leave from a government post abroad. Murray agreed, and the two men evolved a plan: they would begin the immediate formation of an irregular regiment of trained soldiers. It would be a miniature mobilization, an example to the nation.

On page 2 of its Friday evening edition dated July 31st, 1914, the *Pall Mall Gazette* carried a flatly written but mementous announcement:

"IF DUTY CALLS"
MP's INVITATION TO OLD FIGHTERS

With a view to working in unity if duty calls, all Africans, Australians, Canadians or other Britishers who served in either the

Matabeleland, Mashonaland, or South African War and are not connected with any existing military or naval organization and who would be desirous of serving their Empire again are requested to forward their names and addresses with particulars of service etc. to Mr. J. Norton Griffiths, M.P., 3 Central Buildings, Westminster.

Mr. Norton Griffiths commanded the Scouts in the Matabeleland-Mashonaland war and served in a similar capacity in the Commander in Chief's (Lord Roberts') Headquarters staff in the South African War.

The men—tough, bronzed campaigners of experience—began coming forward at once. And each day it became clearer that Norton Griffiths's guess had been sound as the position in Europe worsened.

At four o'clock in the afternoon of August 4th, the mobilization of Army Reservists and Territorials began throughout the country and, at midnight that night, Britain went formally to war. "His Majesty's Ambassador at Berlin has received his passports," the Foreign Office announcement said, "and His Majesty's Government have declared to the German Government that a state of war exists between Great Britain and Germany . . ."

Now, after the days of hesitation, came a rush. Hordes of eager men travelled to London to join the army, swamped the recruiting offices and came back day after day, striving to be enrolled. The confusion at first was appalling.

A great surge of ex-colonial soldiers beleaguered Norton Griffiths's office at 3 Central Buildings, in person and by letter. Some were annoyed when they were not given orders at once. On the 6th, a brief we-are-doing-our-best notice appeared in the *Star* which read, "Mr. Norton Griffiths M.P. states that all applications from ex-colonial servicemen are being dealt with . . . The applicants number many thousands . . ." Although it would have been more accurate to say "several" than "many", the response had indeed been extraordinary.

Next day the first detachment of 500 men assembled for a formal inspection on Horse Guards Parade. The unit was still un-uniformed and unnamed—but an impressive spectacle none the less. The men were "strong and hardy looking", as one observer remarked, "with keen bronzed faces and erect figures". To balance the bizarre assortment of top-hats, boaters and bowlers that they wore on their heads, most also wore campaign ribbons pinned proudly on their chests.

By now the unit—discussed simply as the Colonial Corps—was winning the interest of at least four peers and other important and monied citizens. But it was still a private army with no official approval or resources. The delicate procedure involved in obtaining recognition began.

On the day of the unit's first public parade, Lord Kitchener was made Secretary of State for War. His appointment, although popular with the people, was much less so among some of the Government's ministers and advisers. He brought experience, ability and courage to the War Office—but also prejudice and a certain smallness of mind. His Under-Secretary for War, the Rt. Hon. Jack Tennant, M.P., was astonished at the great soldier's attitude towards already established methods for raising volunteer units. To a remark of Tennant's that "the Territorial Forces Associations are ready to help you to the utmost of their power", Kitchener replied, "I don't want Territorials—I want soldiers." Least of all did he want irregular units of the kind Norton Griffiths and Murray were raising.

Tennant—a close friend of the Murray family—was asked to plead the Colonial Corps' case and probably did so. A rich industrialist, Lord Cowdray, also urged Kitchener to admit the unit to the army. But it was Norton Griffiths who appears finally to have persuaded the Secretary of State to give way.

The two men already knew each other. They had met first in South Africa during the war there. More recently, Norton Griffiths and his wife, Gwladys, had dined as Kitchener's guests in Egypt. At a mid-August discussion, Kitchener relented, and on the 24th the Colonial Corps was formally authorized and named as the 2nd

King Edward's Horse, a regiment of cavalry in the Special Reserve. Norton Griffiths's first important contribution to the war effort had been made. He was rewarded with an appointment as second-in-command and the rank of major.

It was not enough. To begin with, though he took part in regimental affairs quite often, it was somewhat *ex officio* and his appointment was supposed to be more honorary than active; then there was the long period of training that the unit had to face before it could be fit for the front; the men of the 2nd King Edward's Horse were fine warriors but preferred a grand free-wheeling horseman-ship to the refinements of the barrack square. While the tedium of drills went on, Norton Griffiths's impatience mounted. It showed as old-fashioned, red-faced, snort-and-bellow anger. His chauffeur, Benjamin Excell, took the brunt of it.

The two men covered many miles together in Norton Griffiths's car, a Rolls-Royce, technically the property of his wife. It was a huge 2½-ton chocolate and black landaulette which Excell was always required to drive at frightening speed. Habitually, as they set off the command would come: "Drive like hell, chauffeur." Excell did. Sometimes they had distinguished passengers riding with them, but the orders remained the same. Once it was the elderly Field-Marshal Earl Roberts, going with Norton Griffiths to Salisbury. Despite rainswept, skid-prone roads, they drove down at an almost unbroken 60 m.p.h. when clear of the London traffic. As usual, the great car rocked and swayed on a suspension designed for sedater speeds. At Basingstoke they had a violent blowout. Later they ploughed over soft ground and damaged the crankcase. When the time came to go home, Lord Roberts had contrived to leave his host behind and travel alone. "Now, chauffeur," he said very earnestly, "I want you to drive me back *slowly*." For Excell, it was a rare experience.

The rear of the car carried luxurious upholstery, a large table, silk blinds, and a duplicate speedometer intended to warn the owner of too much speed and used now only to warn of too little. Despite so much comfort, Norton Griffiths would sit alert and unrelaxed calling commands down a speaking-tube and swearing at vehicle drivers and pedestrians who forced the Rolls to slacken speed. "Cow's son!" was his commonest curse, shouted with such furious volume that few dared to answer back.

As a Member of Parliament, Norton Griffiths had many opportunities to remind Britons of their duty. He used them all. "Are *you* doing your bit?" he asked from innumerable platforms with an emphasis that was intended to embarrass his audience and usually did. But inwardly he doubted whether he was fully doing his.

It was his fervid, outspoken patriotism that had largely made his name and lifted him—in a phrase of his wife's—from the rank of unknown colonial soldier to celebrity in ten years. When campaigning in parliamentary elections, he always hung a huge map behind the platform to show how much of the globe Britain controlled. Many of his listeners had never seen a world map before and gaped in half-comprehending surprise to find so much of it in red. Norton Griffiths always spoke then with sincere feeling of the country's achievements. Despite an aching poverty that gripped his Black Country constituency of Wednesbury, he made British greatness seem exciting and important.

He always spoke loudly, using many glib superlatives and telling jokes that he bought by the dozen. His methods with hecklers were quick and devastating. Once when a man called out anti-British slogans, Norton Griffiths leapt off the platform, struck him and returned at once to resume his address as if nothing had happened. The quality of his campaigns was always infectiously gay. Even the drunks, the half-starved and the despairing felt it. Sometimes he rode in a carriage drawn by four horses, sometimes on the shoulders of his supporters. There were flags and torchlight processions; there was colour, music and exhilarating noise. Among the nicknames he won for himself were Hell Fire Jack and the Monkey Man. But the name he became known best by—and it spread through the country and beyond—was Empire Jack. It fitted well and he liked it. His devotion to the Empire idea was limitless.

Besides military matters and politics, Norton Griffiths had

extensive business interests to look after. He was entirely a self-created man. At 16 he made his first major decision about life by running away from school—St. Paul's, Hammersmith. He then allowed himself to be articled to a firm of architects but, finding he still hated the role of pupil, walked out again after a few weeks. This time, though not yet 17, he joined the Royal Horse Guards. Once more he found an organized life distasteful. Somehow he persuaded a rich man, Sir Henry Kimber, to buy him out a few months later. Then, with Kimber's son, a youth of about his own age, Norton Griffiths took a boat to Africa. It was here that he found himself. He became many things—a button seller, sheep farmer, prospector and mining company promoter. Apparently he was happy at last. In Africa there was the room, freedom and scope for adventure that he craved.

He drifted to Johannesburg and from there into Rhodesia where he took part energetically in the Mashonaland War of 1893 as a Captain in the British South African Police. Two years later he was fighting again, now in the Transvaal, on the Government's side against Jameson's famous raid. For 11 years he wandered through Africa with hardly a thought of Britain. But then, taking stock, he realized that although he had acquired a number of mining claims, he was far from making his fortune. Also, his father had died and there were affairs to put in order. He decided to return to London.

On March 22nd, 1899, he walked into a courtyard in Zanzibar while waiting for the boat. He was wearing whites—with an open shirt and panama hat; a mongoose clung to his shoulder and a parakeet to his finger. Gwladys Wood, a 26-year-old girl of good family out on a mind-broadening trip to Johannesburg, and now on her way home, saw him through a window. To her he seemed breathtakingly romantic. She fell in love with him on sight and contrived a meeting. It was soon obvious that tender feeling was mutual.

Norton Griffiths altered his booking to travel homewards on the same ship, the S.S. *Kanzler*, and long before they docked they had decided to marry. Not, however, immediately. "I shall make a bad poor woman's husband," Norton Griffiths said, "—and you will make a bad poor man's wife." And six months later he sailed back to Rhodesia alone to try to develop his mining claims there. Then on October 11th, the South African War began and Norton Griffiths had to be in it.

But he and other amateurs were soon advised to leave soldiering to the professionals. In the spring of 1900 he returned to London, confused and depressed about his future. He was incensed to find that pacifist meetings were being held at Queen's Hall and advertised for students to come with drums and whistles to break the movement up. Gwladys Wood was horrified and, fearing that it would harm his name, begged him to stop. He promptly did. Years later Excell, the chauffeur, noticed that she was the only person he would cheerfully obey.

For eighteen wretched and inconclusive months, Norton Griffiths strode the streets looking for something to do. Then his luck changed. A mining magnate asked him to go to New York to select dredging machinery for the Ivory Coast goldfields. At eight on the morning of September 14th, 1901, he and Gwladys Wood were married. Privately the bride wondered if it would last a year (and felt it would be worthwhile even so) but in fact the marriage turned out to be blissfully happy on both sides.

After a four-day honeymoon the couple left together for New York. But soon afterwards Norton Griffiths had to go out to the gold fields, and he went alone. He spent another year tramping the African veld. His method of dealing with natives was traditional. In deciding terms for mining concessions, he would make frequent references to the gods. They would be angry, he would explain, if the terms he offered were refused.

While the matter was debated, a prospector friend armed with a powerful rocket and matches would be hidden somewhere within earshot. When he heard the terms about to be agreed, he would stand by ready.

Suddenly Norton Griffiths's voice would come booming across the bush, "Very well, let the message go up to the gods . . ." Promptly the prospector would touch off the rocket to the terror of the natives who seldom gave trouble afterwards.

After a year Norton Griffiths returned to London to stay. His high spirits, fine physique and tireless drive had given him a good name in the tough world of mining. Also, he had discovered by now that he had an extraordinary skill at making friends. He felt that the time had come to push his way into big business.

Soon he heard that a group of industrialists wanted a railway built from Benguela on the coast into the interior of Angola, Portuguese West Africa. "I'm going to persuade them to give me the contract," he suddenly announced to his wife.

She was alarmed. "But you've never done contracting," she pointed out.

"I know," Norton Griffiths replied. "But I've watched." He was convinced it was enough, and somehow persuaded the industrialists to agree. They gave him the contract. Although it was marred by financial difficulties, it started him in business on the scale he liked. Other work followed. Soon he had so many titled businessmen behind him that he began to refer to his backers as the House of Lords. His firm, Griffiths and Company, Contractors, were taking on costly projects in many parts of the world.

During 1914, Norton Griffiths won a vast new contract in Australia. He had been about to travel out to supervise the job when he foresaw the outbreak of war and paused. After a few days of thought he took his commission in the 2nd King Edward's Horse instead. He told Excell it had cost him "a million pounds"—an exaggeration, of course.

He still had some minor contracts running in Britain. One was a tunnelled drainage system in Manchester, being carried out for the Corporation. The men were driving the tunnels by a method known as "clay kicking" or "working on the cross". It was ideal for the clay subsoil of Manchester. They sat in the tunnels, their backs supported on a wooden backrest (the "cross") their feet pointed at the face. With a light spade-like implement they dug out the clay ahead which a mate passed back for disposal.

In early December the idea came suddenly to Norton Griffiths that these men might have something important to contribute to the war. Already the mud, the waterlogged clay, that clogged men and machines on the front was becoming famous. But to the Manchester sewer diggers—who called themselves Moles—that kind of soil was just right. They could dig quickly out to undermine the enemy.

On the 15th of December 1914, he wrote to the War Office asking that he should be allowed to take "a handful of Moles" out to France. The letter was duly acknowledged, filed under the heading of "Moles" and its contents passed to the Commander-in-Chief of the Expeditionary Force, Field-Marshal Sir John French. A period of waiting, always very trying to Norton Griffiths, began. But soon, on the 20th, the Germans gave new importance to mining by making the first underground attack of the war. It came at the southern extremity of the British line, where Indian troops were entrenched.

The Sirhind Brigade was holding a mile of the front ten miles south of the French-Belgian border, near Festubert. The Indians, already suffering from the rigours of the European winter, were first battered and shaken by heavy artillery fire during the early morning. Then, at ten twenty-five, three mysterious flares were seen arcing high into the air from the German lines. Next moment a loud rumbling crash of sound sped along 1,000 yards of the Indian trench and the ground beneath the soldiers' feet shuddered, split apart and punched upwards with tremendous force. Ten mines had been fired.*

Shocked by the inexplicable nature of the blow and dazed by its violence, the surviving Indians scrambled from the trench and ran rearwards, pursued by deadly mortar fire. Waves of German assault troops then raced over no-man's-land and occupied the position without loss. In the dug-outs they found the corpses of many men still sitting in relaxed positions, undisturbed by the concussion that killed them. The effect on the morale of the already sorely tried

* Eleven were placed but one failed to explode.

Indian troops (and on others as the news spread) was serious. Some units refused to stay at the front, and a few days later the whole Indian Corps was temporarily withdrawn to reserve.

Probably it was not until a week after the Festubert set-back that Norton Griffiths's suggestion reached General Headquarters in St. Omer. By then, Sir John French was already being pressed by his Fourth Corps Commander, Lieutenant-General Sir Henry Rawlinson, to set up a special mining "battalion". Sir John declined. Mine warfare was a long-standing duty of the Royal Engineers, and the C.-in-C. was not in favour of changing the system.

Instead, he followed the attack on the Indian brigade with orders to R.E. Field Companies calling for retaliatory mines to be fired. It was an unrealistic command. The R.E.'s were already over committed and so unable to comply. The engineers simply did not have the large, well-organized labour force that military mining requires.

Nor had they sufficient training in the subject. Their peacetime mining course lasted from two to three days—too short a time to drive more than a rudimentary tunnel. Also the soil chosen for practice was ideal and most unlike the watery clay of Flanders.

At Rue du Bois, near Armentières, the 20th Fortress Company struggled for days in early January to drive a mine. It filled with water faster than the old-fashioned lift-and-force pumps could clear it. Lieutenant Gordon Hyland, R.E., in charge of the operation, fought to keep the men at it. But morale was falling. Then suddenly one day a notice was hoisted from the German lines: "No good your mining," it read in perfect English. "It can't be done. We've tried." Hyland laughed—but passed the Germans' advice to H.Q. The mining operation was promptly stopped.

To help the harassed R.E.s, various brigade commanders soon began forming mining sections of their own—composed, where possible, of men with civilian experience underground. Most of the units were 50 men strong under one low-ranking officer. Often they were attached to R.E. Field Companies and worked with

variable skill. Appalling conditions slowed down the start of digging operations.

January (1915) was a month of rain, snow and flood in Flanders.
The weather alone ensured that the unprotected front-line troops
endured an extreme of misery. Then, on the 25th, more German
mines were fired under the British trench at a point two miles
south of the Festubert attack. Again surface troops followed up
with an attack and quickly captured part of the blown-up line.
British losses this time were slight, but morale sank lower.

On February 3rd it happened again, further north near the
village of St. Eloi. Soldiers of the 3rd East Yorkshire Regiment
reeled back in confusion under heavy fire after being mined from
their trench.

By now insistent demands for protection against mines were
coming from all parts of the front. Shell-fire, the bayonet, machine-
guns, the biting winds and unending wetness were all endurable.
But mines, laid silently below ground and fired without warning,
came into a special category of frightfulness. The troops found the
uncertainty unbearable and began to make their own crude listening
aids in the hope of detecting enemy miners in time. Before 1914
ended, the London Rifle Brigade had one of the first in action. A
petrol tank with the top cut off was filled to the brim with water
and sunk into the mud of the trench bottom. Men already covered
in filth, tormented by lice and enormous rats, now knelt in 12 inches
of ooze, often while snow and sleet fell upon and around them,
dipped an ear into the ice-cold water and kept it there as long as will
power could make possible. Almost any physical distress had become worthwhile to lay the bogey of undermining.

At home, Norton Griffiths grew more than ever obsessed by the
idea of taking his moles to the war. Years later he said of this period,
"I was eating my heart out and longing to get to France." His wife
phrased it even more strongly: "He was nearly like a lunatic," she
said, "frantic for action." As the weeks passed it became steadily
clearer that a stationary war lay ahead. In places the lines were a
mere 30 yards and less apart—at Blangy (near Arras) they were

once barely five. The average separation was 100 yards or so and 300 was rarely exceeded. It had become a strangely intimate war where the two sides could hear each other's shouts and sometimes smell each other's cooking. The situation was ideal for fighting underground, but the chance was being missed.

Then, on Friday, February 12th, 1915, a telegram was delivered to Norton Griffiths instructing him to report to the War Office. He went at once and was shown to the private office of Lord Kitchener.

The Secretary of State, by now at loggerheads with the Commander-in-Chief and certain members of the Government, was at his desk looking overworked and depressed. Kitchener no longer seemed much like a great soldier. He sat in the shabby blue tunic and trousers of a Field-Marshal's undress uniform and wore heavy brown spectacles that gave a studious, civilian touch to his dejection. A number of documents lay on the desk before him which he invited Norton Griffiths to read. They were all communications from Sir John French describing the seriousness of the mining situation. The two men were alone in the room and Kitchener now asked for advice.

"The only thing I can suggest, sir," replied Norton Griffiths, "is that we use moles."

"What on earth are moles?" Kitchener asked.

Norton Griffiths gave a deliberately teasing reply. "Clay kickers—or workers on the cross," he explained. Then, before Kitchener's patience gave way, he snatched the fire shovel from the War Office grate, sat heavily down on the floor and began a demonstration.

Kitchener was entranced by the possibilities. He was usually slow and cautious about decisions. But not this time. "Get me 10,000 of these men," he said. "*Immediately.*"

Norton Griffiths, accustomed though he was to large deals and quick thinking, was flabbergasted. "I don't think there are as many as 10,000 in the country," he replied, adding that in any case he would need to examine the ground to be quite sure this form of mining was possible. Kitchener accepted that and asked him to leave at once—that night—for France. This was a reaction Norton Griffiths understood.

A few hours later, despite high winds and a heavy sea, he set off in a state of high excitement and next day walked eagerly into the office of the Engineer-in-Chief at G.H.Q. in Rue Carnot, St. Omer, twenty-five miles behind the front line.

He was expected. A warning that he was on the way had been wired in advance. The E.-in-C., Brigadier-General George Henry Fowke, R.E., his assistant, Colonel Robert Napier Harvey, R.E. and Colonel James Edmonds, R.E. were ready to receive him.

Edmonds—who later became a brigadier-general and the official war historian—recorded the moment of meeting. Griffiths, he said, "blew in improperly dressed in something between uniform and hunting kit." He was warmly welcomed. Fowke, though not a worrier by temperament, had been under heavy and mounting pressure to find an answer to the destructive German mining. So far he had been unable to offer more than palliatives. He was ready to listen to any sober suggestion.

The welcome was made easier, too, by the fact that both Fowke and his assistant, Harvey, took an immediate liking to Norton Griffiths. Years later, Harvey told of the great relief he and his chief felt when their visitor turned out "to have practical knowledge of his subject and whose forceful character and enthusiasm swept away all opposition".

Fowke was a remarkable officer. Despite his high rank, age (he was 50) and 30 years of army discipline, he could caper about like an undergraduate. He was a big man, humorous and sparkling, with a great guffaw that rang through the officers' mess. He was a fine story teller and often had a crowd of officers around him waiting for the latest. And he loved sport, playing most games with little skill but with the "exuberant energy of a bull"—as a contemporary once recorded.

He was an extrovert, often involved in practical jokes and the most extraordinary accidents. But he was also a brilliant engineer and mathematician.

When he and Norton Griffiths met, there was an immediate exchange of understanding, each in some important ways being a reflection of the other.

Norton Griffiths went straight into his explanation. He said he was a contractor with great experience of the clay kicking method of mining. In his opinion, clay kickers could drive out and under the German lines quickly in very small tunnels without being detected. Once there they could blow the enemy up, spy on them or break out and attack them. The same method could be used to intercept German tunnels being driven towards the British lines. Norton Griffiths was certain that with this method, the mining initiative could be snatched from the enemy.

Fowke and Harvey listened with interest but some scepticism. Both had been instructors at the School of Military Engineering and both had extensive experience of most kinds of field work. Yet neither had heard of clay kicking before.

When Norton Griffiths saw the doubt on their faces he dropped to the floor and gave another dynamic demonstration. Fowke, though still unconvinced, was much amused and found the burly major's enthusiasm irresistible. He turned to Harvey and told him to take the visitor to the Army and Corps H.Q. to see what their engineers thought of the idea. They would have another talk, he promised, afterwards.

At eight o'clock next morning, February 14th, the party set off. Norton Griffiths had brought two of his employees with him—an assistant engineer named Leeming and a foreman, Miles. Harvey steered them in fact to four headquarters, at First Army, First Corps, First Division and First Brigade. At each stopping point Norton Griffiths repeated his performance. Finally they called at the front line at Givenchy. Here, about a mile from the spot where the Indians were blown up less than two months ago, the Germans were still active underground. Strange noises were constantly being reported by the uneasy troops.

Norton Griffiths's foreman dropped to his knees and ran the soil through his fingers.

"It's ideal—isn't it, Miles?" Norton Griffiths asked. Miles looked up smiling, and nodded. "It makes my mouth water," he said.

On the way back to St. Omer, they called again at each H.Q. to give the reassuring news that the soil was suitable. They were back, at G.H.Q., by eleven-thirty in the evening, tired but cheerful. Harvey was now convinced that clay kicking made sense. He promised to arrange a meeting with Fowke next morning to discuss it further.

The meeting lasted all day. In the course of it, the Commander-in-Chief, Sir John French, sent for Norton Griffiths for a personal explanation. Fowke himself needed little convincing, and had probably already decided to give the idea a trial. Most of the time was spent in discussing details of just how the new mining corps was to be set up. During the day a telegram was sent—via the General Staff—to the War Office asking formal permission to form the units.

Notice that "in principle" approval was being given came back the next day. Norton Griffiths had already sent Leeming home with orders to close down the sewer contract and sign on volunteers from the laid-off men for war service. Now he set off himself for England. Everyone knew that something important was starting and he left in an air of some excitement. He promised that the first clay kickers would arrive at the front immediately.

What was later described by Harvey as "the quickest intentional move of the war" was about to take place.

2

THE "KICKERS" START WORK

T HE next few days saw Norton Griffiths at his hustling best. He crossed the Channel by night, arriving in London the next morning, Wednesday, February 17th. He had a letter from General Fowke in his pocket for delivery to the War Office. It suggested how the new tunnelling companies might be organized and asked permission to form eight.

Norton Griffiths's mood was exuberant, now that his idea seemed certain to be adopted. The delays, about which he had grumbled bitterly to his wife and others at the time, were forgotten. His delight with Fowke—whom he began soon to refer to simply as "The Chief"—was great and much in his mind. And there was the intoxicating urgency of the job to be done. It was exactly the type of challenge he most enjoyed. As a child, Norton Griffiths's relationship with his father had not been good. This—or something—caused him to grow up with an insatiable urge to conquer the impossible. The bigger the challenge, and the quicker it had to be met, the more he was drawn towards it.

At the War Office he asked for an immediate interview with the Secretary of State and was shown to Kitchener's room. Inside, he at once began to harangue the silent, weary-looking Minister who sat listening with grave politeness. Norton Griffiths later recounted the words he had used: "The position is so serious for the poor devils in the trenches. You *can't* expect them to be shot at from the surface, boofed at from above *and* blown to hell from below . . ." But Kitchener had already shown that he agreed.

Army chiefs had been badly frightened by the need to accept a sudden influx of untrained, fiercely free-thinking miners. Their greatest worry came from the fact that, to be effective, the men would have to be used in large groups. There seemed a real danger they would turn into undisciplined mobs.

A week or two before, the Commander-in-Chief had agreed to the idea that 200 coal miners should be brought out experimentally. But he demanded of the War Office that it take care to choose only "reliable" men. He was known to be specially against having Scotsmen.

Now, under pressure from most commanders in the line, and affected both by Norton Griffiths's broad promises and Fowke's apparent confidence, he had dropped any limit. The scheme described in the letter Norton Griffiths carried—and which he, Fowke, Harvey and another headquarters-staff engineer, Major Edward Wace, had worked out together—proposed tunnelling units of five officers and 269 men each. They were to be aided by labour forces made up of temporarily attached infantrymen. Norton Griffiths's own role was to be liaison officer between Fowke's office and the tunnellers.

Formal War Office approval was delivered to Fowke at St. Omer on the 19th. The first units were to be designated 170 to 178 Tunnelling Companies, R.E. Each was to be commanded by a regular Royal Engineer selected by Harvey and Wace from R.E. Field Companies. All were to be allotted to Armies (at this time Britain had only two in the field, First and Second) so that however much divisions and brigades moved up and down the line, the tunnellers should—in theory—be left to carry on with their work. It was an unconventional arrangement which baffled many infantry commanders and was not much of a success at first. For months tunnelling companies were to find themselves taking orders from the brigades holding the part of the line they were working. They were to be constantly chivvied also by divisional and corps engineering staffs. In fact, through most of their first year they were in a constant and bewildering state of movement, the very trouble the organization had been designed to prevent.

Norton Griffiths kept his interview with Kitchener short. He gave an account of his activities in France, mentioned that he would like the new type miners to be officially named "moles" (a wish which was ignored) and hurried away. It was clear that he was a full-time soldier from now on and there were pressing business and parliamentary matters to arrange.

One detail he did not overlook was his personal transport. Foreseeing that a liaison officer's duties would involve a heavy mileage through France and Flanders he decided to be as comfortable about it as possible. He asked the War Office to buy the Rolls-Royce for his own use. A War Office official promptly telephoned his wife, Gwladys—the legal owner—and arranged the sale for £750. Within a day or so, the car was shipped to France where its luxurious bulk, slipping and rocking through the mud-covered roads, became quickly famous.

By the time Norton Griffiths left Kitchener's office, his assistant, Leeming, had already reported from Manchester that 20 of the laid-off clay-kickers were ready to join the army. Norton Griffiths replied with instructions to bring them to London at once.

They arrived next day, a shabby, undersized, rather bewildered looking party of men. Norton Griffiths gave them a few heartening words at his office—now about to become an official tunnelling company "depot". He explained that their job would be to tunnel out and under German positions, to place charges there, to wire them to an exploder and then to retire to safe cover. When the plunger was pressed they would have a front seat view of the Germans—as Norton Griffiths used to say—"going up".

The men were medically examined and 18 were found fit. Norton Griffiths signed them on and sent them to Chatham for kitting out. He planned to take them to France himself next day.

These men, all sewer drivers, were the first of the new tunnellers R.E. They were soon to be followed by almost every type of miner including coal, tin and slate miners, and they came from many parts of the country. Some of the newcomers were unusually small, many were middle-aged and a few were white-haired men in their sixties. Almost none had the slightest idea of military procedure or etiquette.

It has often been reported that the regular Royal Engineers were disturbed by the sights they began to see on their immaculate Chatham parade ground. Without doubt this is true. The R.E.'s are fighting soldiers—smart, proud and courageous. They had never before had recruits like some of these that Norton Griffiths began to send them.

His campaigning days as a politician had taught him how to excite a crowd's enthusiasm. From now on he began using every trick he knew to get the volunteers the tunnelling companies needed. Accounts of the sort of inducements he offered are incomplete. But after one commanding officer who badly needed miners had been sought out by Norton Griffiths at the front and promised a delivery of 200 men, his satisfaction was mixed with anxiety. "I wonder," he wrote in his private diary, "how many rules and regulations he has broken—or, worse still, has promised the recruits that the commanding officers will break for them?"

A base camp was hurriedly organized at Rouen where many of the men were again medically examined. The doctor found that although none of the men would admit to being over 35, many had no teeth or so few that they would have difficulty eating the hard tack emergency rations. He referred a number of cases to a mining engineer who had newly joined up, Second-Lieutenant Robert Picken, for his opinion. Picken was much moved by the zeal of these old men all of whom were determined to serve at the front. He gave it as his opinion that every one was fit. Later Picken told how they all flashed big toothless smiles when they heard.

But the attitude of the miner volunteers varied. Some arrived in France with the idea that they were to be mining only near the coast, well away from the shooting zone; a few grumbled when they learned the truth. Others believed they were to be taken to and from their place of work by motor-car. A number even thought that they were to retain their civilian rights. Immediately after 173 Company held its first parade, a protest party waited for the C.O., Major Guy Williams, R.E. Williams, who rose to become a general and a knight, received the deputation (which some commanders might have treated as mutinous) with amiable interest. A spokes-man informed him that "drill or any form of military training was not in their 'contract'—which was to mine *only*". Williams listened gravely, then suggested that they should all talk it over quietly. He held several informal meetings with the company and eventually convinced the miners that it was better for their own safety to know a little about soldiering. They then agreed to be drilled.

Most of the tunnelling company officers, other than the com-manding officers, were as unmilitary as the men. Second-Lieute-nant Arthur Lumb, a very reserved man, found himself at Chatham a few days after stepping off the boat from Nigeria. He had come home to volunteer and found the Royal Engineers desperate to have him. He was commissioned immediately and sent hurrying to Chatham to pick up a draft. His instructions were to take the men to France at once.

Several times Lumb pointed out anxiously that he had had *no* military training. "Never mind," a major told him. "Just get the men out there—that's all we want."

He arrived at Chatham on a Sunday and next day was standing in front of the squad, which he had been assured would be a small one. In fact it numbered 120 men aged between 20 and 60. They had spent three days at Chatham and were leaving for the front that morning.

Lumb was relieved to find that an experienced sergeant was to assist him as far as Southampton. He understood that he should march the men off towards the station and then, in some military manner, take up a position at the head of the column. Uncertain how to go about all this, he told the sergeant he would hold him responsible for getting the draft to Southampton. "Furthermore," he added, "you will walk in front. I shall walk behind to be sure there are no stragglers." The sergeant saluted and began to bellow the proper orders. The squad moved off. Lumb followed bash-fully in the rear.

To his dismay he found the sergeant had instructions to leave the party as soon as it arrived at Southampton station. Lumb seemed to be faced with shepherding the men to the quayside and up the gangway alone. Then to his relief he spotted a solitary, uncertain-looking lance-corporal among the men. Lumb at once put him in charge but this time decided to march in his proper place at the head of the column.

As they approached the ship, marching two-deep, its captain began loudhailing them impatiently from the bridge. Lumb halted the men in renewed embarrassment. The captain's irritation grew. "Come on, sir!" he bawled. "You're holding up the whole ship." But Lumb was quite unable to decide what order to give. At last he raced to the back of the column and told the lance-corporal that he was again in charge, adding that the men must be put in single file and marched aboard.

It was the N.C.O.'s turn to look stricken; he was equally unsure of the proper commands. Slowly, he walked round to the front two men, then suddenly grasped them by the arm and began silently man-handling them one at a time towards the gangway. So the party stumbled aboard and journeyed safely to France.

Ashore again, there were more misadventures. At Le Havre, Second-Lieutenant Lumb, once more marching in front of the column, was dismayed to see a funeral procession approaching. He knew there must be some military drill to follow for such an occasion, but had no idea what. Then, just before the two parties met, he saw a side street and sneaked his sappers into it. After the funeral had passed he gave the about-turn order and resumed the march.

In Rouen, the party puffed up a long hill with Lumb still at the head. On the top he looked back at the column to see some of the men climbing out of a bus. They had jumped aboard at the foot of the hill and ridden up.

When the party eventually arrived at its destination (near Ypres) the roll was called. Two men were missing.

Norton Griffiths seemed to have double vision on the subject of his miners' military smartness. He knew better than most the material his men were made of and he defended them against any kind of military disapproval. Yet he seems vaguely to have wished they could be better parade-ground soldiers. Towards the end of March he travelled with one batch on the crossing to Le Havre. Shortly before the miners were put ashore he searched out the officer temporarily in charge—a young Northumbrian, Lieutenant Cecil Cropper—and gave him a reminder about marching etiquette. "Don't forget the compliments, Cropper," he said, meaning such refinements as the "Eyes right" and "Eyes left" courtesies given to high-ranking soldiers or civilians who happened to pass by. Cropper was astounded. He knew his men would never have heard of such commands and he ignored the advice.

Many of the tunnelling companies did become proficient drillers eventually. An unnamed senior officer is said once to have mistaken a party of marching tunnellers for a unit of the Guards; but that was more than a year later.

Not all the new sappers enlisted as civilians. Many ex-miners already serving transferred from their units. On February 17th (1915), the day Norton Griffiths first returned from France, a War Office request for miner volunteers had arrived at the headquarters of the 8th South Wales Borderers, then stationed in Hastings That afternoon a special parade was called and an officer, Captain L. T. Thorp, asked for men with mining experience who were willing to be transferred for special front line duty with the R.E.'s to step forward. From D Company alone, 50 men did so. One of them was a young private, Garfield Morgan; he noticed that the officer seemed embarrassed by the response and in a moment the volunteers were told to step back into the ranks. Immediately afterwards the parade was dismissed and the men went off to their billets for tea.

Half an hour later, while Morgan was still at tea, the quarter-master-sergeant walked into the billet and asked if he would like to be one of the men transferred. Morgan, puzzled by the way the affair was being handled, hesitated. "Your money will be six shillings a day," the quartermaster added persuasively. It was high pay in 1915 and Morgan's moment of doubt promptly ended. He agreed to volunteer.

The quartermaster asked him to find eleven miner friends and to report to his billet at six o'clock. It was an easy task and the party assembled on time. The quartermaster announced that at seven they were to go before Captain Thorp at the regiment's head-quarters in the Palace Hotel for interviews. Then he became con-fidential and explained that the men to be signed on at the six-shilling rate were supposed to know something about a special method of mining. He described roughly how clay kicking was done, then held a light heart-shaped spade up. He told them all to have a good look at it and to remember that if the Captain asked them what it was, the proper answer was "a grafting tool". Down at the Palace Hotel Morgan's men found 24 other ex-miners assem-bled, from sister companies. Morgan was the first of his batch to go forward for interrogation. Captain Thorp asked a few questions about mining—then pointed to a grafting tool and asked what it was. When Morgan gave the right answer, the Captain asked him to name three friends who would go with him and had the remain-der dismissed. Two other groups of four men had been selected, from A and B companies. The twelve were told they would be going by train to London next day to be interviewed by a certain Major Norton Griffiths, a clay-kicking expert.

A sergeant-major escorted the party to Westminster. On the way he warned the men that they *might* be asked to sign for two-and twopence a day (the standard sappers' pay) and advised them to stick out for the higher rate.

The party marched down Whitehall to Norton Griffiths's office at 3, Central Buildings. Then, one by one, the men went in to be interviewed. The first to go was Private Dave Evans. But he was back almost within seconds and quickly told the others what had happened.

As soon as he had entered the office, the red-tabbed major had thrust a piece of paper into his hand and said, "Sign here."

"What's the rate, sir?" Evans had asked.

"Two-and-two."

"I'm not signing, sir."

Norton Griffiths had stuck his chin forward in anger. "Then get out," he had said.

It was the same with every man. One by one they walked in, defied the Major and were promptly ordered out. Norton Griffiths went doggedly through the list. When the last man came out, the sergeant-major paraded the party on the street and gave the order to quick march. It was a cold day. London looked at its greyest and most sombre. Gloomily the miners began the journey back.

Before they had taken more than a few paces a stentorian voice called out from behind, "Halt the men, Sergeant-Major! Send them back up." Norton Griffiths's bulky figure was standing in the doorway. He needed men badly and had decided to stifle his anger. He signed them all up at six shillings a day—and added one-and-ninepence ration money for that day's lack of food.

It was the start of a pay muddle that disrupted the tunnelling companies throughout most of their time. Trained clay kickers were supposed to be rewarded with the six-shilling rate, while the others, classified as mates, took two-and-twopence. In practice much confusion and discontent were caused by what were often arbitrary classifications.

The next day, Garfield Morgan, Dave Evans and the others left the 8th South Wales Borderers and entrained for Chatham. Simultaneously, twelve miners were on their way from the 11th Welch Regiment and another twelve from the 8th South Staffordshires. They all met at Chatham just as the first party of Manchester sewermen—the real clay kickers—were leaving, escorted by Norton Griffiths and another officer. The Manchester men went off looking as much like soldiers as possible. They were even armed. Norton Griffiths had been taken aback to discover that regulations required them to carry rifles and 150 rounds of ammunition when leaving for active service overseas. But he learned also that they could be disarmed immediately after landing in France and he at once gave orders that this should be done. Later he admitted that he had "felt something approaching terror" while he wondered "if each man would be shooting the other before we got them to the other side".

The turn-round routine at Chatham had been speeded to the limit. Garfield Morgan's party of 36 had been swelled by 30 clay kickers Norton Griffiths had found and persuaded to enlist. All 66 were equipped and on their way to France within three days, on February 22nd (1915). As they left, news was coming out that the day before a violent explosion had taken place beneath the feet of the 16th Lancers, then holding "Shrewsbury Forest", a wood three miles south-east of Ypres. Many officers and men had been pitched high into the air and losses were serious. As the dazed survivors picked themselves up the German infantry had attacked and taken the crater. The British line had been pushed back about 40 yards in another mining victory to the Germans.

Morgan's party escorted by a South African mining engineer, a new lieutenant, Lionel Hill, crossed by night from Folkestone to Boulogne. There they were divided into two equal parties and one was put aboard a train bound for Bethune, near the Givenchy part of the line where Norton Griffiths and the first 18 clay kickers had already arrived.

The rest—including Garfield Morgan and Lieutenant Hill— went by open-top, solid-tyred lorries to Ypres. It was a terrible journey of 60 miles. For most of the way heavy snow fell and the men, particularly the older ones, suffered from exposure. They were also battered almost beyond endurance as the lorries jerked and jolted for hours over the badly rutted roads. And the sounds of battle grew louder with each mile.

At about two o'clock in the afternoon they arrived and were shown to billets—a large building formerly used as a convent. At seven they were paraded and told they were to march to the front line at Hill 60, a fighting zone which already had an ugly reputation.

A sergeant guide arrived to lead the way. He explained first that there was danger just in going to the line and described how and when to dive for cover. Eventually, in almost complete darkness, the party set off. The countryside was still spread thickly with snow and slush and now, since nightfall, the night had grown even colder. Flashes of gunfire showed on the black horizon and dazzling green flares soared repeatedly into the sky. Guns of all calibres roared and rattled round about, and when heavy shells landed near, the ground beneath their feet shook with the shock.

The miners were following the guide in grimly silent single file when, without warning, he fell sideways to the ground. They all gathered round to see how badly he had been hurt. He was dead— shot through the head by a cat-eyed sniper. The men crouched together in utter confusion. Nobody knew the way forward and now, the more they discussed it, the less sure they were of the way back. They were lost.

Suddenly there was more of the blinding green light as another flare arched through the sky. They dropped flat on their stomachs but glimpsed a haystack and decided to head for it when they dared. As the light burned out they broke into a shambling run and arrived breathless but unhurt. They settled down for the night behind the stack, pulling hay over themselves for warmth. At least they were out of sight of the Germans. When dawn came they scrambled rearwards to a brigade headquarters where Lieutenant Hill reported what had happened.

The men were sent back to their convent billet for the rest of the day and were glad to stretch out on the straw-covered floor. But that evening they were again sent up and this time reached the squalid trenches of Hill 60, a mean, misshapen triple hummock that was on its way to immortality for the multitude of young men who were to die there. Already it was thinly littered with decomposing, foul-smelling British, French and German bodies.

An hour or two after they arrived in the trench, the noise of gunfire grew to a sudden frightening crescendo and men came running down the trench snatching at rifles and ammunition. Word flashed along that the Germans were attacking and every available man was wanted on the fire step. Morgan found himself a place and saw German soldiers sprinting towards the trench. He loaded and fired, loaded and fired as fast as his fingers would move. Despite losses, the Germans pushed forward to within 15 yards of the trench and then fell back.

As the battle subsided, Morgan looked round to see what had happened to the special intake men. They were crouching where they had been put—out of everyone's way. Even in the emergency no one had dared let them handle weapons. Some were shaken by their sudden immersion into war. Morgan heard them say that if they had known what it meant they would never have volunteered. But he noticed, too, that although there were a few grumbles, there was no panic.

The party was soon taken over by Lieutenant Wolfred Cloutman, who already had a little trench experience.

Two days later, on the 27th, 80 miner volunteers and two officers arrived, drawn from the 1st and 3rd Battalions of the Monmouthshire Regiment. The mining party was now growing to a useful strength and began to be known by its proper name, 171 Tunnelling Company. There was the inevitable confusion at first as the various batches were converted into a unit and not much work was done.

There was time to gaze at the snowy desolation all around and to wonder where this was going to end.

3

DRAMA AT HILL 60

IN 1915, the front line ran more then 400 miles through Belgium and France to the Swiss border. For much of its way it was an unimpressive system of ditches, holes and sandbag breastworks. It started on the Belgian coast—half way between Dunkirk and Ostend—and ran due south towards Paris. Fifty miles outside the city it swerved east along the banks of the Aisne river—then jogged slightly south to Verdun and Nancy. From there onwards—more than 100 miles—it straggled south-east through wild mountainous country where organized fighting was hardly possible. Primitive and flimsy though the line was, it stood up to tremendous battles for three and a half years—until the closing months of the war— with nothing but minor changes of position.

Of this long line, the British Expeditionary Force at first held a mere 20 miles. But as the size of the British army grew, their line was extended. At the start of the war Britain could only muster about 150,000 soldiers. But within five months, nearly 1,000,000 men had enlisted and Britain had two armies plus two cavalry corps in the field. Piece by piece the British line was extended until by March, 1916 it covered a continuous 60 miles. And they were brutal miles, densely packed with troops on both sides and of almost non-stop attack and counter-attack.

The northern-most point was the ancient cloth-making town of Ypres, by no test a natural defence point. It forced a huge forward bulge in the British line—as prominent and vulnerable as the nose on a person's face. And half encircling the town, two to three miles out on the German side, was a dangerous 15-mile spine of high ground—the only break in the vast flatness of Flanders. Whoever

stood up there, on what the Allies called the Messines Ridge, commanded Ypres—and miles of the British line.

In late October, 1914, the ferociously fought First Battle of
Ypres broke out. On the 31st, the British line was broken and the
Germans were free to pour through. A major defeat seemed certain. Then a gallant force of Worcestershires raced to the spot and
closed the line again with barely minutes to spare. Bloody fighting
continued. And day by day the Germans increased their hold on
the vital high ground of the Messines Ridge.

Then, on November 11th, they made a massive all-out attack
intended to send them smashing through into the town and beyond,
perhaps, all the way to Calais. But the defence was just as determined. By now French reinforcements had arrived and non-
combatants were armed. Every man who could hold a rifle was
ordered into the windblown, rainswept line. Cooks, batmen,
clerks, drivers and sappers piled into battle beside the infantrymen.
Between them they fought twelve and a half highly trained German
divisions to a standstill.

The effort cost 50,000 British lives. Also, the most vital parts of
the high ground had been lost. Then a bitter winter set in and
clogged further movements. The war quietened down. The town
had been held, and now became a symbol of defiance for its defenders.

Unhurriedly, the Germans wheeled up their heavy guns, took
casual aim from the ridge and, on November 22nd, began the slow
murder of Ypres by shell-fire.

Most civilians remained for a few more months. Despite the
siege there were cafés, shops, dry billets, band concerts in the
market square and pretty Flemish girls to make the soldiers' rest
periods worth having. But the rate of British—and for a while
French—losses around the Ypres salient became high—in fact about
the highest of the whole front line.

A single track railway ran out south-east from Ypres to the small
red brick town of Comines on the Franco-Belgian border. Where
it crossed the Messines Ridge, a cutting had been carved and the

unwanted soil dumped in three heaps near by. Beside the largest of
these stood a painted board bearing the figure 60, for 60 metres
high. This was the soon-famous Hill 60, named by its height.

It stood to the east of the track and was the highest point of the
whole Messines Ridge. The two lower heaps, known as the Dump
and the Caterpillar, stood on the opposite side of the track. Astounding sacrifices were made for the view this minute range of
man-made peaks could give. From the summits the spires of Ypres
could be clearly seen. So could the British-held hamlet of Zille-
beke—a mere three-quarters of a mile away.

French troops had fought first for Hill 60 and, in December, 1914,
lost it and the Caterpillar to the Germans. When the British army
took over that part of the line the Commander-in-Chief decided at
once that the hill must be retaken. From then on the Messines Ridge
was seldom out of the thoughts of British commanders for long.
Villages, tiny townships and other landmarks that had existed unknown to the world for centuries took on a dramatically quick
importance.

The eyes of British generals swept ceaselessly up and down the
ridge, starting at Hooge—a point due east of Ypres—and scanning
southward to Messines and beyond. Hooge was hardly more than a
château and stables. Next came a copse of poplars and willows
christened Sanctuary Wood. From there the line curved south-
westward through Hill 60, on through a canal embankment named
The Bluff to the once quiet village of St. Eloi. Here the line
changed direction again to run due south through the townships of
Wytschaete and Messines. All this the British soon decided they
must have at whatever cost.

As early as February 8th, 1915, Lieutenant-General Sir William
Robertson, then Chief of the General Staff, was urging the capture
of the ridge. But all field commanders knew that the German defences on it were frighteningly—or as Sir William himself put it,
"abnormally"—strong. Yet the conviction grew that this year,
next year, or just sometime, the ridge would have to be taken.

There were obvious opportunities for attack by mining, and

orders went out from G.H.Q. for a start to be made at St. Eloi
and Hill 60. Colonel Henry Jerome, the Commander, Royal
Engineers (C.R.E.) of the 28th Division, then in that part of the
line, was put in charge. He passed the job over to his chief assistant,
another regular soldier, Major David Griffith, R.E. Griffith was
still planning the mines as Garfield Morgan and the other volunteer
tunnellers began arriving in half-organized and sometimes bewildered batches at the front.

One very early group, the first members of 173 Tunnelling Company, was dumped from a train at Estaires, fifteen miles south of
Ypres. A vast pile of mining equipment was stacked on the platform beside them and Sapper Harry Mosley, a Yorkshireman, was
detailed to guard it. The others moved off and left him. He filled
in time by examining the gear; some of it astounded him. At 34 he
already had nearly 10 years of civilian mining experience behind
him, but he had never seen digging tools, water and air pumps like
many of these. The vital air pumps were the most extraordinary
items of all—they were heavy, crude and antiquated. It was later
admitted that these, and other pieces of gear, were leftovers from the
Crimean War that had lain in stores since 1854.

Hours passed with wearisome slowness, and Mosley decided to
look for the others whose prolonged absence was beginning to
make him suspicious. He found them, as he thought he might, in a
nearby *estaminet*—by now rather drunk. They made him welcome
so he joined the party. Nobody cared about the equipment any
more; or the technical point that a sentry had deserted his post. To
Mosley's sober eyes it looked for a while as if nobody cared about
the war any more.

That night they were ordered to carry some of the mining equipment into the front line trench near by. Mosley was put in charge
of a section and told them to advance in single file, ten paces being
left between each man and his leader. Suddenly a vicious bombardment was started by the Germans. Shells and bullets shrieked and
crashed around the confused men as they blundered wildly through
the mud in search of cover. One man, Sapper "Taffy" Davis, lost

contact with the file ahead of him. Soon he and the men following were lost. Mosley, coming up from behind, was utterly perplexed when he saw what had happened. He had never been under fire before, never even been in the area before, never even been in charge of men before; he crouched for a moment in a nightmare of indecision. Then he decided to go in what seemed to be a forward direction alone, in search of the others. Almost at once he met an infantry officer who angrily ordered him back, out of the way, and said that a German attack was likely any minute. While Mosley was wondering how to obey, a star shell went up and illuminated scattered oddments of mining gear jettisoned by other members of the party who had made their own decision to retire. Mosley found his way to the rear by following the trail of tools.

Further north, the Hill 60 party had been having little to do for its first week at the front. Ten Monmouthshire men were assisting with survey work on the hill and an abortive attempt had been made to dig a shaft on the orders of a Major Pollard of the R.E. Company. The porridgy earth oozed back into the hole as each shovelful was removed. The work was soon abandoned.

For Sapper Garfield Morgan and most of the others the time was spent going into the line for trench experience at night, returning before dawn to the convent at Ypres. Through most of the day-light hours, the men rested on the wooden floor. On the third day, a sapper found a trap-door in a corner of the room which had been hidden by straw. He pulled it open and was amazed to find a large group of silent nuns in hiding there. In embarrassment he slammed the door shut. The news went quickly around—and language be-come more restrained. As the days slipped away, exposure to mud, bitter weather and gunfire became familiar and more bearable.

At last, on March 8th, three sites named M1, M2 and M3 were chosen and orders for serious work to begin were issued. Tunnels M1 and M2 were begun from a curving section of the line known as Trench 40 at points about 40 yards apart. M3 was located in Trench 38—a short, dangerously exposed and very forward posi-tion. It was here that Garfield Morgan was put to work. The aiming point was the German trench lying 50 yards away and dead ahead.

Orders were, first, to dig a narrow pit 16 feet deep through the saturated sandy-clay subsoil. In daylight, Garfield Morgan and another sapper, Albert Rees, started work. As they scraped away the surface soil they discovered the decaying and odorous body of a French soldier. They tried to lift it clear, and the body broke up. Although neither Morgan nor Rees considered themselves squeamish, they were badly shaken by the experience. They asked for instructions and were told to put the body, and any others they might encounter, into sandbags. During the first hour or two they uncovered three more bodies, all French and all in the same state of decomposition. Morgan and Rees were several times almost overwhelmed by nausea but loaded all the bodies into bags and, after dark, dragged them back behind the trench. There the four unknown Frenchmen were buried in quicklime. They were four of many and from now on the caustic smell of quicklime began to hang over the whole Hill 60 area. (Forty-five years later an officer who was there, Captain Percy Abbot, still found that it was the smell of quicklime that brought memories of the hill flooding back to his mind quicker than anything else.)

Despite the frightful conditions and the non-stop crashing of shell-fire, the shafts began to grow. The men had been sorted into eight-hour shifts (further divided into periods below and above ground) and work went on continuously, day and night. They spent between six and nine days at a time in the line, sleeping and resting in support trenches, followed by three days off in Ypres.

When the shaft was down 16 feet, the tunnel that was to end directly beneath the German line began. At this depth the wet sandy-clay pressed inward with great force and the tunnel had to be stoutly cased with timber. Even then it was far from dry. The wood frames met each other in simple butt-joints without tongues and grooves. A constant struggle had to be waged against mud jets which squirted through every chink.

At a point twelve feet into no-man's-land the tunnel took a right-angle turn to the left. From here it became very small—about three feet high by two feet three inches wide. Men laboured in pairs at the face by candlelight, one crouched immediately behind the other. The front men clawed out the dripping clay with grafting tools, bayonets and hands, then passed it back to his mate. The mate packed it into sandbags and tied the bags to a rope held by men at the open end who dragged it to the rear. In M1 and M2, which were dug slightly larger in size, simple trolleys were used to transport the heavy bags.

In any case it all had to be done in silence. Noise would help the enemy to locate the tunnels, and the men had been warned what would happen then. The Germans would set off a mine near by to shake the tunnels down, burying the occupants alive or dead. So the men talked, and even swore, in whispers; tools were handled gently and timbers were patted into place by hand.

Almost from the outset there were ventilation problems and these soon became acute. The Crimean blowers, although hand-cranked, made a loud humming noise and had to be discarded at once. They were replaced by blacksmith-type bellows blowing through toughened hosepipe. The hose was taken right to the face but still the men working there found themselves seriously short of air.

After a few minutes' exertion their chests heaved and they began to notice the eerie sound of their own heavy breathing; in the unnatural quiet it made an extraordinary roaring noise. Then the candles would dim and sometimes go out from lack of oxygen. Even a match when struck burned a cherry red without flaming. Men came off shift exhausted and some were ill with agonizing headaches. Garfield Morgan's sight was permanently damaged. A Monmouthshire man, Sergeant David Evans, nicknamed "Dusky" for his dark colouring, turned white-haired in six weeks. Two Royal Flying Corps pilots being shown round the front lime once arrived at M2 and peered inside. One made a gesture of distaste, then turned to the other. "I wouldn't go down there for a ruddy pension," he said. But the tunnel went forward about ten feet each day.

The weather remained cold and raw as winter dragged interminably into spring that year. But still the men finished their shifts soaked in sweat, and muddy water. There were no fresh clothes to change into so they had to dry out as they were. A large tot of rum given to each man as he came from the mine helped to make life endurable and was said to prevent chills.

After six days in the line most tunnellers spent their three-day rest periods in Ypres, living uproariously to forget the squalor they had just left and must so soon return to. They bought beer and cognac from private householders and at one time almost every inhabited house seemed to be open for business. Yet relations between soldiers and the civil population were not good, and at times were positively bad. Garfield Morgan was walking once with a group of soldiers near the village of Dickebusch—about two miles west of Ypres and more than three from the front line—when one man fell from a sniper's bullet. He was only slightly hurt. Some near by infantrymen and an officer investigated and found that the sniper was a Belgian boy of 17 or 18 sitting in a tree with more than a dozen British identification tags strung round his neck. Although caught, he remained unrepentantly anti-British. The officer ordered a trenching tool to be brought and the boy was told to dig a hole. Trembling visibly, but in silence now, he obeyed. Two soldiers then held him over the hole while the officer drew his revolver and, walking close, shot him through the head.

It was not Morgan's idea of justice, but in the salient, where life grew cheaper every day, it did not seem a matter of great importance.

*   *   *   *

The tunnels at Hill 60 were not the only ones 171 Company was supposed to be driving. A party of men had been sent to the near by front line village of St. Eloi on the night of March 1st to start mining there. They found the whole area so ravaged by gunfire that it was scarcely possible to move from cover. The ground was also about as bad for tunnelling as it could be. Dawn came without a spade being used.

About 500 yards south of the village, standing between it and the Germans, was a shallow, half-acre mound rising 30 feet into the air. German gunners ranged on to the rise and kept it and the ground near by under such heavy fire that British soldiers called this the "Mound of Death". They had good reason—for the casualty rate was consistently high.

The following night the miners came back to the roaring shambles of St. Eloi. Again movement was impossible and they passed the night crouched in trenches listening to the non-stop crescendo of noise around them and feeling the quiver of the ground. Again no digging was done.

The third night was worse than the other two. A miner, Nat Lewis, was hit in the leg before they reached the front. They took his boot off and found it filled with blood. Later the shelling became so violent that the officer in charge decided to withdraw the men. While leading them back he also was hit and seriously wounded by a bullet that smashed through his ribs. St. Eloi seemed altogether too active a part of the line to mine from. Poor subsoil made it less suitable still.

On Sunday, March 7th, Norton Griffiths blew in to Jerome's office in Ypres to be told that the decision to concentrate on Hill 60 and suspend work at St. Eloi had been taken. He was also told why. But seldom satisfied with other men's views, he went at once to Fifth Corps headquarters in Poperinghe where he arranged permission to visit St. Eloi that night. There he met Lieutenant-Colonel Lord Lock of the 28th Divisional Staff who told him that the St. Eloi situation was a cause of much anxiety. Lock said that it was most important for successful mining to be carried out there.

At about midnight, Norton Griffiths arrived at the scene to make his own examination. He saw for himself that conditions were bad—and made worse by a surface litter of dead bodies, barbed wire, abandoned rifles and other objects. But he reported to Fowke that mining *was* nevertheless possible.

Half-hearted attempts were made during the next day or two from trenches on the mound but as soon as a hole was dug it filled with water and running sand and before long the effort petered out.

Because brigades of the 27th and 28th Divisions were still reporting sounds of German mining from the St. Eloi mound, a few miners were detailed to keep a listening watch in two small and badly sited shafts inherited from the French. Lance-Corporal Robert Leonard spent many hours crouched in one with the only listening aid available—a short length of stick. He was told that if he pushed one end into the ground and held the other with his teeth, he would feel the vibrations from below. He found it was not so simple. As the mound rocked under the pulverizing bombardment, vibrations jarred and shook his teeth most of the time. How to distinguish the ones that mattered had not been explained.

After a few days he was withdrawn from St. Eloi and ordered to M1 tunnel at Hill 60. He was given a large shovel known in army jargon as a number three. It was unwieldy enough to be almost useless. He was conscious of an air of confused hesitation as the days passed and no new orders came. Fatigue parties went into the woods and cut timber for use in the mines but apart from that there was little to do. Then, on March 10th news came up the line that units of the First Army, under General Sir Douglas Haig, had attacked the village of Neuve Chapelle 15 miles to the south. Haig's troops had been entrenched in the waterlogged valley of the River Lys and this was their bid to climb out on to higher and firmer ground. For four days disturbing accounts came in of British and Indian infantry struggling to attack through thigh-deep mud; of soldiers dropping asleep from exhaustion in the shrapnel-filled openness of no-man's-land, and of terrible casualties. But ground had been taken and by the 14th the battle was being talked of as a victory.

Then, in the late afternoon that day there was a sudden violent eruption at the St. Eloi mound. Three plumes of debris rose from the British trenches and soared high into the air. Moments later, the shelling stopped and a horde of shouting, gesturing German soldiers began to run across no-man's-land towards the craters.

The attack was a complete surprise to the battered and dazed men of the British 80th Brigade who turned to face it.

*   *   *

One of the charging Germans was a young N.C.O., Sergeant Michael Schneider, of the 23rd Bavarian Regiment. He had sat for hours watching the German sappers on guard over their electrical exploder and waiting for the moment when the plunger was pushed.

A little before five o'clock an order was passed down the line. "*Fertig machen!*" The men were extremely tense now as the minutes ticked away. Then, on the hour, the mines went off with a loud rumbling sound and a wild-eyed major was racing down the trench shouting "*Herans! Herans!*" to hurry the men out. Schneider raced up a short trench ladder and over the top in time to see the debris still high in the air. A vivid picture implanted itself in his mind of British soldiers—as he described it—"bursting like fat toads".

As the Germans ran across the torn and soggy ground an extraordinary loathing gripped them. "Poisonous ulcer!" was one of many insults they shouted, more at the hill than at the bewildered Britons defending it. That mound, they believed, had enabled the British to see for "thousands of yards" and had cost them many lives as a result. They were exulting now in the idea of revenge. They pounded through falling lumps of clay and hardly noticed.

A furious hand-to-hand struggle began the second the Germans reached the British line. Schneider saw one of his men drop a grenade too close to himself and go reeling back, bleeding from the head. A frenzied-looking Englishman, weirdly dressed in a pullover, sprang out of the trench and was immediately shot in the stomach. Another British soldier peered over the parapet just inches away from Schneider, shot a German private through the forehead and was killed himself a second later. The men were smashing at each other with everything they could use, including dirt aimed at the eyes.

Very soon the British went into retreat. As they ran back to the support line, the whooping and shouting Germans dropped to their knees behind the wrecked parados of the trench and raked them with fire. Scores of men fell. Schneider and about 30 comrades became so excited that they began running after the retreating British. Schneider covered a few yards, then was hit and fell to the ground. He raised his head and in front saw the village of St. Eloi and the charging Germans being shot to pieces as they ran towards it. Looking behind he saw the mound, heavily cratered now by the mines. He heard orders being shouted to entrench in the British position; the objective had been reached.

After a perfect example of combined underground and overground warfare, the hated mound was German. The British counter-attacked late that night but failed to recapture it.

*   *   *

News of the St. Eloi disaster reached Hill 60 almost at once. It was yet another big mining success to the Germans and clear proof that they were far ahead in underground war. Almost immediately afterwards, 171 Company tunnellers began hearing what they had dreaded since work began. They knelt in their tiny tunnels at the face end, pressed their ears against the sides and floor and, in quiet moments between exploding shells, listened to the muffled but unmistakable sounds. The Germans were digging too. On the 16th it was officially confirmed that enemy countermining was taking place. The tunnellers were told that their mines must now be "forced" to win what had become a terrible race. The stakes were the highest—life or death—since the losers would inevitably be buried.

Suddenly the British tunnellers found astounding reserves of strength. Panting, coughing and sweating, they clawed at the clay with almost desperate vigour. The rate of driving went up to twelve, sometimes fourteen feet a day. Once it reached sixteen and a half. Each day the sounds of German work grew clearer.

They were loudest of all where Sapper Garfield Morgan still laboured at M3 shaft. From it two galleries, M3 and M3a, running 12 feet or so below the surface were being pushed towards the German line on the extreme right of the attack scheme.

Morgan and his mate, Sapper Albert Rees, were working in M3a. Suddenly one day Rees felt his grafting tool break through into a void in the left hand side-wall of the tunnel. He grabbed Morgan's arm and pointed to the spot. Morgan looked for a moment at the sinister, ragged hole, then quickly put out the candles. For a moment the two men crouched together in silence, listening. A foot splashed heavily into water on the other side of the breakthrough—and it could only have been a German foot. The moment was one of extraordinary, unnerving intimacy. "Come on, Albert," Morgan whispered. "We'd better go back and report this." They scrambled homewards along the tunnel and up the shaft.

In the officers' dug-out they found Second-Lieutenant Thomas Black and told him the story. For some time, an hour or more, Black sat discussing the situation and considering it. Then he said he must go to have a look, and told Morgan and Rees to come too.

Silently, with racing hearts, the three went down the shaft and along the darkened tomb-like tunnel. Visibility was nil—they advanced feeling their way by the timbered sides. After covering many yards, Morgan put his mouth close to Black's ear and whispered that they ought to be about at the spot. They stopped there and Black switched on his flashlight.

There was an immediate explosion—the sharp, single, stunning crack of a bullet being fired in a confined space. It ripped a piece out of the sleeve of Black's tunic and sent them all stumbling and scrambling back towards the safe end of the tunnel. There they crouched by the entry shaft to catch their breath and decide on the next move.

They sat for at least another hour of uncertainty and strain. Then, with outward cheerfulness, Black said, "We'll go back now. Remember the Jerries are just as scared of us as we are of them."

Cautiously they returned to the danger spot. There were no Germans there this time, but a light canister of explosive had been placed in the tunnel. They cut a pair of wires leading from it and replaced it with a 250-lb. guncotton charge of their own—and climbed gratefully out into the cold fresh air of the trench again. Work on the gallery was then stopped but was resumed a week later and completed. Both galleries, M3 and M3a, were eventually charged with 500 lbs. each of guncotton in time for firing with the other and bigger twin charges of M1 and M2, to the left.

On Saturday evening, April 3rd, Norton Griffiths arrived in Ypres and hurried to the office of Major David Griffith, the officer still in charge of 171 Company affairs and the Hill 60 operation, for what proved to be a strained and unhappy meeting.

Seven weeks of hardship had left Norton Griffiths as ebullient as ever. Despite a recent brief but incapacitating bout of stomach trouble, sleepless nights and almost non-stop travel by horse, car, train and boat, he was in his usual breathless hurry. He was not satisfied that 171 Company was being quickly enough organized towards independence. His plans were first to ask searching questions about the Company's strength and efficiency, then to go up that night to inspect the Hill 60 tunnels.

But when he met David Griffith, he ran into the human equivalent of a stone wall. Besides being a regular R.E. of 26 years experience, Griffith was the son of an R.E. officer. The accepted principles of military engineering and military behaviour were in his blood and he was gravely affronted by Norton Griffiths's ideas on both. Although a capable officer, he was a traditionalist, tough, determined and, at times, aggressive. And he could not have forgotten that the last time Norton Griffiths came by, it had been to disagree with his and his colonel's opinion that St. Eloi was unsuitable for mining.

He refused point blank to answer questions that night and said that the earliest time he could arrange a visit to the tunnels would be Monday. Norton Griffiths, not at all used to being thwarted, was angry and surprised but accepted the position for the moment and left. In fact, he was not as sure of his authority as he would have liked. The disagreement had shown the muddled state control of tunnelling companies was in. In theory each company had its own commanding officer and was answerable to the chief engineer of its army, an officer of not less than brigadier-general's rank. In practice tunnelling companies were still attached to R.E. Field Companies, and in turn came under the orders of the local divisional C.R.E., an officer usually carrying the rank of colonel. The truth was that no senior officer could quite define the limits of his authority over these new units. This uncertainty continued long after the tunnelling companies had acquired commanding officers and become independent of the Field Companies.

Norton Griffiths spent the night at Poperinghe, seven miles west of Ypres and was back at David Griffiths's office the next morning by nine o'clock. He said he believed that two sections of the company had little or nothing to do and he would like to know if this were so. Also, he wished to know if any unskilled men had slipped through as fully fledged tunnellers. Again he was bluntly rebuffed. Griffith was emphatic that he would not discuss the two sections, nor the calibre of his men, nor any other details of 171 Company organization.

Norton Griffiths, now furious, went at once to Brigadier-General Petrie, Chief Engineer of the Fifth Corps, for advice. The Brigadier-General promised to intervene and later persuaded David Griffith to climb down. Norton Griffiths called again that day and this time was civilly, if still coolly, received. Griffith showed him the Hill 60 mining scheme and to some extent discussed it. He said work was being delayed by want of air pumps and electric lighting gear. Norton Griffiths decided not to press his request to visit the tunnels and left in the early evening for a second night in Poperinghe. Next morning he rose long before dawn and set out for another part of the line to investigate new reports of German mining.

By Saturday, April 10th, digging at Hill 60 was about finished and six mines were ready for charging. M1 and M2 ran singly and roughly straight out under no-man's-land for more than 100 yards.

Then, just before reaching the German trench, each became two by forking right and left to form the shape of badly proportioned Y's. The arms, just a few yards long, were slightly widened at their tips to form four gunpowder chambers. The other two tunnels, M3 and M3a, which had been in such special peril from German countermining, were charged as they were—without the enlargement of the ends into chambers.

When he came to calculate the charges, Major David Griffith found himself hampered by inaccurate figures. He was working strictly to the formula shown in the Manual of Military Engineering, which took the depth of the mine as an important factor. Now Griffith discovered that nobody quite knew what the various depths were. This was because when Hill 60 was surveyed it was under heavy fire. Some of the levels taken were mere approximations as a result. Eventually he decided to take M1 as 20 feet down, M2 as fifteen feet and M3 as twelve.

The formula in the Manual was for gunpowder, an old-fashioned, rather inefficient explosive. To blow a good crater—Griffith was aiming at 60 feet across—he found that a massive 2,700 lb. charge would have to go into each of the M1 chambers. M2 would need two charges of 2,000 lbs. each. M3, because it might be entered any moment by the Germans, required lighter, more portable charges which could be dumped quickly and left. Griffith decided on two 500-lb. charges of guncotton here, one for each face. He gave the order to Lieutenant Lionel Hill to go ahead with the charging at once. Hill, the officer who had brought Garfield Morgan's party out, was a soldier now of about seven weeks' experience. But he was already in full charge of day-to-day operations on the hill.

The men had new dangers and fears to face now. The gunpowder came parcelled in unwieldy 100-lb. bags. Ninety-four of them would have to be manhandled up to and through the communication trenches, then winched down the shafts and hauled along the tunnels. In the open air, the men staggered forward with a bag slung over a shoulder. They made macabre jokes about what would happen now if a ceaseless shelling and machine-gun fire happened to ignite a bag. The officers carried the detonators in their pockets and were actually in greater, though less obvious, danger of being blown up.

As the first charges were being placed, Norton Griffiths came speeding into Ypres again. He avoided David Griffith but called at once at the 27th Division headquarters for news. He was excited to learn the size of the coming Hill 60 explosion, which he seemed inclined to credit entirely to Lionel Hill. Cheerfully he reported to General Fowke that Hill had made an extraordinarily good job of running out the mines; later that same day he sent a second and even more exuberant message outlining his views on how the infantry assault should be made. He wanted the men to go forward *without* waiting for flying debris to land. In typically coloured language he suggested that it was better to have a few men hit by falling Germans than a large number hit by machine-guns.

The charges were all ready by April 15th. They had been laid in waterproofed boxes, double-fused and wired back to three plunger-type exploders assembled in a single dug-out. In case some calamitous electrical fault should suddenly develop, each pair of charges was again double-fused with primitive burning fuses. Now four firing systems all but guaranteed that the mines would go off on time. To make sure that all the blast went forward and up towards the Germans, M1 and M2 tunnels had been blocked solid in three places for ten feet at a time with sandbag tamping. Between each barrier a ten-foot, shock-absorbing airspace had been left. So behind each of the two main pairs of charges stood a massive 50-foot dam. Slamming the exploder plungers home was all that remained to be done.

Two miserable and frightening days then followed. The mines were to be part of a complicated assault by the 13th Brigade of Infantry. The Brigade was undergoing special training and was not due into the line until the following night. Zero hour for firing the mines was fixed for the evening after that—April 17th, 1915 at about seven o'clock. It left a 48-hour interval of acute suspense.

Lieutenant Hill ordered that the fuses must be checked at the gallery faces every two hours throughout the waiting time. The men took it in turns to go with tautened nerves down the shaft and away along the dark, wet, narrow tunnels to the end, inspecting each inch of wiring and fusing by flashlight. In the uncanny silence, the sound of Germans moving about near by was quite distinct. They were directly overhead. And it was almost certain that by now they had laid heavy charges too. They might yet press their plungers first. As the hours passed and nothing happened, the tension grew.

Conditions on the day of the big blow were extraordinary. After a long and bitter winter, spring had arrived and the 17th was a balmy day of sunshine and breezes. As evening approached the routine firing by both sides subsided and, to everyone's surprise, eventually stopped. The last hour was theatrically still.

At five past seven, Griffith, Hill and one other officer were standing side by side in the dug-out, each with a hand on his exploder. Griffith nodded, murmured the order to fire, flicked his exploder handle a short distance up and down at speed—then pushed it hard into the box. The others followed on almost at once. Griffith was slightly deaf and at first heard nothing. "My God," he suddenly exclaimed, "—it hasn't gone off!" But it had: dramatically.

The eruption in the heart of Hill 60 spread itself out over a ten-second period. It flung debris nearly 300 feet into the air and scattered it for some 300 yards around. One British infantryman who peered over the parapet was hit violently in the face by some of it and killed. As the mudlumps, sandbags, trench timbers and shattered German bodies were still spinning through the air, a tremendous bombardment began from the British side. Besides three British artillery brigades and two batteries, French and Belgian guns joined in. The fire was aimed to the sides and rear of the hill.

Simultaneously an attacking party of Royal West Kents and Home Counties Company Field Company sappers with bayonets fixed scrambled out of the front trench and raced towards the hill.

The regimental buglers played loudly throughout the thrilling and terrible moments of the charge.

From its strange mood of peace, the evening had become a dreadful farrago of noise. But there were uglier sounds still to come as the assaulting party closed with what was left of the German 172nd Regiment holding the hill. The dazed Germans screamed in agony as bayonets sliced intotheir stomachs and chests. About 150 died— and only 20 lived to be taken prisoner. Total British casualties, so far, were seven.

Hill 60's topography was now drastically altered. The craters were all larger than had been expected. The middle pair of charges had ripped a single gigantic hole nearly half an acre in size. This was despite the fact that a large amount of gunpowder had evidently become too damp to explode and had been seen fountaining upwards, blackly, in the centre of the debris.

A German mine was discovered charged and ready wired to its exploder. It was later found out from prisoners that German sappers planned to blow on the 19th—just two days too late.

One-seven-one Tunnelling Company had won the day and almost immediately afterwards became an independent unit. David Griffith handed over control to Captain Edward Wellesley, the new O.C. The men, though still sappers, were now becoming known as tunnellers. Hill 60 had shown that a new and important force had been created.

4

SOME LESSONS LEARNED

For one glorious and misleading hour, the Hill 60 operation looked like a great success for the British. But as the Germans recovered from their surprise it became increasingly obvious that a costly tactical blunder had been committed.

Because it jutted into the enemy line, the hill was exposed to fire on two sides. German gunners saw their opportunity and began a pulverizing fire. It went on hour after hour destroying trenches, sandbags, dug-outs, wire—the whole paraphernalia of defence. Whenever the fire eased, it meant always the same thing: a counter-attack. There were four that first night. Somehow, the shocked and shattered British forced them back each time.

Three days later the battle the defenders could not win was still being fought as bitterly and pointlessly as when it began. By now, seven fresh battalions had gone into action to support the West Kents, four V.C.'s had already been won—and Hill 60 had secured a place in military history for ever. The hill had become, as the Official Historian described it later, "A rubbish heap, in which it was impossible to dig without disturbing a body." In fact the bodies often sprawled several deep, British, French and German, in an extraordinary and loathsome muddle.

On April 22nd, a lovely spring day, new fighting started which faced Britain with a second and bigger crisis. The morning began with a specially heavy bombardment of Ypres. A number of im-mense 17-inch shells not seen before by the British landed on the market square and exploded with uproarious noise, killing about a dozen people. Now, as the whole town appeared to be falling, the civilian population began to go. The movement spread in a rush and soon the streets were jammed with refugees heading west. Some went so hurriedly that they left their doors unlocked, valuables in the houses and money in shop tills. A Canadian unit trying to move against the flow had to put six large men in front with bayonets fixed to force a passageway through.

Then, at five o'clock that afternoon, the Germans began the first gas attack ever made.

Five miles north-east of Ypres, at a part of the line still held by French troops, a bluish-green mist was seen to be drifting slowly downwind towards the town. It was chlorine—a gas that attacks the eyes, nose, throat and lungs. Newly arrived French Algerians were first to breathe it. At once they clambered from their trenches and fled, running through the cloud, choking, vomiting and crying "Gas asphyxiant!" while they went. As the gas cloud spread, other units followed. The Canadian 3rd Brigade, next to the French and less affected by gas, held on. But there was a gap in the line nearly four miles wide. The Second Battle of Ypres had begun—badly for the Allies.

Some of the gas drifted to Hill 60 to make the terrible conditions there worse. But by then it had thinned out and was no longer disabling. The struggle went on. By May 4th, the British were still on the hilltop, battling blindly, heroically, for their lost cause. Next morning, during a rare lull in the German fire, many of the men fell into an exhausted sleep. At a quarter to nine, a sentry saw what they all now feared—another cloud of gas. It was coming densely this time, right across the hill. To this the defenders, with nothing but cotton pads to protect them, had no answer. Fifteen minutes later, the Germans had followed up and were on the summit again, digging in to stay. With the hill they took three new mine shafts 171 Company had been sinking.

The gas had swirled down into the trenches and shafts, affecting an officer and about 15 men—including Garfield Morgan. Those who had the breath to do it, fled to the rear. Morgan tottered towards Ypres, clawing at his throat and throwing up bright green vomit on the way. He reached a clearing station and was rushed from there to hospital at Etaples, on the coast, where he lay for eleven weeks recovering.

When the gas cleared, the British counter-attacked sporadically, then faced the truth. The hill—for which such monstrous efforts had been made below and above ground—could not possibly be held. The full cost of that lesson was staggering. Some 2,000 British soldiers lay dead on a hillside little bigger than a large back garden. Hundreds more were wounded. More still were struggling with the after-effects of gas.

While Hill 60 was being lost, 171 Tunnelling Company was facing a private crisis about money. Some of the men were being paid at six shillings a day, others were drawing two-and-twopence. Norton Griffiths felt strongly that clay kickers working right at the face should be paid more than tunnellers' mates. He was determined to distinguish between the two grades. In practice it was proving most difficult to do.

Some men without previous experience of clay kicking had wangled a six-shilling rate. Many others, paid as mates, claimed that they were taking a full share of face work and deserved the pay for the job. Most of the mates also argued that they had been specifically promised the higher rate when they signed on for mining. As the desperate race under Hill 60 went on, the grumbling grew steadily louder and more bitter, and ended at last in an astounding document which was suddenly put forward for the Commanding Officer to read. It was a bluntly written strike notice demanding six shillings a day for all miners if further work was to be done, and was signed by most of the aggrieved men. None had realized that this was mutiny—a most serious crime in wartime for which the penalty could be death.

The reply came swiftly. The men were told to parade at once in a nearby barn. They obeyed, hoping to be told that the demand would be met. Instead, a furious Lieutenant walked in and announced that if their ringleader could be found, he would be summarily shot. In shocked silence the men listened to a blistering rebuke that followed. For the first time they realized exactly what it meant to be in the army. In fact, the ringleader was never searched for and officially the incident was not acknowledged.

The fracas was a symptom of muddle and discontent already widespread in the still very young tunnelling service. Norton Griffiths decided early that too many men were being promised the high rate—which was intended as a special reward for a special contribution. He was much concerned by the fact that, despite his immense energy, he could not check the skill of all tunnelling recruits himself. For one thing, officers and men were soon coming in at the rate of more than 100 a week—some from civilian work, others as transfers from infantry units. For another, he was attached to G.H.Q. in St. Omer and much of the recruiting had to be done in England.

An R.E. Lieutenant, Ernest Homer, was deputizing for him at his Westminster office, now the tunnelling companies' official depot. He wrote Homer in early March urging that transferred men should only be signed on at the lower rate, and that skilled civilians were the men most urgently wanted. Homer apparently took offence. He replied that he was stopping the transfer of serving men as from that day, the 11th. And he asked that someone else should seek out civilians, since he had "no personal knowledge of the principal sources of this kind of labour".

Homer claimed also that "with few exceptions" the men he had signed up had been worthy of being included in the draft. On the matter of pay, he said, "I have told all the men that they would receive pioneer pay R.E., i.e. one-and-twopence plus sixpence and am not aware that any mention has been made to any of these men— before proceeding to Chatham—of the six shillings a day tunnellers' rating except for that first draft of men which came to this depot (whilst you were here) before February 19th."

At about the same time the War Office attempted to end the trouble by laying it down that, without exception, all transferred men were to start at two-and-twopence. If and when they qualified as proficient tunnellers, they could apply to be regraded and paid the six-shilling rate.

Norton Griffiths determined that wherever he could find proof of a six-shilling man's lack of skill, he would have him removed. On the 29th he sent the first few unqualified men back to their regiments—despite pleas by their more skilled comrades that the rejected men should be allowed to stay as mates. Norton Griffiths was adamant. In what he vaguely described as "the interests of work" he decreed that any men who were not expert clay kickers would go and "must not be allowed to remain a day longer than necessary". Gradings were not the only causes of grumbles among tunnellers —lack of tools was another—but they were having by far the greatest effect on morale. He was convinced that the unrest could only be checked by ruthless readjustments.

Immediately after the Hill 60 mines had been blown, Norton Griffiths arrived to see the men. All the clay kickers in the company—about 50—were assembled in a large barn that had become the makeshift drill-hall. Norton Griffiths sat in a corner with Lieutenant Hill. One by one the six-shilling men were called over for a quick, blunt interview. Norton Griffiths wanted to know on what they based their claims to be skilled. He turned for an opinion on each man to Hill. Two of the company, a corporal and a sapper, failed the test. They were told to pack up for transfer back to their units.

Afterwards, Norton Griffiths came forward to speak to the whole assembly. He said good work had been done and that he was pleased and proud. Immediately afterwards, he left in his mud-drenched Rolls-Royce for other parts of the front. Just before the car drove off he handed several bottles of whisky out for the men.

For a while, that evening, 171 Company forgot its grumbles and worries.

5

FIRST OF THE BIG ONES

LIEUTENANT GEOFFREY CASSELS of 175 Tunnelling Company and his C.O., Major Hunter Cowan R.E., (a regular soldier) hurried through lunch together, then called, as they had been instructed to, at some commodious cellars beneath a convent in Ypres. They were received by Brigadier-General A. R. Hoskins, Commander of the 8th Brigade. The General was friendly. He handed round glasses of apricot brandy before explaining the purpose of the meeting.

The Brigade's front line included the tiny village of Hooge with its vast château and stabling, two-and-a-half miles east of Ypres and just north of the main road to Menin. Most of Hooge, including the château's stabling, was in British hands. But the ruin of the château itself was held by the Germans. Hoskins had orders to drive them out; he was to be assisted by mining, and this part of the operation had fallen to 175 Company as the nearest to the spot.

Hoskins explained that what he was asking would be dangerous and exceedingly uncomfortable. The rival trench systems were somewhat confused in the area and close together; they were also wet. Worse, they were shallow; the tunnelling party would have to work from an unpleasantly exposed position, often under heavy fire. Two officers would be required to take charge of 40 men. So far one had been named—Lieutenant J. Warnock; there remained the matter of the other. In Hoskins's opinion, it was essentially a job for volunteers . . .

The glasses were passed round again and Cassels became aware of the strong, comforting apricot brandy inside him and of the General's expectant attitude. He volunteered at once. Hoskins seemed pleased and said he would walk up with the two of them, Cassels and Cowan, to within viewing distance of the site that afternoon, June 9th, 1915. A colonel and two orderlies joined the party and soon they were all stalking towards Hooge in open order, 200 yards between each man. On the edge of a cornfield, the General stopped and gathered them all together to point out the scenery. Far off to the right, Hill 60 could be seen; ahead and to the left was Hooge with, behind it, part of the Messines Ridge known here as Bellewaarde Ridge. Beyond the cornfield were some trees. This was Sanctuary Wood which the General said they should head for, explaining that he and the Colonel would now have to turn back. He stressed that from this point on, they must take special care; the danger was acute. "If necessary," he warned, "get down in the corn and crawl."

But Cassels, Cowan and the two orderlies arrived in the shell-swept copse without incident. They found it already fully occupied by troops. Someone offered to escort them the rest of the way up and soon they were in the watery trenches of the Hooge sector, peering through a borrowed periscope at the target area 50 yards away. It began to rain heavily—the start, as it was to turn out, of a long wet period. A nauseous smell filled the air; when Cowan mentioned it, soldiers familiar with the sector put it down to "dead cow". But there were also many human corpses lying about and Cassels observed with distaste that they were turning black. Grimly the two officers searched about for a suitable site to start the tunnel, eventually deciding on the inside of a stable. The thick brick walls would give some protection as well as screening operations from view. By the time the decision had been made, darkness had fallen and they were both wet through.

Next evening Cassels—who by now had learned that he was in charge of the operation—led the first dozen of his sappers towards Hooge. They were new arrivals snatched into the army and rushed (as usual) through fitting-out at Chatham and to the front without a moment to catch their breath. As Cassels tried to steer the men forward, a new type of high-speed shell nicknamed the "whizz-bang" began to fall, scaring them badly; they fled repeatedly. As patiently as possible, Cassels rounded them up each time and turned them again in the direction of the front; most insisted on advancing on their stomachs despite laughter and jeers from hardened infantrymen who were looking on. Eventually, after what to Cassels seemed an unbelievably long time, they arrived in Sanctuary Wood and he put them to work building and repairing dug-outs.

After their hesitant start, Cassels was impressed by how quickly the men settled down. It was true that their dug-outs in the wood, standing half below and half above ground in a sheltering hollow, offered fair protection. But the comfort inside them was slight and life generally was full of hardship and stress. The men were permanently wet and no fires could be allowed to dry their clothes; they were worked very hard due to constant difficulty (from water) with the tunnel; the roaring racket of shell-fire around them beat at their nerves; they went exhaustingly short of sleep; and there was the constant tension just from being always so close to the Germans and their watchful snipers. But they kept going. Cassels helped them with generous tots of rum. It amused him after they had been there a while to reflect that most of his stores indents seemed to be for rum: stone jar after stone jar of it came up. He supposed Cowan must wonder if they were tunnelling in a stupor, and felt glad that he had a Scot for a C.O. "who liked his dram" and would understand.

By far the greatest strain fell on Cassels himself. He spent most of each night at the front with the men directing and advising, and giving them confidence. At about two each morning he would make his way down the trenches, over the Menin Road (by means of a flooded culvert if the Germans were in a shooting mood), back to the wood to receive rations and stores from the supply wagon, checking them off and arranging their safe keeping. Most mornings were spent on surveys, measurements and routine paper work. Only the afternoons were left for sleep. Then he would sling a garden hammock he had had sent out from Harrod's between two posts inside his own dug-out which happened to be unpleasantly exposed; this way he obtained some insulation against the noise of bullets whacking into the sandbagged walls. He was often disturbed by visitors. The local C.R.E., monocled Lieutenant-Colonel Charles Wilson, arrived one afternoon unexpectedly, woke him up and accused him of scrimshanking. Wearily Cassels explained the position—not for the first time. Cowan, at least, was very considerate and avoided afternoon visits.

The days of effort dragged by with little to show for them. Soil conditions beneath the stable could hardly have been worse for tunnelling. Wet running sand came almost to the surface. The men had to force special sand-retaining piles into the ground, using complicated levers instead of hammers to prevent the Germans hearing the work. Even then, pumps had to be kept continuously at work inside the beginnings of the shaft, but soon they were sucking sand from under and behind the piles, threatening the stability of the whole structure. Cassels tried to cure the trouble by stripping the kilts off dead Highlanders and stuffing them in behind the piles. But they, too, were sucked through, and eventually the truth had to be faced: with the equipment available, no tunnel could be driven from here.

Now Cassels moved his men 200 yards to the west, to the ruins of a gardener's cottage. This time they had better luck. The cellar itself was deep which gave a good start. Also, the ground was drier and before long the shaft had been sunk 35 feet into blue clay. Work was beginning on the tunnel proper when it occurred to Cassels that the château had ceased to be the best target to aim at. For one thing, it no longer seemed to be so strongly held; for another, shelling ought to be able to smash up what was left of the structure efficiently enough. But most important of all, he had spotted a better target ahead and slightly left of the new shaft site: twin concrete redoubts. They were being built, apparently, with the help of civilian labour. Contractors' top-hats could actually be seen at times bobbing ludicrously above the German defences.

He reported his feelings and was promptly invited to attend a staff conference to elaborate further. After lengthy discussion, the change was agreed and a date for the action set—July 19th. That was a mere three weeks, or so, away. By now Cassels had two officers assisting him, Warnock and Lieutenant Arthur Lumb. He sped back to give the news to them and the men. An all-out effort now had to be made to surprise the Germans in their new position.

The length of the main tunnel was calculated at 190 feet. About one-third of the way along, a branch left was to be broken out and pushed something like 100 feet towards the second strongpoint. It was a heavy programme to undertake in the time available, especially in view of the need to do it quietly. Clay kicking began at once. For its first yards, the tunnel was cut to a comfortable size of about seven feet by two feet six inches, but it shrank further in, ending up a cramped four feet by two. It was neatly close-boarded the whole way.

Progress was hindered by frequent pauses for listening checks. During these periods, all work ceased; even the bellows-type air-feed—which made a steady, rhythmical "woof-woof" as the air surged through the pipe—had to be stopped. Cassels often went down to do the listening duty himself; he preferred to be quite alone, which he found helped his concentration. Once he described these lonely moments underground:

> Forehead pressed to the face, side or floor of the gallery, one stood, knelt or lay—listening, listening, listening. Some sounds would be heard, dull and muffled. There was always that fraction of a second of doubt—when it *might* be enemy mining. One's pulse rate would quicken and fright push to the fore in one's whole being . . .

But on these occasions the sounds all turned out to be innocent enough—exploding shells, infantry hammerings and other surface disturbances. Later, noises were traced to the Germans holding the right hand redoubt. They were heedlessly at work overhead. This was a good moment for the tunnellers; the main drive had arrived on target.

However, the branch tunnel was not going so well. Finally, with only a few days in hand, Cassels discovered it had run so badly off course that it would miss the left (and smaller) redoubt altogether. Was there time to make a correction? Cassels pondered the question anxiously and decided the honest answer was No. For a moment the situation seemed hopeless. He cursed the primitive surveying instruments and poor sighting conditions that had caused the error. Then an alternative plan occurred to him—one that he admitted was "bold and risky": If he placed a very large charge beneath the right redoubt, it should heave enough material into the air to bury the other post near by.

Urgently he talked the idea over with Cowan, a much more conservative officer, and persuaded him to back it. For Cowan it cannot have been an easy decision. Cassels had to admit that he was not sure of his depth and had no idea of the weight and quality of concrete in the redoubt above him; nor was he entirely sure, even, what the effect of a large charge at a shallow depth would be. But a desperate situation called for a desperate remedy and Cowan said Yes—subject to approval from the 5th Corps H.Q. And while making one experiment they decided to dare another: they would use an explosive seldom (possibly never) used before by the army, though it had been known about for 15 years. This was ammonal. It had three-and-a-half times the lifting power of gunpowder. After further anxious discussion they decided to use 3,500 lbs. of it—if as much could be supplied by stores in time.

Fifth Corps gave its permission and the rush to put the scheme into practice began. Cowan sent a written requisition to the Quartermaster-General at G.H.Q. for the ammonal while Cassels set off to complete his arrangements at the tunnel face.

Unknown to either of them, a minor drama broke out in the Q.M.G.'s office at St. Omer on receipt of the requisition slip. Nobody there had ever heard of ammonal and a check was ordered. A message was sent to the 5th Corps Quartermaster asking:

Can you please say if you have made any use of ammonal and if so, whether the results are satisfactory?

But the 5th Corps Quartermaster was equally at a loss and passed the inquiry on to his Camp Commandant who, after a brief pause for thought, replied:

This is not understood. For what purpose is ammonal used, please? Is it a drug or an explosive?

Helpfully the 5th Corps Quartermaster signalled back:

Perhaps the Medical Officer attached to Corps H.Q. will be able to give you all required information.

The Camp Commandant took the advice and a period of silence followed. Then came the reply:

In accordance with your Minute 4 I have consulted the M.O. . . . He informs me that ammonal is a compound drug extensively used in America as a sensual sedative in cases of abnormal sexual excitement. So far as I am able to ascertain this drug is not a medical issue to Corps H.Q. . . . At the present moment the M.O. states that no cases have occurred among 5th Corps personnel indicating the necessity for administering the drug.

Both G.H.Q. and 5th Corps had confused ammonal with ammonol.

Meanwhile Cassels, tense and impatient, was beginning to give up hope of receiving the charge. When the 16th came and there was still no sign of it, he rushed messages to everyone he could think of who might have some kind—almost any kind—of explosive to spare. From Maple Copse, another 175 Company post, he obtained 500 lbs. of gunpowder; from the company's H.Q., 700 lbs.

of ammonal; from neighbouring R.E. units, 200 lbs. of guncotton. It was ludicrously insufficient. Next day he came down for break-fast and a frantic word with Cowan, to learn with astonishment that the full load of ammonal had gone up to him by wagon the previous night and ought to have arrived before dawn. Cowan was horri-fied to hear that it had not appeared and sent a number of search parties out at once.

But when Cassels got back to Hooge later that morning, he found the wagon there, waiting. The driver had had a broken wheel, or some such trouble, and had been delayed. With extra-ordinary coolness he had carried on when he could, though it was by then full daylight and he was easily visible to the Germans. Cowan said later that in his view only the rain, which happened to be falling heavily at the time, had saved the load from being "whizz-banged". He greatly admired the nerve of the driver.

Cassels waded eagerly into the newly arrived ammonal, stacking it in with the rest of the charge, placing and wiring 24 previously prepared detonators in batches of six and running two sets of firing leads out to a dug-out a safe distance away in a communication trench. He also placed two shorter instantaneous fuses to be ignited in case of a double electrical failure—and reflected ruefully at the time that if he was unlucky enough to have to light them, he would almost certainly be buried before getting clear. Then several tons of clay and sand tamping in bags were hauled into place.

By soon after half-past two next afternoon, July 19th, 1915, the heaviest mine yet laid in the war was ready for firing. Cowan arrived almost immediately and tested the leads. Later he with-drew 1,000 yards and joined a 3rd Division Brigadier whose men were to make the surface attack, to watch.

As seven p.m.—zero hour—approached, Cassels tested and re-tested the circuits with a weak torch battery and lamp for con-tinuity. He and Lumb were both standing by an exploder waiting eagerly for the moment. Then, just minutes before seven, a Ger-man shell crashed into the ground near by. Cowan, watching from the rear, saw it; as he later admitted, his hair "stood on end for two centuries". Cassels was full of the same fear: Had it affected the mine? A quick test revealed the truth with sickening certainty. It had. The continuity test showed a break.

Frantically, the two officers and a corporal ran back along the wiring. It was the corporal who found the damage—a clean cut in both sets of wires near the newly formed shell crater. They repaired it crudely and dashed back to the dug-out. The continuity test showed that all was well again. Cassels looked at his watch. There were four and a half minutes to go.

It was a beautiful evening now, quite quiet and with the sun setting peacefully to the left of them. There was nothing but dried mud and ruins in sight but from somewhere birds were singing; a little black cat that had earlier been sitting on Cassels' knee came over and rubbed itself against him.

Then, at seven precisely, the two plungers went down and the mine exploded. Gazing up at the fountaining debris, Cassels made out a whole tree gyrating like a match stick. Human limbs fell near them and then, as German artillery opened up in the first reprisal, he and Lumb ran for the rear. The job had been done and it was time to get out.

In a minute, they paused to look back at the scene, still one of smoking confusion. No British troops seemed to be moving and, as they hurried on to the dug-outs in Sanctuary Wood, they began to wonder in alarm whether the whole British assault force had been buried with the Germans.

In fact, men of the 4th Middlesex and 1st Gordon Highlanders went forward as planned, captured the crater, which measured a full 120 feet across, and joined it to the British line. But it later became known that ten of the Middlesex men who had been crouching well forward really had been buried by the debris and lost. So had two advanced store dumps.

Cassels expected that there would be trouble, even though from 200 to 600 Germans had been buried in their redoubts. He made his way down to the Company H.Q. in Vlamertinghe feeling too over-whelmingly tired to care. The long weeks at Hooge had caught up with him. After a drink with Cowan, he turned in. His head barely seemed to have reached the pillow when he was being roused again. It was morning and a motor cycle and sidecar had come to take him at once to see a general, apparently Major-General H. de B. de Lisle, but he was never entirely sure.

Still dazed with fatigue and feeling muddled in his senses, he was driven to a distant H.Q. There a captain and lieutenant told him to take off his hat and Sam Browne and to consider himself arrested. A minute later he was standing in front of the General struggling to answer angry, jabbing questions about the death of the men from Middlesex. Then the door opened and the huge figure of Lieutenant-General Sir Edmund Allenby, Commander of the 5th Corps, walked in. Cassels was dismissed but told to wait in the hall and soon Allenby came out. "Go inside," he said, "salute the General, say thank you—then get out and into my car." A few minutes later Cassels found himself being driven to a lunch party with Allenby and the C.-in-C. himself, Sir John French, and their staffs. Allenby congratulated him warmly on the mine; it had all become a little hard to believe.

That evening Cassels learned he had been awarded the M.C. and Cowan laid on a champagne and port dinner for him in the mess. On the 21st, Allenby came over with his A.D.C. to inspect the Company and make a speech of congratulation. It was an unusual honour and Cowan called it "the proudest day of my life".

By then, Cassels was on his way home to England on ten days' special leave granted by Fowke. He supposed he could assume by now that his arrest had been forgotten.

A curious thing about the great Hooge mine was that it was almost entirely overlooked by the historians. Even the Official History of the War spared it only one passing sentence; and it gave the charge weight as 3,500 lbs., when in fact it was almost one-third as much again.

But, of course, Cassels alone knew that.

6

THE MUDDLE WORSENS

NORTON GRIFFITHS had unshakable faith in his own ability as a man manager. He judged men quickly—often instantly—and seldom changed his opinions later on. In describing someone he disliked he was frank, sometimes so much so that he alarmed his seniors at headquarters—Harvey and "the Chief", General Fowke. He described one officer as "fat and round and liable to go off in his own tunnels". Of another, who had not arrived at the front when expected, he said he had been "left at Southampton, sick, presumably from an epileptic fit—but his brother officers say D.T.'s was the real cause". It was reckless comment and, in a written note, Harvey advised him to "watch it". But Harvey and Fowke also learned to depend on these judgements, and most would-be tunnellers who failed to please Norton Griffiths were posted away. Years later, in an after-dinner speech, Harvey said, "His powers of judging a man were remarkable . . . He rarely —if ever—made a mistake . . ." Once, Harvey had asked Norton Griffiths how he did it, and had been told, "I look a man straight in the eye." Remembering the keen, unblinking eyes that Norton Griffiths turned on a man's face, Harvey described the ordeal as "no mean one".

By mid-1915, Norton Griffiths was still the only effective link between headquarters marooned in the 28-miles-to-the-rear remoteness of St. Omer and the front-line war of the mines. Harvey, who had become steadily more interested in tunnelling affairs, was by now convinced that there was no better man to do the liaison job. Norton Griffiths was still covering a tremendous daily, and often nightly, mileage. A non-stop flow of telegrams (most of which read simply: ENEMY MINING SEND GRIFFITHS) followed him. Wherever he went he gave technical advice, listened to complaints, and above all recruited without let-up in his own unorthodox manner.

A young Canadian corporal serving with the first Canadian Division was resting in a tent a few miles south of Ypres one evening when a soldier dived through the entrance flap with extraordinary news. "There's a bloody general out there looking for you," he said. The corporal, Basil Sawers, could scarcely believe it but hastily straightened his clothes and went out to investigate. There he saw the huge Rolls-Royce and Norton Griffiths standing, an impressive red-tabbed and banded figure, beside it. Word that in civilian life Sawers was a McGill University undergraduate in mining had somehow reached Norton Griffiths. He had come to know if he would like to transfer to a tunnelling company. Sawers said he would. After a conversation lasting ten minutes, or less, Norton Griffiths told him he should certainly be an officer and said he would arrange to have him commissioned. "You'll hear in a day or two," he called as the car drove away.

Three days later a chit arrived at the orderly room saying, "Second-Lieutenant Sawers to report to R.T.O. Steeenvoorde for transportation to 177 Tunnelling Company R.E." But for six days Sawers was not told of it—while his Commanding Officer checked up on the arrangement which he had heard nothing about and which he considered most irregular. But the transfer and promotion were both properly authorized and Sawers was eventually released.

It was a typically Norton Griffiths swoop. He was disdainful of regular officers—he once even told his own chiefs that neither they nor any other regular R.E.'s could do the job he was doing—and liked to do his negotiating with potential tunnellers directly. This was improper military procedure and most commanders resented it. There were repeated rows. Norton Griffiths cared little, but carried cases of good port in the car which he gave away to the more incensed of the officers.

A gas specialist, Lieutenant Alan Reid, once witnessed an argument between Norton Griffiths and an annoyed brigadier-general supported by two colonels. The general began by asking "what the hell" Norton Griffiths meant by taking officers from their battalions. Norton Griffiths replied, mildly, that tunnelling was very important. The general became extremely angry and retorted, among other things, that the infantry were *more* important. When the opportunity came, Norton Griffiths suggested that the brigadier should take his complaint to Sir John French, the Commander-in-Chief. This had a calming effect and Norton Griffiths followed up with an immediate invitation to join him for a drink.

To Reid's surprise the party, held in a wooden hut Norton Griffiths had commandeered, was soon convivial. Norton Griffiths was capable of extraordinary charm and he was using it to the full now. The party ended with vague though cordial concessions on both sides. The general promised not to complain so long as not too many of his men were taken, and Norton Griffiths promised not to lure too many away.

Whenever he called at St. Omer, Norton Griffiths was cheerful and informative. No amount of fatigue seemed to subdue his spirit. He was conscientious also about filing regular reports. Harvey has told how they awaited them eagerly at G.H.Q.—not only because they were informative (which they were) but also because they were often entertaining. They became known in the office as Punch. Yet it remained true that for all the energy of their liaison officer, G.H.Q. officers had only a vague idea of what their steadily expanding tunnelling force was doing. No one man could cover the whole fighting front efficiently.

The only other fragments of information to reach Fowke and Harvey were diary reports written by the tunnelling companies. Each was keeping a diary composed in terse, engineering jargon—but commanding officers seemed unsure where to send their reports once written. Many were signed for by any senior staff officer who happened to be handy, and then were lost. Those that did travel right through the slow hand-to-hand journey to G.H.Q. arrived too late to be of value.

The year 1915 was, in many ways, a year of trouble and disappointment for the mining force. It was a new, hurriedly set-up affair that nobody understood. Tunnelling companies tended to be thought of as the familiar R.E. Field Companies which were attached to divisions and controlled by a senior engineer—the divisional "Commander, Royal Engineers". Some of these laid mines too, on a small scale, as part of their normal duties; but they were an adjunct to a division, travelled with it when it was moved and existed to help the division fight effectively.

The object of the tunnelling companies was not the same. They were supposed, as far as possible, to work independently as fighting troops. Although few people understood it during the early months they were evolving into a private army engaged in their own war—a war within the main war; a claustrophobic, uncomfortable and often terrifying, hard-fought war underground.

Tunnellers were alternately courted and spurned by the surface troops. When front-line units suspected that German mines were being placed beneath them, the tunnellers were sent for, warmly welcomed and given every assistance in carrying out tests and taking counter measures. But in quiet parts of the line the reception was sometimes much cooler. There was always the fear that the start of tunnelling work would attract German fire. The risk was real. Tunnel entrances were important targets that artillerymen on both sides searched for.

Viscount Elibank, then Major the Hon. Arthur Murray and commander of a squadron of the 2nd King Edward's Horse (the regiment Norton Griffiths helped to form), has recalled how he reacted when he was told that tunnelling operations were to start in his part of the line. The regiment, by then dismounted, had been in bloody and frightful fighting, which had included the horror of Festubert in May. It was recuperating in a quieter sector opposite Messines, about seven miles south of Ypres. One day Elibank was confronted by a tall officer of the Canadian Engineers, Tom "Foghorn" Macdonald, who explained that he had orders to start a mine. Elibank was furious. "To Dante's inferno with your cursed tunnel!" he had replied, adding that the Germans would spot what was happening and would "blow you and your men and me and my men to Timbuctoo".

Foghorn MacDonald, who once as a junior officer told a be-ribboned brigadier-general that he looked like a "bloody tart at a wedding", was not put off. As it turned out, he managed to keep his work secret and there was no increase in the shelling of the area. It was unusually good work—and luck.

Front-line soldiers remained extraordinarily jumpy about the possibilities of being mined. After the war, Harvey★, by then a Major-General, revealed that for a while the whole of the 1st Army was ready to go back if the tunnellers eased their defensive efforts underneath. The other armies shared its fear. Tunnelling officers were constantly being asked to make dangerous, wearisome journeys to investigate sounds that turned out to be harmless. Most often the noise came from wood being chopped in a near-by dug-out. Sometimes it was rats nesting or foraging. But the infantry were slow to accept such explanations. Cassels, of 175 Company, invented a bogus wooden box fitted with battery and impressive looking headphones that he used for difficult cases; it helped him to sound convincing. Tunnelling officers were increasingly inclined to delegate the job of checking up to N.C.O.'s and sappers. One-seventy-seven Company went further and appointed two elderly coal miners, Sappers Laughton and Bickley, as visiting listeners. They were chosen mainly because their hearing was poor, and are said to have originated a coarse joke that spread widely through the British army and was even picked up by the Germans. To anxious infantrymen they would say, "Yes, we hear them. They're there all right. They seem to be fornicating." The hoped-for reply was an astonished, "What—the Germans?" to which Laughton and Bickley would say, "No—not the Germans—the rats." And walk away.

★ At an after-dinner speech on November 26th, 1926, General Harvey said (of the 1st Army): "The men would not stay above unless the miners were underneath. That is a fact."

On the other hand, the infantry often felt that genuinely suspicious sounds were ignored. Relations between surface and below-ground troops were sometimes strained as a result.

Tunnelling affairs were causing trouble in London also at this time. Homer, who had first taken over recruiting duties from Norton Griffiths, had been transferred. Norton Griffiths had recommended a successor, a civilian named Miles Bailey, who was duly appointed and whom he hoped to keep under his control. But Bailey resented being given instructions and the two men were soon at loggerheads.

Norton Griffiths found it unbearably vexing that Bailey, sitting in his office and appointed on his say-so, should insist on making independent decisions. The trouble, as usual, centred on the quality of the recruits being signed up. Early in May, Norton Griffiths sent written instructions to Bailey to go very slowly on signing up men at the six-shilling rate, and to accept as many at two-and-two as he could. Because of the discontent there had been over pay rates, he was more than ever determined to promote men in the field. But Bailey replied that the War Office was still banning the transfer of men already enlisted and no longer wished him to recruit mates at two-and-two. He had been told he could still enlist clay kickers at six shillings.

The position seemed nonsensical and Norton Griffiths felt—and said so openly—that Bailey should sign the cheaper men and send them to France too quickly for the War Office to realize what was happening. It was what he would certainly do himself. Instead, Miles Bailey carried on recruiting at the higher rate. By about the 17th of May, Norton Griffiths's patience ran out and he left for London. He was determined to bring at least 1,000 men back with him as tunnellers and mates, and to establish a better understanding with both Miles Bailey and the War Office.

He went at once to the depot—his own office—and with characteristic bluntness put the position, as he saw it, to Bailey. He had three main points to make: First, that authority given to Bailey by the War Office was subject to his control. Second, that he was going to annul arrangements Bailey had already made to send seventeen miners to France as six-shilling tunnellers. Third, that Bailey was to stop signing men at this rate. Having said all this, Norton Griffiths departed on a visit to the mining centres of England in search of recruits. In the Midlands, he traced the names and regiments of twenty-one serving men who all had the right sort of experience to be tunnellers. Ignoring the recent War Office ruling on the matter, he wired the Adjutant-General asking that the men be all transferred. The nonplussed Adjutant-General's department referred the wire to Kitchener, who approved it. Norton Griffiths heard the decision on Monday, the 24th. He was delighted and described it as "the thin edge of the wedge". He told Bailey to keep on wiring names in batches of ten or twenty at a time in the same way.

The next day he called on the Stoke colliery owners. They gave off what he later described as "a considerable amount of hot air" but pointed out that men were not easily spared. Eventually they promised to call a special meeting the following day to see if they could raise a draft of a hundred.

That day the harassed War Office announced a new ruling—that the tunnelling companies could have up to a maximum of 100 men transferred so long as no more than five were taken from any one battalion. Norton Griffiths was scornful of the decision and wrote bitterly to Harvey about it. He mentioned that a general he had spoken to at York had said that 500 men could be spared and not missed. If true (which Norton Griffiths would not have bothered to check) it made the trouble and delay doubly exasperating.

There was worse trouble coming. Miles Bailey's irritation with what he regarded as interference by Norton Griffiths, had been mounting. On Friday, the 28th, he wrote to the Director of Organization at the War Office giving his version of what was going on. He asked for a ruling: was he correct in believing that he was to carry out War Office instructions, and only War Office instructions, or not?

The War Office reacted swiftly. An immediate letter was sent to Fowke stating that Norton Griffiths was "causing complications", had no credentials and was behaving irregularly. His recall to France was bluntly demanded. After a three-day delay, the War Office wrote a further letter to Norton Griffiths pointing out coldly that he was attached to G.H.Q. and that the tunnelling depot was under the control of Bailey who was not to be given instructions by him.

Norton Griffiths was flabbergasted at these events. He denied that he was interfering and claimed that after thinking it over Bailey regretted having made the complaint. To Harvey, who was sympathetic, he confided that he was up against a "swollen head", which he described as a dangerous complaint. "My only consideration," he added, "is not to let the Chief down." But the Chief apparently wrote that he should return to France at once and Norton Griffiths replied on the 31st that he was making arrangements to do so. Probably he was glad enough to go. He hated what he used to describe as the "War Office frills". In passing, he added that it was not easy to "pick up a thousand men suitable for our work". To the last minute he was recruiting as hard as he could go. On the 2nd of June he started back for the front.

His rumpus was only one of many that were bedevilling the Allied war effort at that time. Nineteen-fifteen was a year of bad generalship, bad luck and (at unfortunate moments for the Allies) bad weather. As a result, it also became a year of bad temper. In a moment of bitterness, Sir John French sacked his senior Army Commander, General Sir Horace Smith-Dorrien, giving no clear reason. Sir John also became involved in bitter arguments with his French counterpart, General Joffre. Joffre, in turn, nagged at the British authorities for not taking enough of the war burden into their hands. The British and French High Commands squabbled over strategy and the disposition of troops in the line. Throughout Britain there was much private and public unrest as the casualty figures climbed from thousands to tens of thousands—and there still seemed so little to show for it all. At the two battles of Ypres, precious ground and an enormous number of lives had been lost. When the first big British push—the Battle of Neuve Chapelle—

ended in mid-March, only trivial gains had been won; on the other hand losses had been spectacular and alarmingly poor staffwork had been revealed. Festubert, which had followed in May and was fought just a mile or so south of the Neuve Chapelle fields, had brought another poor result: nearly 17,000 men lost—again for a trivial advance. But the most serious revelation about Festubert was splashed in *The Times* of May 14th: British soldiers had been hopelessly hampered by a shortage of shells. Anger swept through the country. It was echoed in a Cabinet conference held that day which Winston Churchill attended as First Lord of the Admiralty. He later described the mood of the meeting as "sulphurous". Within two weeks a new coalition cabinet was formed.

The stress of a complex and brutal war was certainly beginning to show. From the Russian and Italian fronts, the news was also bad. Britain's and France's fighting friends were in serious trouble. And the Gallipoli venture, for which so much had been hoped, was in a terrible state of muddle. There was still a further serious blow to come for Britain before 1915 ended—the Battle of Loos. It was fought to support an enormous and unsuccessful French offensive further south in Champagne. From the beginning nearly everything that could go wrong, did. The weather, as usual, was adverse. Gas was being used for the first time by the British and the breeze dropped, fluttered and backed so much as zero approached that an attempt was made to cancel the attack. Later, drizzle fell and a ground mist developed which hindered the troops as they attempted to advance. But there were grave errors of generalship on the part of the Commander-in-Chief also, and General Sir Douglas Haig, in command of the 1st Army, protested about them later to the War Office.

When Norton Griffiths returned to France in June, French and British army chiefs were already holding the talks that were to lead to the disasters of Champagne and Loos. Another subject being discussed was Britain's share of the war. Joffre was painfully frank. He felt—and said—that the British should be holding much more of the front line. He won his point. Orders were given to the 2nd

Army to spread itself to the north, above Ypres. The move took place on June 7th, five days after Norton Griffiths arrived back. It meant that his already impossibly long beat was suddenly two miles longer. At about this time he apparently began to feel that too much was being asked of him, and he was heard to say that the tunnellers should be "overlooked by a general".

There was a much greater shock to come. Joffre was still dissatisfied with the British effort and now badgered the War Office and the C.-in-C. to take over a 21-mile stretch of the line down near the River Somme. Sir John French was angrily opposed to the proposal. The Somme was more than sixty miles south of Ypres. Any British force down there would be cut off from the rest of the expeditionary force. But again Joffre had his way. The British 3rd Army was formed in mid-July and moved down to take over its part of the front in August.

Between it and the rest of the British front line was a fifteen mile gap manned by the French 10th Army. Norton Griffiths's liaison task was much more than doubled by the decision. Besides sheer distance, he would have to talk his way through the French sector each time he made his way down to the 3rd Army tunnelling units. He was poorly equipped to do it. Despite two French expressions that he loved to tack jestingly on to his everyday speech—"*n'est'ce pas?*" and "*absolument*"—he could hardly speak a word of the language. It was becoming clear to tunnelling officers everywhere that drastic changes in the control of mining operations were needed. Norton Griffiths's own view that the job required a general (with presumably a general's staff) was already beginning to be shared both at G.H.Q. and the War Office. By early August, 13 Tunnelling Companies had been authorized. Before the end of the month Fowke was recommending another seven. The strength of each company, with attached working parties drawn from near by infantry units—fluctuated up to about 1,000 men. The consumption of man-power had become frightening. Was it worthwhile? Many senior commanders were beginning to ask the question. There is evidence that among them was the Chief—General Fowke.

And it had to be admitted that so far the bulk of the mining work had consisted of defence rather than attack. It had been a matter of burrowing out to meet approaching German miners, then firing small charges—known as camouflets—designed to destroy the enemy workings without making craters on the surface.

There was no concealing that the Germans were still achieving much better results; always they were turning up somewhere under the British lines. While Norton Griffiths was in London, the 5th Battalion the Lincolnshire Regiment was busy listening with mounting anxiety to sounds from below their trench—"E.1 left" in the Mount Kemmel sector, about four miles south of Ypres. Muffled thumps and even voices had been heard.

At three o'clock in the afternoon of May 20th, a young officer of the regiment, Lieutenant Eric Dyson, was sitting in a dug-out talking by telephone to another officer in the rear when it happened. The conversation was never finished. Suddenly Dyson was aware of darkness and a crushing weight around his body. Gradually the truth sank in as his mind cleared. The German mine had been blown. He was deeply buried under many tons of debris. Though, as it was later discovered, he had been flung a distance of more than 20 yards to the side, the corrugated iron roof of the dug-out had travelled with him, wedging itself over his head on hitting the ground. Because of it he could breathe. But he was jammed in the debris doubled up like a jack-knife, his head forced over his knees in a position of frightful discomfort. He found he was still holding the telephone in his hand. It made a useful weapon for tapping a roof timber in the hope the noise might be heard. Fourteen hours of seemingly endless loneliness and darkness passed, and then the rescuers dug through. Dyson was permanently injured— but alive. Fifteen other unfortunates had died. Four were never found.

Shortly before leaving on his visit to Miles Bailey in London, Norton Griffiths had had an idea that excited him. It still did, whatever bad news there might be from the front. Through all the worries of the following weeks, it occupied his mind.

The idea came to him first while he stood in heavy rain during the evening of Wednesday, May 12th, inspecting the two-mile length of front facing Wytschaete and Messines on the German-held ridge. He stayed in the area that night and spent part of it studying trench maps. Wytschaete was on the foremost tip of a sweeping bow projected towards the British. The rim of the bow started in the north at St. Eloi and ran about three and a half miles through Wytschaete to Messines. As Norton Griffiths studied the maps before him, he became sure that the bow could be mined and the Germans blown cleanly off it. Here was the sort of opportunity the tunnelling companies needed. It seemed a fine chance for the tunnellers to do a serious attack—the sort of undertaking he had always foreseen and which had somehow never happened. Even the one major mining offensive that had been made (at Hill 60) had ended in failure. This time, Norton Griffiths was sure valuable ground could not only be taken with the help of mining, but held. Success would shorten the British line and would drive the Germans off an important vantage point.

At once he sent the idea—which he described as a "most useful mining programme"—to Harvey for consideration by the Chief. He explained that six mines at strategic points might do the job he had in mind, but it was most important that these points be well chosen. He hinted that the selection should not be left to local R.E. commanders. Instead, he suggested, he should study the possibilities most closely, then pass his views on to the Chief so that he, in turn, could "discuss" the proposals with the local engineers. With the proposal, he sent a crude, diagrammatic sketch. It consisted simply of an arc like a large Capital C with three crosses for St. Eloi, Wytschaete and Messines in line to the right of it.

Brigadier-General Fowke—the exuberant sportsman who broke his rackets, fluffed his catches and roared with laughter at his "rotten luck"—reacted unexpectedly. He was furious. Colonel Harvey was with him when he cast an incredulous eye over his liaison officer's proposal. He rejected it at once with, as Harvey later said, "contumely".

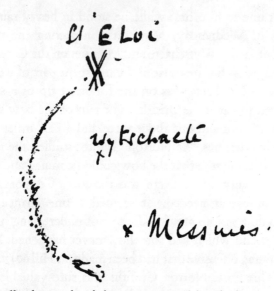

The hurriedly-drawn sketch by Norton Griffiths which started the idea of
a great mining attack against Messines Ridge

There were almost certainly two reasons why Fowke threw out
what was in time to turn into one of the most momentous ideas of
the war. There was first the knowledge that British tunnellers were
not even able to fend off their German counterparts, and could
hardly therefore afford ambitious offensives. Second—and more
personally—Fowke's good humour and immense reserves of common sense had made him everyone's consultant at G.H.Q. He was
grossly overworked and dealt with many non-engineering, purely
military matters as the months passed. By the next February his
ability as an all-purpose administrator was to be recognized. He
was then knighted, promoted to Lieutenant-General and appointed
Adjutant-General to the Forces.

Norton Griffiths, as indefatigable as ever, was not put off by his
chief's reaction. He began talking with great persistance to Harvey
about the idea of combining heavy mines with a general action at
Messines. Harvey became interested and grew increasingly so as
time passed.

Meanwhile, there were more immediate matters that had to be worked out. In the main they were the old ones of recruiting and tools. It seemed impossible to obtain enough men of the proper calibre. During September, three experienced miners joined as tunnellers' mates at Ossett Town Hall. Two were drunk at the time. The third, Sapper Hubert Leather, saw them a few days later in Rouen. One of them was acutely depressed. His wife did not know where he was, he explained, and there was no way he could tell her because he was unable to write. Leather was going on a short leave and promised to tell the man's wife that her husband was now in 185 Company. The other man was quite cheerful. He was over 50 and had lost his false teeth. He said he had asked for a medical board and would be discharged. Soon afterwards he was.

French miners were still manning some of the mines down near the Somme because the British simply could not produce enough men at the time of the take-over. Parts of the rest of the front were also inadequately protected and infantry units, in desperation, were still transferring men to the extemporized Brigade Mining Sections. Norton Griffiths disliked this trend, which had absorbed many men he might otherwise have had, and was becoming very anxious to take all the amateur sections over.

The matter became more complicated by the fact that as the Brigade Mining Sections grew they developed an *esprit de corps* of their own. They were proud of their contribution. However, it remained obvious to Norton Griffiths that these "amateur" miners would eventually have to be absorbed. By mid-September he had evolved a take-over scheme which, he said, would make the Chief "smile with joy at the quiet way the deed would be done". And a few months later it was to come about. But some Brigade Miners refused resolutely to make the switch. One of these was a 49-man Brigade Tunnellers unit under Lieutenant Aubrey Moore. This little section twice met the Germans underground in the Ypres-Messines area and fought with exceptional verve. When asked to transfer to the Tunnellers in the spring of 1916, Moore and all but two of the others declined, and returned to their original units. The two who did so changed their minds and left again later.

About lack of equipment Norton Griffiths was at times close to despair. In July, he put it to the Chief most earnestly that mining required prompt delivery of materials, and he complained that at present it was taking weeks and often months for anything ordered to arrive.

Much of the gear that was delivered continued to be useless. During or about the month of August a 178 Tunnelling Company officer, Lieutenant Edmund Pryor, went to book in special ventilating equipment that had arrived by lorry from England. It had come specially quickly because it was so urgently needed at the front. When he saw what the lorry was carrying, he stared for a moment in disbelief. There were four immense underwater diving bells for use on the sea bed. They were quite useless. A preposterous mistake had been made. After exhausting months of quite desperate fighting underground, of no leave, little sleep and almost non-stop action, it was too much for Pryor to bear.

He sat down beside the lorry and wept.

7

BITTERNESS IN THE SOUTH

EDMUND PRYOR reported to the newly formed 178 Tunnelling Company in late summer, 1915. Though only 21, he was a full lieutenant with nearly a year's active service behind him.

Pryor, a student mining engineer, had joined up at the outbreak of war and been gazetted a second-lieutenant in the 8th Battalion the Norfolk Regiment, then with the 53rd Brigade. The Tunnelling Company was being set up in the village of Meaulte, near the Somme, where the Brigade was also organizing its headquarters. It was part of the British army's frantic rush to take over this part of the line from the French. An intricate though badly constructed mining system was part of the inheritance, and had to be manned. At the time of Pryor's transfer, 200 miners went with him—all from the 53rd Brigade.

The Officer Commanding the new company was a dashing and handsome grandson of the Duke of Wellington, Captain Edward Wellesley, transferred from 171 Company. He, too, was a very young man—of 26. From the beginning, Pryor was greatly impressed by his daring and powers of leadership.

By now the tunnelling companies were beginning to take on a discernible character. They were lusty, cheerful, extremely efficient at their work and still determinedly unmilitary. Pryor found that Wellesley was running 178 Company like a civilian engineering firm. Rank and standing were much less important than knowledge and ability. Pryor, the boyish lieutenant, was made senior trench officer and was at first surprised to find that he had three much more experienced engineers beneath him.

In fact, he had no cause for uneasiness. The older men, who

were already serving happily under their young captain, were content with the arrangement. They were treated—and respected—like civilian consultants. There were moments when Pryor found it difficult to believe that he and the others were really all serving soldiers, subject to the exactitudes of military discipline. Drills were unheard of, the word "Sir" was rare and saluting seemed even rarer. Officers were free to wear what they liked while on shift. Pryor's own standard rig was a dirty white sweater, stores-issue slacks and tennis shoes with, usually, a caged bird in his hand for gas detection. Some officers wore gardening gloves and knee-pads—and crawled through the workings with their caged canaries dangling from a string gripped in their teeth.

A tremendous air of urgency was at once detectable at the Company's headquarters. The Somme front at this time was active in places, quiet in others. Certain French and German units had developed an amazing cordiality—and were even said to share sleeping quarters in one convenient village.* But Pryor's company took over a small, dangerously exposed and very active nib of highish ground known as Tambour du Clos, by the village of Fricourt. A few yards away, one of the most experienced of the British companies—174—was also starting work.

Tambour du Clos was a valuable viewing-point from which the important cathedral town of Amiens could be seen. German sappers were pressing furiously to win it. A 174 officer, Lieutenant Laurence Hill, has told of how a French soldier showed him round, pointed downwards at several spots and said, "*Tres dangereux. Boche mine. Poof!*" Each time he made an upward gesture with his hands. Hill wryly observed that the Frenchman, who was due to leave the sector, was very cheerful.

Such good humour was not shared by the senior French commanders. They were anxious to be off to other parts of the line and were exasperated by what looked to them like British slow-footedness and muddle. But the British seem to have been rushing their arrangements as earnestly as they could. Two new officers sent to

* *A History of the World War.* Liddell Hart.

174 Company were not allowed time to buy uniforms and arrived dressed as privates; they were at once put to work by an N.C.O. cook and such an angry scene followed that Norton Griffiths decided to send them on to another company. Men were still being recruited in frantic haste and many arrived at the front unattested. Pryor was given the unusual job of swearing a number in on the battlefield.

His company and another—179—were brought officially into existence on July 10th. By mid-September, authority had been given for 10 more to follow at once—eight of which were destined for the Somme regions. And, of course, there was 174 Company of longer standing already there. But units simply could not be set up as quickly as the precarious situation required. As it turned out, the French were obliged to leave sapper units in the area for months longer, working alongside their ally. As late as spring next year, the British General Staff was forced to make a humiliating appeal for five companies of "*sapeur-mineurs*" to be left for a further month with the 3rd Army.

Pryor's first examination of the front line was a shock. The trenches were very shallow and had the bodies of French soldiers lying two and three deep on the bottom. There was great reluctance to dig through this human putrescence for greater depth and so the trenches were left as they were. Pryor, six feet two inches tall, found that the parapet top came only to about his chest level. Yet the Germans were a mere 30 yards away and to be seen was almost certainly to die. After long stretches of up to 8 hours, stooped either in the trench or tunnel, he was often nearly frantic with fatigue.

Mining in the Tambour du Clos-Fricourt area was done in solid chalk which lay below a shallow layer of surface clay. It called for techniques that differed greatly from the ones used further north in the deep clay of Flanders.

Chalk was better for mining work in some ways. It was cleaner, much less sticky material than clay and required little timbering until it had been broken up by repeated mine explosions. But chalk brought special hazards, too. Mining operations were unavoidably noisy and each side had to accept the fact that the other could hear it coming. There was also the problem of what to do with excavated material; its dazzling whiteness meant that any lying loose could easily be seen by German airmen who would know what conclusions to draw. Above all, there were gravely increased risks of gas poisoning. Carbon monoxide given off by mine explosions was found to linger in cracks and pockets of chalk, seeping slowly and continuously into the workings. A day seldom passed with less than three men in Pryor's company becoming gas casualties of varying seriousness. Sometimes the number rose to fifteen. And there were constant risks of explosion.

Once, after an enemy blow, an officer, Second-Lieutenant Robert Mackilligin, hurried to the shaft top planning to go down to the help of sappers trapped below. The workings were in total darkness. Mackilligin struck a match to light his candle and a tremendous blast of hot air drove past him at that instant. Brilliant popping flames were left dancing around him—then consciousness went. He woke up on a stretcher and thinking back realized the explosion had saved his life. Had he ventured down into such a concentration of gas, he would have died in moments. When workings were so heavily soaked in gas it took days to clear them.

The company had three combat orders to obey. First, the high ground of Tambour du Clos must be held. Second, all enemy tunnels must be intercepted and destroyed. Third, every effort must be made to mine the Germans from their trenches so that British surface troops could advance to take them.

To 178 Company's engineers, the French system they had inherited seemed full of Gallic unreason. Tunnels went at varying depths and in puzzling directions a few yards towards the enemy and stopped. Some had a charging chamber at the end, some had not. Many had already been blown in and were unsalvable. There were suspicious signs, too, that some of the tunnels were not where the French drawings showed them. The British engineers set about overhauling and improving the system.

The existing forward trench followed round the perimeter of the Tambour. At strategic points, holes were cut into the front wall or the trench to become entrances. They were extended into tunnels about five feet high by three feet wide which ran outwards towards the enemy, sloping down as they went. Each stopped about 12 feet out and became a vertical shaft plummetting down some 30 feet into the chalk bed. Access was by ladder or, in some cases, merely a rope. At the bottom, the shafts were linked by a sideways-running, candle-lit gallery which followed exactly the line of the front trench.

Little fighing tunnels were then poked out as needed like pointing fingers from the subterraneous gallery towards the Germans. They could be used simply as advanced listening posts—or packed with a small charge and fired when the enemy was heard coming near. Most of the mines fired were camouflets which collapsed the German tunnels and flooded them with gas.

Pryor found the pace extremely fast from his first moments at the front. The Germans had pushed several headings towards the British line during the take-over period and had to be fought back. Three shifts were formed to keep the effort going 24 hours a day, each under the control of a senior trench officer. After every four days in the line, shifts were given two off for recuperation.

As a flow of listeners' reports telling of suspicious noises came in, Pryor—as "Senior Trench"—with Wellesley and the consultants—had to make hurried, on the spot decisions about how best to act. The narrow finger-like tunnels would be forced out towards the sound at top speed, loaded and fired.

A nerve-shaking blind-man's-buff developed as the sweating miners on both sides strove to out-think and out-work their enemies. Victory came to the man who knew when his opponent was going to blow. The danger signal was a sudden silence—the usual sign that digging had stopped and a charge was being laid. It was then that a grave decision had to be made—whether to stay at work in the hope of charging and blowing a counter-mine first or to withdraw for the moment, abandoning the tunnel to whatever fate was waiting. Officers took great pride in guessing well and the sappers quickly came to know whose judgement to trust and whose to fear.

Artificial digging noises were sometimes made to hoodwink the enemy while a mine was being charged. After the war, Laurence Hill of the neighbouring 174 Company told how a young unnamed Second-Lieutenant did this successfully on this Tambour-Fricourt front. His mine had been charged with 1,000 lbs. of ammonal, had been tamped and wired ready for firing when the Second-Lieutenant realized that German digging had stopped. He concluded that the German sappers had guessed the situation correctly and withdrawn to safety. The young officer determined to lure them back to the mine.

Alone, he returned to his own dark tunnel and began picking energetically at the sides. For variety, he shouted, threw digging tools about and hauled a clattering train of tin cans up and down the gallery. After a while the Germans were reassured and resumed their digging.

As soon as he heard them, the sweating, panting Second-Lieutenant raced out of the tunnel to the exploder already set up in the trench and threw himself on the plunger. At the moment the mine went off, the Corps Commander, Lieutenant-General Sir Thomas Morland, was passing along the trench with an escort of senior officers on a rapid inspection of the front-line system. The sudden heave of the explosion dislodged a number of sandbags from the parapet which spilled on to the General. The usual reprisal for a mine-firing was an immediate increase in the shelling rate and it began now—while the General was still being brushed down by his staff. As the ground shook and quivered from the bombardment, the inspecting party hurried round into a traverse in some confusion. There they met the Second-Lieutenant dressed in the usual tunneller's rags, covered entirely in chalk-dust and still standing beside the exploder box. He bowed gravely towards the party. "All my own work, gentlemen," he said.

As senior trench officer, Pryor's duties were supposed to be mainly supervisory. But such was the excitement and challenge of the situation that he found himself constantly down at the mine faces. Much of the time he spent listening for the enemy. There were still no scientific aids available although some officers had begun to try out stethoscopes. Pryor, gifted with excellent hearing, preferred to rely on his own unaided ears pressed hard up against the chilling chalk.

He became accustomed to the sounds of enemy work. Sometimes, in fissured ground, he heard German voices quite clearly. The knocking of timbering, the clonk of hand picking and even the muffled bumping of chalk-filled bags being dragged away were common sounds. There were times, too, when flakes of chalk fell from the roof due to enemy vibrations while Pryor crouched, still and listening.

Great care had to be taken that lighted candles and explosives never met. The danger was much increased by the fact that charges were always laid with burning type fuses as well as electrical ones. Once Pryor was making his way up from the face after laying a charge when he saw with horror that a candle was alight immediately below the orange burner fuse pegged to the gallery wall. The fuse was already connected to the charge—a heavy one laid in two chambers. He rushed at the candle but found that the fuse had already started to burn on the outside. When the inner core of gunpowder ignited, the flash would race down to the charge at 88 feet per second. And his sappers were still down there, tamping the charge with bagged chalk.

Pryor knocked the candle aside then, grabbing the stout fuse a few feet lower down, tore at it with his hands and teeth. In a frenzy of effort he parted it in time. But disaster had only been averted by a second.

A strict order was in force that candles were not to be lit when charging was in progress—electric torches were to be used instead. Pryor never found out who had placed this one where it was. There seemed little doubt that someone had come down from above to do it deliberately.

Besides being in constant danger from mine attack, the Tambour du Clos was probably under the heaviest sustained fire of any part of the 3rd Army front. This was a serious additional hazard for 178 Company sappers since they had to scramble to and fro between the mine and Meaulte—where they were quartered when off shift. Working parties constantly carrying away heavy bags of chalk for disposal had an even worse time of it from the shells and bullets. Casualties were often very heavy. At one time the Germans appeared to have pulled up some heavy artillery in support of the usual lighter howitzers and mortars. One day while the trench rocked and trembled under the barrage, an enemy aircraft joined in, ripping the line up and down with machine-gun fire. Pryor was making his way along the front at the time and met a cheerful looking infantry sergeant. "How are you keeping, Sergeant?" he asked with dry humour. "Are you worried?"

The sergeant cocked an ear jauntily towards the German lines and laughed. "Worried, sir?" he replied. "If I worried enough to do justice to this bloody mess I'd go mad. No, I'm just carrying on." Pryor left him feeling curiously moved by his indomitable good humour.

At about the same time, Autumn 1915, he witnessed some unforgettable bravery on the part of one of the "consultants", Second-Lieutenant Alfred Mackilligin.* The two men had been touring the mine and emerged in daylight into the trench leading to Pryor's dug-out. Pryor came first and reaching down to an old tree root near the foot of the rear wall of the trench, pulled himself out. Mackilligin followed. At that moment Pryor heard a sharp crack from behind but, thinking little of it, walked on, talking as he went.

As they entered the dug-out, Mackilligin—who had been following closely—murmured, "Spread a paper for me, Pryor." Pryor looked round. Mackilligin was very white and very calm. His lower forearm and right hand had become a shapeless jelly, hit by a rifle grenade the moment he left the tunnel. There was surprisingly

* Brother of Robert Mackilligin mentioned on page 96.

little blood. Pryor picked off the shreds of flesh and urged him to lie down while he sent for a stretcher party. But when the stretcher arrived, Mackilligan refused to use it and walked to the casualty clearing station without help, the stretcher following on behind. Pryor knew he would always remember the courage and coolness of this man.

As the months passed by, much deeper tunnels were dug. These varied from about 70 feet to well over 100 feet down. Fighting continued at the 30-foot level also and, at both levels, conditions became increasingly hideous. The constant collapsing and re-opening of tunnels broke the chalk into finer and finer particles. As these mixed with water seeping down from shell craters on the surface, a stiff, glutinous liquid resulted. It was extremely difficult to mine through. And when sappers were killed underground and their bodies pulverized by explosions, the chalky water oozing through the tunnels became discoloured with blood. In places the spectacle was overwhelmingly ugly.

The ooze also made the rescue of trapped miners dangerous and slow. Once a rescue team heard indistinct tapping noises coming from a cut-off portion of a deep mine after an enemy blow. More usually, trapped men were quickly killed by the concussion or gas, but this time there seemed a chance of survivors. An all-out effort was at once started to clear the tunnel.

The chalk was in so liquified a state that it had to be close-timbered all the way. After the rescue party had dug and strutted their way through about 30 feet, shouts for help could be heard and there was now no doubt that some of the men were living. But the sounds were muffled and it was clear that a considerable distance still had to be travelled. The rescuers now began to doubt whether, at the present rate, cut off from fresh air, the trapped men could live until help arrived.

The other Mackilligin—Robert—was the officer in charge. He ordered a pilot hole, very narrow and unsupported by timbering to be pushed with the utmost speed towards the men. The rescue team took it in turns to wriggle forward on their stomachs, clawing at the putty-like chalk with their hands, passing it back as best they could. The tiny, treacherous tunnel had gone 20 feet when, suddenly, the man at the face called that he could see two survivors by the light of his torch. They were 10 feet ahead and lying pinned down on their faces by shattered timber.

Mackilligin ordered the rescuer back and himself wriggled forward through the ooze to encourage the men and see how best to save them. With him he took an air line.

The men had a dazed look in their eyes but were fully conscious and now hopeful. Mackilligin observed that the timber pinning them down was also what had saved them—by keeping the crushing weight of fallen chalk off their heads and chests. But close behind was a rapidly rising pool of water dammed back by the debris and almost ready to overflow. As Mackilligin studied the situation in dismay, he felt the tunnel tightening round his own body. It was closing up and he knew that he had only a moment until it swallowed him completely. He began to fight his way back. Already he had delayed too long and movement was difficult. Fortunately, a miner had come gallantly up behind him and helped now by hauling at his feet.

Before he lost sight of the doomed men, the flood broke free and swirled round their faces. While still wrestling with the slippery chalk for his own life, Mackilligin saw them gulp the chalky water and die. At least the end was quick.

Edmund Pryor found that he was a successful trench officer, good at the guessing game. But the strain on his nerves was enormous. He became slowly aware of mounting tension and an often intolerable fatigue.

It was not only the non-stop gamble with death that strained a tunneller's endurance. There was also the lack of sleep, hard physical work and the repeated small doses of carbon monoxide. The gas was a great trial to all the men. In small amounts it caused giddiness, breathlessness and headaches, followed quickly by painful vomiting and retching. Often victims struggling up an escape shaft were suddenly hit with muscular paralysis, and in some cases fell to the bottom as a result. There they almost invariably died. Sometimes they appeared to have recovered, then suffered unexpected relapses and died. Ironically, due to the action of the gas on the blood, victims always looked in rosy good health.

Towards the end of the year, Pryor detected noises that he was sure could be only one thing: a German tunnel dangerously far advanced and headed towards the most forward British observation post in the area. Immediate action was essential. He sent word to the Commanding Officer—Wellesley—at base, asking permission to drive an emergency tunnel towards the sounds. Wellesley gave permission at once and work began.

Pryor went below ground with the men and demanded the utmost speed. Already he was sure he could hear German tamping going into place—which meant that the charge was laid and might be fired at any time. The men, well aware of the game they were playing with fate, responded superbly. At this time it was accepted that the fastest driving rate through chalk for a normal sized, timbered gallery was about one foot per hour. Pryor's men now began to drive forward nine times as fast. The tunnel was only two feet square and untimbered, but it was still an astounding pace.

When they had gone 45 feet—and as far as they dared—Pryor himself wriggled down the tiny tunnel which was little larger in girth than a coffin. He went feet first, face uppermost towards the Germans, with the clear knowledge that the heavy chalk just inches above his nose would drop to crush him at any moment if they fired their mine.

At the end of the tunnel he called for gelignite. It was pushed down to him in 50 lb. sacks. He hauled it, sack by sack, over his face and down his body to his feet, then kicked it into position. He placed five tons this way, lodged it as firmly as he could by ramming chalk-filled bags after it, then wriggled out with aching arms and caked in a mix of chalk-dust and sweat.

Parked near the safe end of the communication trench, Pryor had a motor-cycle. He scrambled out of the mine, raced to the machine and sped away towards headquarters to seek permission to fire the charge. It would have been quicker to telephone, but the Germans seemed somehow to be intercepting calls, and Pryor knew that if they overheard this request they would certainly fire their mine at once.

At base in Meaulte, Pryor had a shock. Wellesley refused permission for the charge to be fired. Often when a mine was ready, infantry and artillery commanders were consulted to see what support they could give it. To Pryor's astonishment, Wellesley had plans of this kind in mind.

Pryor pleaded and argued his case. The mine was a small one and purely defensive. It was 40 feet deep and not likely even to crater. Above all, if it were not blown *now*, he was sure the Germans would blow theirs first. But Wellesley had made up his mind. He told Pryor not to be "windy" and to return to his post to await further orders.

It was four in the afternoon. Pryor sat in his dug-out in a state of torment. He was confident, to the point of certainty, that the Germans were going to blow. In the past he had guessed rightly as a rule and the men had trust in him. They were down there now, carrying on with the usual shift work and in—as Pryor believed— the gravest danger. At ten that night he risked a telephone call to Wellesley. The reply was blunt: If he interfered in any way, or bothered the C.O. any more about the matter, he would be court martialled. As Pryor put the telephone down, it seemed he had gone as far as he could.

But by three in the morning Pryor, frantic now, decided he could bear it no longer. A court martial, almost anything seemed better than just waiting for what he *knew* must happen. On an impulse, he scrambled down the nearest shaft and through the main connecting gallery shouting for every man to leave the mine at once. As they began to come up from their tunnels he explained that he had urgent work for them to do on the surface.

He was standing in the trench with all but three of the 22 men who had been down the mine safely on top when the Germans fired. He heard the crumping sound—not very loud but extremely menacing—and felt the ground shake. Simultaneously, the German guns opened up on the area to hamper mine rescue attempts. But this time no rescue work was needed. A heavy wad of chalk had crashed up the tunnel at enormous speed killing the men still below ground with such force that their bodies all but disappeared. The only trace Pryor could find when he was next down was one hand sticking partly out from the tunnel wall.

After the incident was over, Pryor found that his admiration for Wellesley was not diminished. He realized that a commanding officer had more than one crisis to cater for and, at a time when false hunches were commonplace, the decision had not been unreasonable. And in fact the Germans had blown prematurely, too short to damage the observation post they were presumed to be after.

Another harrowing incident followed soon after. Pryor was at work in his dug-out, plotting the day's progress and the suspected positions of enemy mines, yawning with weariness and rubbing the sleep from his eyes, when a soldier rushed in breathless and excited. He brought news of a breakthrough into a German tunnel.

Pryor no longer felt tired. He dashed along the trench to the mine entrance and was underground in seconds. By the usual flickering candlelight he could see that the report was evidently true.

The main gallery connecting the vertical entrance and exit shafts had recently been damaged by an enemy blow. In repairing it the tunnellers had uncovered a quite unsuspected tunnel beneath them. It was already tamped with heavy lumps of chalk and was therefore —presumably—charged. They had seen at once that it was heading accurately towards the British front and support trenches. Pryor sent a runner at the double to headquarters five miles away to report the news. Then he cleared the mine and notified the local infantry commander to remove his men from the danger zone.

There remained only one immediate thing to do—the investigation of the tunnel. Inwardly, Pryor dreaded this more than any other duty. He was sure that when the Germans heard or saw their mine being dismantled, they would blow it at once. If for any reason they could not, they would surely be waiting for him, armed and ready, underground. But it was a job he knew he had to do himself. With a revolver in his pocket, two Mills bombs beside him and three strong, unmarried sappers standing near in the main gallery, he began to drag out the heavy tamping with his hands. He dug like a dog at a rathole. Soon his fingers were torn and bleeding but he laboured on for two agonizing hours of suspense. By then he had cleared the tunnel and found that it seemed to be an abandoned section that started nowhere and ended nowhere. There were fuse leads in it—but no charge. In utter perplexity he crouched gazing at the mystery when his mind began to float and a moment later he fainted.

When consciousness returned, he was lying on the firestep of the trench, out in the open air, gazing into the pale moonlight of the night. Wellesley was bending over him. "I *am* sorry, Pryor—I'm *damn* sorry," he was saying. The C.O. went on to explain that a French surveyor had taken a bad bearing and set his sappers to work digging a tunnel in the wrong direction. Out of deference to French feelings, it had been filled in and not shown on British maps. Pryor was being told that he had endured his worst two hours for nothing.

Wellesley now made him an offer—the Military Cross or two weeks' leave. Pryor found it an easy decision. He asked for the leave which he felt he badly needed and, soon after, left for home. Precious days followed—of nourishing food, hot baths and regular sleep. He soon felt physically and mentally much the better for the rest.

On his return to the front, he found he had been posted as a staff officer to a nearby C.R.E.'s office. For a while the fighting war seemed to be over for him. But when he called in at 178 Company headquarters to say good-bye, he was immediately asked if he would do one more tour of duty in the mine. The Company, he was told, was extremely short of officers. Pryor gladly consented.

Another senior trench officer had meanwhile been appointed and Pryor now took his orders from him. He was put on listening duties in one of the new very deep shafts in an area that was said to be safe. To his trained ears it was quickly apparent that the tunnel was far from safe. He was convinced it was in danger of being blown at any minute.

The new senior trench officer—a man of comparatively slight experience—was not impressed by Pryor's diagnosis. He refused to take any immediate action and when Pryor went off shift the tunnel was still intact and outwardly secure.

But he remained intensely worried. It was another occasion when he was certain disaster was coming. He attributed feelings of this strength to certain fey-like qualities inherited from his Welsh ancestry. True or not, his acute hearing was undoubtedly another factor. It had been found that tunnellers varied greatly in their ability to hear and interpret enemy sounds. An American known as "Texas" Tobin who served as a 174 Company officer proved that he had almost miraculous hearing once during an underground test. A group of British sappers shouted and sang at a tunnel face while Tobin and other listeners stationed in another tunnel many yards away reported on what they could hear. With the exception of Tobin, the most they could say was, "Faint shouting heard." Tobin reported, "They are singing Samuel Hall." He was correct, to the astonishment of his comrades.

Pryor felt equally confident of the sounds he had interpreted. At four in the morning he stretched wearily out in his dug-out for a catnap and willed himself to waken at six-fifteen for a further listen. Instead he woke earlier, allowed himself to doze off again— and finally overslept. It was eight o'clock when his batman shook him into consciousness. Pryor, dismayed by the time, scrambled from the dug-out and ran towards the mine. As he arrived, he felt the ground give the familiar slow-motion heave and judder of a heavy camouflet exploding. He had come too late.

The senior trench officer, now very agitated, sent all the company's available trained rescue men underground to give help. They were equipped with complicated anti-gas equipment known as Proto sets, and only they were allowed down into the gas and flame-swept chaos of the mine. Then came a second disaster.

Almost as soon as the rescue men had gone below, the Germans blew a further heavy camouflet. Pryor was busy dealing with a few survivors who had staggered out dazed and gassed—some flailing their fists like men who were fighting drunk. The situation was desperate now—the rescue men would almost certainly have been killed or hurt themselves. Pryor raced to the rescue equipment store, grabbed a Proto set, ran back to the shaft top and there— although he had little idea how to control it—put the set on.

He was half-way down the long, inclined shaft and could see a sapper lying a few feet further on when he began to have difficulty in breathing. The run to the store and back had increased his respiration rate so much above normal that the demand valve was unequal to his needs. He went on as far as the inert man and had started trying to rope him when his own distress became unbearable. Close to suffocation, he scrambled back up the shaft and snatched the face-piece off as soon as he could poke his head out into fresh air. At that moment the Germans blew their third mine. The ground shook so violently that Pryor lost his footing and began to roll and bounce down the steeply raking shaft. He fell nearly 80 feet, crashing from side to side, battered by broken timbers and still wearing the disconnected 32-lb. Proto apparatus round his waist. Somewhere on the way down, consciousness faded.

He came round in a dug-out with three other survivors, one of whom was raving. His pulse thumped in his ears most strangely— fast for a while, then very slowly. In time the attacks of fast beating stopped and his heart went slower and slower and he had the impression of a second or two between beats. He decided he was about to die and, soon after, slipped again into unconsciousness.

Pryor was not alone in anticipating his death. Later that day they took him out in bitter weather, dressed only in one gumboot and a pair of trousers and threw him over the rear of the trench with a number of corpses for burial. A shrapnel shell burst and a heavy lump of metal smashed into his half naked body. It was December 21st, 1915.

Eventually, Pryor's batman came along hoping to find some

memento he could send home to relatives. He was astonished to see the eyes of his supposedly dead officer open feebly for a moment —and then close.

Days later, Pryor's father, a schoolmaster, was interrupted while reading the lesson in church to take a message that his son had died of wounds in France. But by then, Pryor was already safe in England, his fighting days over. For two years he walked on heavy sticks, for years more he felt less than normally fit. But in the end his recovery was complete. Pryor had been lucky. During his five months at the front more than 300 of his comrades in 178 Company died.

*   *   *

While mines and camouflets shook the ground at the Tambour, the front less than five miles away—at Suzanne on the river Somme —was quiet.

Members of the newly formed 184 Tunnelling Company took over this sector in September, 1915, but after weeks of listening began to doubt whether German miners were anywhere near. One young officer, Lieutenant Arthur Eaton, went on leave with a silent promise to himself that as soon as he was back he would find out for certain. The way to do it seemed obvious: he would simply cross into the German lines for a look.

The promise was kept. In the small, cold hours one morning, Eaton began to splash his way through the belt of marshland at the Somme river's edge. He was fully clothed and heavily greased all over underneath. When he reached the water, which was unpleasantly soiled by shell-fire, he plunged boldly in and struck out eastwards. He had intended to swim silently but found this impossible to do. The noise he made began to remind him of an elephant taking its bath.

In about a mile, he came ashore unchallenged. He was now well behind the German lines and started to make his way north. It seemed strangely quiet everywhere. His first discovery of interest was an ammunition dump which seemed unguarded. The flag of the 23rd Infantry Regiment was flying from it and he snatched

it down as a trophy. Then, immediately afterwards, he saw a
sentry walking his way. Eaton had brought a few Mills bombs
and a truncheon with him. He crouched in the darkness, waiting, and when the sentry came near, sprang out and smashed the
truncheon into the back of his neck. The German fell with a
heavy thud which was apparently overheard. Other soldiers came
running.

Eaton climbed frantically into a tarpaulin-covered wagon that
happened to be near by. He lay there for some time, listening to his
thudding heart, reluctant to emerge. Then suddenly two Germans
climbed on to the wagon and began to drive it off; now there was
no choice and Eaton slipped out. Nobody saw him.

He continued walking north and found an artillery battery con-
cealed before a little wood. The flash as it fired gave its position
away accurately; he noted it carefully for passing on to his own
gunners, and continued walking. Swinging left, he found himself
approaching the German trenches from the rear. Still nobody had
noticed him. He passed a dug-out and paused. There was a lot of
chatter from inside; over the door was a name: HAUPMANN.
Eaton pulled the pin from one of his grenades, waited several
seconds, then lobbed it inside. There was a shout, then the explosion, screams for a moment and finally silence. Nobody seemed
to be coming to investigate. It was amazing. He walked on, soon
actually entering the trenches.

He crept unobserved through a labyrinth of trenches, looking for
signs of mining. As he had expected, there were none. By now
there was a hint of dawn in the sky and he feared he had left his
return too long. While wondering what to do, he spotted a commotion down the line. A patrol was going out. The idea flashed
into his mind that he could join it and next moment he had done
so—as the rearmost man. Half-way across towards the British line
he branched off south and arrived again at the river. He swam back,
arriving on the British part of the bank with the dawn, "cold and
weary", as he put it, "but not downhearted".

He returned to his dug-out, drank a large amount of warming

rum, made out his report and sent it to the C.O. That seemed to be the end of the matter.

But next day he was instructed to report at once to G.H.Q. There he was taken before the C.-in-C. who looked at him gravely and asked, "What do you mean by leaving your post without permission—and above all by going into enemy territory? Are you aware that had you been captured, valuable information would have been given away?"

While Eaton was trying to think of something to say the C.-in-C. smiled. "I should be glad if other young officers had the same initiative," he went on. "I am pleased to award you the D.S.O. as an immediate reward in the field." Eaton was amazed.

Then the congratulations began to come in, among them a delighted letter from Norton Griffiths. Later, a French Order of the Day granted Eaton the Legion of Honour and Croix de Guerre with Palm.

The object of Eaton's expedition had been to have his company moved to a real fighting front. In due course this was done. One-eight-four Company went to Arras. Now Eaton felt he could be sure the effort had been worth while.

8

CRISIS AT THE BLUFF

As 1915 drew towards its end, mine fighting went on in the 2nd Army's part of the line—along the sharply curving sector just south of Ypres—as bloodily and furiously as ever.

By July, Norton Griffiths was describing the situation underground at Hill 60, as a "regular rabbit warren" of galleries. So many tunnels and counter-tunnels had been driven that both sides were losing track of the position. It became almost common to break suddenly and unexpectedly into an enemy mine. Usually, a tunnel discovered in this dramatic manner was empty—but not always. At noon on July 31st, a very daring 175 Company Officer, Lieutenant Euan Tulloch, crawled into a German mine and found it loaded with three-quarters of a ton of high explosive, ready wired, detonated and tamped. Very quietly he cut the wires and laboured to remove the complete charge and detonators which he then had carried to his own company store.

News of the operation reached 175 Company's C.O., Major Hunter Cowan, just as he was reaching what he later described as the "toasted cheese" stage of his dinner at Vlamertinghe. It was eight o'clock.

The news was given him flatly, by the Second in Command, Captain Freddy Harris. Cowan reacted with great excitement and set off at once to visit the mine. He rode by motor-cycle to within half a mile of Hill 60, then parked it and ran most of the rest of the way. But by the time he arrived Tulloch* had cleared the mine. Cowan was delighted with the success and wrote his wife, saying, "Oh, it was great and it showed nerve, too. I hope he'll get the

* Tulloch was awarded the M.C.

Cross I mean to recommend him for . . ." Tulloch re-entered the German mine later, re-charged it and blew it as a safety precaution.

In fact, 175 Company was so hard pressed that Cowan grew worried at the effect the sustained effort seemed to be having. Some of the officers were growing jumpy and the men were tired. It became increasingly difficult to keep the listeners awake throughout their wearisome eight-hour shifts. Once two lieutenants, Arthur Lumb, and Euan Tulloch, found a young sapper asleep at his post and told him off. As they were leaving, Lumb turned to the man casually and said, "You will be shot at dawn." Then they dismisssed him and his lapse from their minds and completed the tour of inspection. Afterwards they returned to their dug-out, relaxed over a large rum, sang a duet and went to bed. In the morning they were told a sapper was waiting to see them. It was the sleepy listener from the night before. He was in a state of collapse. Lumb and Tulloch were flabbergasted when he began begging them to reconsider their sentence. The two officers (inwardly feeling mean and guilty) conferred gravely for a moment, then announced that they had decided, for once, to overlook his offence. They gave the man a glass of rum and sent him to bed.

For a few mid-summer weeks, the company was under orders to carry out no big-scale offensive mining—in the hope that the Germans would slow down their effort also. The lull was short-lived. To the disappointment of British Commanders—who were preparing for the 1st Army's major assault at Loos and so hoped for a quiet time on the 2nd Army front—the German Sappers were soon attacking again. Cowan's company was fully extended just keeping them in check.

Then, on August 13th, the Company was given new orders—to start work on four big offensive mines to be blown up under the German trenches at the start of the Battle of Loos in September. It was to be part of a sizeable diversionary move, a good 25 miles north of the Loos fighting and officially named the Second Attack on Bellewaarde. The idea of dropping the no-offensive-mines rule

appears to have come out of a rather strange discussion between
Norton Griffiths and Major-General Glubb, Chief Engineer of the
2nd Army. The two men met for a talk at Army Headquarters on
August 3rd. Glubb, who was looking tired and seedy, explained
that the present plan was to lie quiet. Minutes later—perhaps a
result of Norton Griffiths' infectious love of action—he showed a
change of view by suggesting that four heavy mines should be
fired. He wanted Fowke to suggest to the Army Commander,
General Sir Herbert Plumer, that this should be done to shatter the
tangle of enemy workings. But Norton Griffiths became most un-
characteristically formal and replied that the initiative should come
not from the Engineer-in-Chief, but from Glubb's own 2nd Army.
Very soon, Plumer did adopt a four-mine plan, but switched it a
mile and a half to the north of the Hill and gave it new importance as
part of the diversionary attack.

It involved a heavy extra load on the already glum members of
175 Company. On the 14th of August (1915), Cowan went to
break the news to Lieutenant Arthur Firebrace, who was to be in
charge of the work. There were to be two long tunnels, one of 220
feet, the other of 320. Each was to have two explosives chambers at
the end. Firebrace listened in such gloomy silence that Cowan
asked irritably if he ever felt any enthusiasm for anything. Firebrace answered in a word: "No." Cowan confided later to his
wife that he could nearly have wept. But the orders were given
and despite his cool reaction, Firebrace was soon pressing the work
ahead.

This offensive work inevitably increased the risk that the Germans
would slip through unnoticed. On August 25th, late at night, they
were found to have done it. Firebrace telephoned Cowan to say
that he had checked on sounds coming from beneath the front line
and that he was satisfied they were from German sappers placing a
mine.

Cowan told him to bore an eight-inch hole down 10 feet into the
ground immediately over the noises and added that he would be
over at once. He planned to ram some high explosive down the

bored hole and set it hurriedly off in the hope of collapsing the tunnel on the Germans. It was going to be another race for life.

By the time Cowan arrived, the boring tool was seven feet down and had run into an obstructive layer of flinty pebbles. The mining noises were still audible—but were now loudest 15 feet further back behind the British front line. Apparently the Germans were not yet aware that they had been detected—but the situation was terribly dangerous.

One of the men held a pointed iron bar in his hand and Cowan decided that it should be used to punch the pebbles loose if possible. Great force was needed—and Cowan later confessed that the method was noisy enough to have been heard in Berlin. Certainly, it must have been heard by the Germans below. But repeated punching with the bar did smash through the layer and the boring tool was then successfully forced down to 12 feet.

Cowan decided to stop it there and ordered 50-pounds of ammonal to be pushed into the hole and roughly tamped down from above with clay. Then a timed fuse was set off and they all retired to cover. Nothing happened. After a lengthy pause, Firebrace and Cowan returned to the charge and pulled out the fuse. To their surprise, it had burned right through quite normally. The most likely explanation now seemed that the Germans had heard the charge being placed over their heads—and had simply removed it. Both men well knew that if this were so, retaliation would be coming swiftly.

Cowan decided that the only thing that could now be done was to reopen the hole for inspection. Laboriously, and while expecting the Germans to press the plunger at every moment, this was done. Peering down the narrow hole, they could see a zinc canister that had contained the charge; but there was still doubt whether the ammonal was inside it. Cowan called for the bar again—and a hole was punched in the top. To everyone's relief, the point of the bar came up covered in white ammonal powder. So at least the charge was still there.

This time they installed three electric detonators, bedded them down with an additional 25-pounds of ammonal, retired 30 yards to cover—and fired the charge. The result was swift and dramatic. First came a powerful sounding rumble—followed to everyone's surprise, by a spout of sandbags and huge quantities of earth, which flew high into the air, spreading over a wide range. For many seconds the party was occupied with avoiding heavy debris.

When the eruption subsided, a massive hole 30 feet across, and 12 feet deep had been left. It was an astonishing result in view of the small amount of ammonal that had been fired. Then Cowan realized what must have happened—the small charge had detonated a larger German one being hurriedly made ready for them. It was a puzzling situation, because two heavy British camouflets had been blown in the area during the last 10 days and should have destroyed all nearby enemy workings. The important thing was, they had won the race, close though the finish had been. Cowan recommended three sappers who assisted, for D.C.M.'s and the awards were made in each case.

On September 25th at nineteen minutes past four on a wet morning, Firebrace's four mines were successfully fired. But only just. The Germans had known that an attack was coming and opened up a furious shell-fire at the very moment the exploders were being connected and blew the lights out in the firing dug-out. Cowan was relieved to hear that even so they had gone off on time, forming four good craters in exactly the places intended. About 150 yards of German trench had been destroyed and Cowan wrote to his wife later saying that captured Germans from the area had estimated that about 150 of their comrades had been buried.

As the Company fought desperately on, the grumbling continued. Morale was further affected on October 1st, when two of the Company's second-lieutenants were killed—Arthur Fletcher and Frank Thomas. The incident began with an infantry report of enemy mining noises. There had been many such scares in recent weeks and, as on other parts of the front, they were usually bogus. Once it had been a sentry clicking his heels; another time a window

was banging in the wind; and there had been the scratching of rats—
by now an almost routine diagnosis. But the two officers began a
conscientious investigation.

While Thomas—a new man who had joined the Company that
week—stayed listening on top, Fletcher ran down into a nearby
gallery to hear what he could from there. At that moment the Germans blew. Fifteen feet of the front trench went up and an advance
post but none of the infantry who were standing clear. Thomas's
body was soon found buried deep in debris. Fletcher's, far down
underground, had to be left until later. The loss of both men was
felt with special keenness. Fletcher had been one of the most popular
officers in the strength, and Thomas was a new and promising man
who had only been with the Company a week.

Cowan worried a good deal about the low spirit of the Company. "What am I to do when extra work is ordered to be done?"
he asked, when recording his thoughts on the matter. Two days
later, he confessed that "Life in this Company is harder than in any
other I know of". He felt that the weary grumblers blamed him
personally for their situation. "I'm afraid they think I ask for extra
work to be given so that I may acquire *personal* kudos," he wrote.
"It's sickening to me but . . . I've got to put up with it for the sake
of the show."

And, in fact, Cowan was begging for more officers and men to
help share the load as earnestly as he dared. Norton Griffiths, himself straining to find more and more men, was even annoyed by this
commander's persistence—and was characteristically frank in saying so. He was unfair enough to suggest to General Glubb—and
later to his own Chief, General Fowke—that 175 Company was
slacking. It was an example of the less satisfactory side of Norton
Griffiths's impetuous character. These reports were undoubtedly
harmful to Cowan's reputation—particularly in his dealings with
Glubb. The unfortunate commander was put in the position that
officers under him were complaining vigorously about overwork,
while certain others over him passed it around that his effort was too
slight.

Such casualties were inevitable when Norton Griffiths was in action. He was a grand-concept man who seldom had time, or the inclination, for detail. He could be ruthless also. He never seemed to care deeply for anyone, except members of the family. To them —and particularly to his wife—he was devoted. When one of his daughters was let down in a love affair, he was seen to weep. But he never, or seldom, allowed outsiders to reach his heart. Once he told Fowke and Harvey how, when a contract went wrong in civilian life, he would sack not only the man running it, but the man's chief assistant as well. His theory was that the number two man must have allowed the job to go wrong deliberately—out of jealousy of the number one. Harsh and arbitrary though this justice may have been, it was a short cut to decision. Because to Norton Griffiths, that was what mattered most, double-sacking became a rule of thumb.

While 175 Company groaned and sweated to hold its present ground, Norton Griffiths's mind was still filled with his hope for a spectacular mining offensive up here by the Ypres salient. He still foresaw the possibility of an underground convulsion big enough to have a real effect on the whole war. One man in the Chief's office— Colonel Napier Harvey—was encouraging him to keep the idea alive. Otherwise, the reaction from above remained cool. Fowke himself, after his burst of irritation when confronted by Norton Griffiths's first crude sketch, now behaved as though the matter had been dropped.

But Harvey, who knew his chief very well, believed that he would still be willing to give the plan fair consideration. He advised Norton Griffiths to work it out in greater detail, offering that he would then suggest such modifications as seemed necessary, and would finally resubmit the finished plan to the harassed and over-worked Fowke.

On Tuesday, September 2nd, Norton Griffiths finished off a draft scheme and delivered it to Harvey as arranged. For security reasons he referred to the series of deep and powerful mines pushed far under the miles-long ridge from St. Eloi to Messines as "Wells".

From then on, he and Harvey used this substitution in discussing the scheme whenever there was a risk of being overheard. One thing was clear from the beginning—that secrecy would be essential to the success of any elaborate mining scheme. If the enemy commanders had the good luck to find out when and where to expect a major blow, an almost absurdly simple remedy would be open: They could withdraw their troops just prior to zero hour, then send them racing back to occupy the craters immediately after the blow. The whole mining effort would have been wasted.

Even at this early stage, Norton Griffiths named a few of the officers he wished to see put in charge of operations. He divided the front line into three sectors—north, south and centre. In the north he wanted Lieutenant Horace Hickling, in the south Captain F. Gordon Hyland. For the key central position he named 37-year-old Captain Clay Hepburn, Commander of 172 Company, then mining immediately to the right of Cowan's unit.

Hepburn was physically tall and slender, and in outlook a man of considerable culture and refinement. In many ways he was Norton Griffiths's opposite. Hepburn, a colliery manager from Monmouth, had found himself thrust unexpectedly into command of his company when the original C.O., Captain William Johnstone, V.C., surprised him one day early in May, by saying, "Look here— I don't know anything about these tunnels. You do. Take over." Johnston, though a regular R.E., was an infantry-man at heart with an extraordinary contempt for enemy fire. He had won his V.C. ferrying men and supplies across a bullet-swept river in August 1914, and now, as he strode about the St. Eloi front, seldom bothered to take cover. He left almost at once. But only five weeks later news reached the company that he had fallen to a sniper's bullet and was dead.

Hepburn became one of the very few civilian soldiers holding a command at that time. He quickly settled down to his unexpected responsibilities and by July was awarded the D.S.O. for his achievements.

Mining conditions at St. Eloi were filthy and the tunnellers were

unpopular for making them worse. Water had to be pumped continuously out of the mineshafts to discharge in the already squelch-
ing trenches. On May 6th, 1915, one of Hepburn's subalterns,
Frederick Mulqueen, was intercepted while on shift duty by a
colonel of the Northumberland Fusiliers who demanded that something better be done with the mine water. Next day Mulqueen,
with just two weeks' active service behind him, set out to comply.
In what appeared to be safe ground, screened from the enemy, he
found the remains of a neglected ditch and took two men over to
clear it out for use as a drain. He lingered for a while, explaining
exactly what was to be done. But the ground was not the "dead"
area it looked; while the three were bending over the ditch discussing it, a grenade arrived, plopped between them into the
muddy water, sank at once and then exploded two feet from Mulqueen's head; the explosion hurled him on to his back. He
struggled to his feet concussed, scratched and soaked in mud but not
seriously hurt. The other two men were stretcher cases who had to
be temporarily dressed in the line and taken out that night. The
mine water continued to slop into the near by trenches after that.

The bad conditions became indescribably worse when the
sappers found themselves tunnelling into an old cesspool. Even certain of the shell-holes in the area had been used by troops as latrines.
In mid-May, Hepburn was showing Norton Griffiths round and
took him across one of these by means of a narrow plank bridge.
Heavy rain had made the plank greasy and so Hepburn—who was
going first—warned his visitor to take care. Norton Griffiths retorted with some impatience that he would be all right. But before
they reached the other side, Hepburn heard a loud splash and looking
round saw Norton Griffiths struggling and swearing in the filth
below.

To escape unclean seepage, Hepburn and Hickling decided to go
60 feet down into the firm, blue Ypresian clay to be found there.
By doing so, they made military mining history for as mining grew
more scientific, the value of depth became apparent. Various companies and individuals were later credited with going deep first. The

names of these two men have never been among them—but it is to them that the credit belongs.

The first of these deep mines was started on May 7th—the day Mulqueen had been blown on to his back by a grenade; and he was put in charge of the job.

A special collar to form the top of the shaft had been built and Hickling came over to explain how it was to be fixed. He was grimly earnest about it all, explaining that the timbers lining the shaft would be hung from the collar and that it was *most* important it be correctly placed and secured.

But Mulqueen's head was aching intolerably and became worse each time he bent forward over the collar; at last he put an intelligent-looking sapper in charge and went off to lie down for three hours. When he came back, the job had been bungled; the collar was grossly distorted. Frantically he laboured for the afternoon and evening to undo the damage. But when Hickling appeared to check the work over that night, Mulqueen, crestfallen and wretched, had to admit that it was "a hell of a mess". Hickling, himself tired and tense, was furious.

The rest of the work went ahead satisfactorily. In June the Company had the almost common experience of breaking through to a German mine near Hill 60. Hepburn raced to the spot as soon as word reached him and there found two north-country sergeants crouched 50 feet along the tunnel calmly studying their find by candlelight. Well over 1,000 lbs of explosive powder compacted into pebbles lay around them. Hepburn feared that a spark from the candles would send it all up—but no other light was available. For two days a party worked under Hepburn and the second-in-command, Lieutenant Gilbert Syme, removing the charge and its eleven detonators.

Hepburn already had a use for the explosive in mind. At St. Eloi he had a five-mine system advancing towards the German front line. By July the mines had been laid and loaded—apparently without being detected. Among the charges was the German one removed from Hill 60.

The Company suffered from little or none of the discontent that was upsetting 175 Company immediately to the north. Hepburn believed that part of the trouble there was Cowan's solemn militarism. It had already earned him the name of "Dog-face" among his men and he, in turn, used to complain of what he called the "civilian mind". Hepburn, by contrast, was relaxed and tolerant, concerned far more with results than methods. When one of his new officers raised his hat to a superior and later to the sergeant-major, Hepburn simply smiled.

Having laid his mines, Hepburn was anxious to extract the utmost benefit from them. He walked over to see General Glubb at 2nd Army headquarters to ask for artillery support. Glubb heard him out, then put his own position frankly. He explained that he had only 10 rounds for each gun and that that was going to have to last a full week. Artillery support would be impossible. "You must blow up the mines," he said grimly—"and that's that."

It was disappointing but quite believable. The scandal of the shell shortage, which had ruined British chances at Festubert, was still in everyone's mind and the newly created Ministry of Munitions was barely four weeks old. Argument was clearly useless. Hepburn returned to his unit.

On July 10th at half past three in the morning, Hepburn gave the order to fire the first mine. He and Horace Hickling walked from firing point to firing point, carrying the exploder box with them and attaching it to each set of firing wires in turn. The inevitable delay was part of the plan—Hepburn felt that the waiting and wondering if each blow was the last would do extra harm to German morale, and to strain it further they dodged from mine to mine at random, instead of working systematically along the line.

Hickling pressed the plunger while Hepburn watched results over the trench parapet. He gave his commands quietly and undramatically. "Let this one off now," he would say—and then wait while Hickling wired up and fired. He was rewarded with a fine view of his plan succeeding. As the last of the debris was settling, the Germans came out of their trench and ran widly towards the rear, going right and left of the dreaded St. Eloi mound in the background. Hepburn swung himself up on to the parapet and sat silhouetted against the skyline to watch, judging rightly that not a shot would be fired towards him. Apparently Glubb had given orders for some slight support to be given after all, because ten rounds of shrapnel burst noisily over the Germans' heads. Machine guns also started to rattle away from some British position and about 20 of the running men tumbled into the mud and lay still. In a few moments, it was over. The front became suddenly quiet.

Hepburn and Hickling were fully satisfied with results—which had been all that could have been hoped. So, as they later heard, was Norton Griffiths. He was particularly pleased with Hickling—who had supervised most of the digging and charging of the mines —and expressed his admiration in a report to Fowke. By October, Hickling had been promoted Captain and given command of his own tunnelling company, the newly formed 183.

The position at St. Eloi gradually improved for 172 Company after the first big blow there. For a while the Company had been the only defence across a narrow front between the village and a cross roads just to the south. Surface fortifications were dug and manned now and the line became moderately secure. But other grave worries were developing near by.

Almost exactly half way between St. Eloi and Hill 60, the British and German front lines were cut at right angles by a high banked canal, a full 120 feet wide. In carving a way through the Messines Ridge for it, engineers had thrown the spoil up into embankments north and south. The north bank was particularly steep, rising to about 30 feet above ground level and ending abruptly in an almost cliff-like face which stood squarely opposing the German line. It was a specially fine observation point—perhaps the best on the Ypres front. The British—who held the position— named it the Bluff. To the Germans it was *Die Grosse Bastion*.

The Bluff was part of the long front that 172 Company—aided by a smattering of Brigade Mining sections and R.E. Field Companies

—was protecting underground. In May that year, 1915, Hepburn had had an elaborate underground listening post dug in front of a 700-yard stretch of trench to the north of the Bluff. Five vertical shafts had been sunk, then linked together underground by a gallery. From the gallery, the usual very small and lonely listeners' tunnels had been run out beneath no-man's-land. But between this system and the Bluff proper, stood a gap about 200 yards broad. The soil here was loose, sandy, and very wet, the most difficult kind to tunnel through. To the relief—but also surprise of 171 Company officers, the local infantry commander made it clear that he wished no protective tunnelling to be carried out beneath it. What his reasoning was has never been made clear. Almost certainly, he hoped —as other infantrymen were simultaneously hoping a mile or so further north at Hill 60—that if they stopped the underground war, the Germans would do the same. And for a while, through the mid and later weeks of summer, the front was quiet enough both above and below ground. The Germans struggled to dig a gallery which ran into water and which they drained into the canal—but it also was defensive.

By August, 172 Company's gallery had been all but abandoned. In theory, infantrymen were running guard and inspection patrols through it and were responsible for keeping the system dry. But in practice, the gallery was seldom, if ever, visited and was soon half full of water.

In September, the lull ended—abruptly. A Brigade Mining Section of Sherwood Foresters, acting apparently on its own initiative, began to push a tunnel towards the Germans at a position 400 yards north of the Bluff. Retribution came swiftly. Within a few hours, the Germans blew a pulverizing camouflet that smashed the Foresters' gallery and entrance shaft to pieces.

Then, just a day or so later, infantrymen holding the Bluff began to hear sounds which they interpreted as mining work going on beneath them. They raised an alarm. Trained listeners who came over to make tests, denied that there was anything to fear. But on September 30th, another German mine went off at exactly the spot where the sounds had been heard. Almost all of a Sherwood Foresters platoon (of the 5th Battalion) were killed.

Next day, it happened again. And once more it was the Sherwood Foresters who were caught. This time an officer and 14 men from the 10th Battalion died, and still more violence from below was soon to come. The Bluff front had come viciously to life. On October 15th, two explosions crashed out in the night. At half past one in the morning, a mine was fired, 200 yards north of the Bluff, under the 5th Cameron Highlanders—and caused heavy casualties to the Scotsmen. At four, an even more terrible explosion convulsed the Bluff itself, killing and injuring some 70 of the men of the Argyll and Sutherlands and badly shocking dozens more. Total mine casualties for the night were close to 100.

This last mine had been almost prevented the day before by Lieutenant Napier-Clavering of the 64th Field Company, R.E. The Lieutenant had been surprised when walking through a Bluff trench with his sergeant, to see a sentry stabbing a bayonet into a hole near the foot of the parapet. Napier-Clavering and the sergeant investigated. The man had some cheese on the bayonet point and explained that he was just trying to catch a rat. But the sergeant's attention had been attracted to this hole. He looked closely in for a moment, then told Napier-Clavering that he felt sure it was a mine. He was an experienced ex-miner and said he could tell by the smell.

As soon as it became dark, Napier-Clavering and a party climbed over the trench top and began digging down to the tunnel, planning to collapse it by exploding a small charge a yard or two ahead of their own line. But they were soon seen and heavy machine-gun fire then forced them back into cover.

Now the front trench was cleared at the danger point and the garrison waited tensely through the night for what it knew almost for certain was going to happen. And before dawn, the shock had come. Most of the men it killed had been back in the support trenches where it had been assumed they would be safe.

All this time, no serious counter-mining effort was called for

from 172 Company. Hepburn was concentrating his effort at St.
Eloi, where more than 20 tunnels were being energetically forced
past towards the enemy. In the spring this threat was to erupt in
such a display of destructive violence that the Germans would be
forced to re-think their whole mining approach and organization.
But in the meantime, the situation grew daily more desperate for the
British perched in fear on the Bluff.

It was not until late November—when a change in the garrison
brought the 3rd Division to the sector—that the tunnellers were
asked, urgently, to give help. They moved into action at once, to
face an almost impossible position. German sappers were at work
in several places and were so well established underground that there
was no time to evolve a coherent plan to meet them. The weather
added to the difficulties—heavy rain which had started before the
end of October, now poured steadily on for weeks. The subsoil—
unstable, sandy and wet—could hardly have been worse for tunnelling. It did at least allow the boring tool to be used with comparatively slight effort. So the sappers slithered over the drenched
ground and down into the German craters where they bored towards the nearest suspicious sounds, rammed charges in and fired
them as fast as they could. Work was also begun on a defensive
gallery, despite the unpromising conditions. From this gallery, the
useful boring tools were also used to probe ahead for the feel of
German mine timbers. During the next few weeks the position at
the Bluff began to look more hopeful to the British. Although the
weather remained very bad, it hampered both sides equally, and
during November the Germans managed to push only one important mine through. During December they had no success with any,
and, where direct encounters between the two sides took place
underground, the British tended to be the winners. This was
largely due to a remarkable second-lieutenant, Richard Brisco, whose
exploits soon became famous in the sector.

Brisco first made a name for himself on November 9th. Sappers
down in a British gallery slightly north of the Bluff, had been probing ahead with boring tools when they struck something that felt

like German mine timber. Brisco ordered them to enlarge the hole
—using a bayonet as a slow but silent digging tool—then wriggled
along head first to examine the situation for himself. The sappers
had been correct; they were hard up against an enemy mine. Brisco
quietly removed a few pieces of the German timber and slipped
through into the darkness beyond. He had a revolver with him—
which by now was standard issue to tunnelling officers.

Soon an unsuspecting party of German sappers approached and
Brisco began to shoot. The noise in the confined space was terrific
and the shocked Germans began to retreat at speed. One sprawled
dead or unconscious on the gallery floor and was left by his comrades. Now Brisco scrambled back into his own tunnel, collected a
portable charge and, before the Germans had time to return in force,
pushed it through the hole and lit the fuse. When the charge exploded, the German gallery was safely sealed off—at least for a
while.

On December 30th, Brisco carried out a similar underground
raid. At seven-thirty that morning, the rain-soaked sides of a
crater suddenly subsided revealing an entrance to another German
gallery. Brisco crawled immediately into the crater and once more
went exploring enemy territory. Again he met a party of
Germans—and this time he withdrew to the entrance before opening fire down the narrow tunnel. The Germans, greatly hampered
by their cramped conditions, fired back. They had—apparently—
done some sandbagging of the crater sides and Brisco now hauled a
number of the bags over and jammed them into the entrance. At
six-fifteen that evening, after Brisco was safely back in his own
trench, the Germans blew a camouflet in their own gallery to close
it.

These adventures were exciting and good for British morale, but
had little effect on the military situation. And the Germans were
wasting time.

At two o'clock on the morning of January 22nd, 1916, they exploded the biggest single mine of the war to that date. With
terrifying suddenness, a six-ton charge ripped open the south-east

face of the Bluff. A black column of earth shot skywards carrying men, ammunition boxes, trench timber, and other materials with it. Bodies and debris were scattered over hundreds of yards. A new surface defence system which had just been dug on the Bluff, disappeared and in its place stood a barren crater about 20,000 square feet in area and 40 feet deep. About 100 casualties resulted, mostly Suffolk men from the 2nd Battalion. Many of the dead had been buried alive.

In February, 172 Company listeners heard another gallery approaching to the north and feverish work began to intercept it. Again it was Brisco who was running the operation and after having a short tunnel driven, charged and tamped, he decided not to blow it. Instead he waited for the Germans to arrive. A day or two later they did so. It was the 10th, when a listener reported that he could hear them removing the sandbag tamping to the British charge. At once, Brisco crept forward and began to do the same, but very quietly. For four hours the German and the Englishman crept towards each other through the sandbag barricade—with the difference that only the Englishmen knew what was happening. When he estimated that the wall between them was only one bag thick, Brisco stopped work and drew his revolver, waiting. In a moment a hole appeared and the German came into view. Brisco promptly shot him—and looked for the next. But nobody seemed to be following, so once more the cool-nerved, hard-fighting Brisco stepped into a German gallery. He placed another charge and set it off. So a further German thrust was checked.

That same day, yet another German tunnel entrance was observed inside a crater close to the Bluff. Word was now sent to the Divisional Commander that the situation was critical, and that the enemy would probably blow another mine. But in the evening of the next day, February 11th, Brisco moved into action again. He crawled out over no-man's-land to the crater, entered the German tunnel and went exploring. Forty feet along it, he came to a corner. As he went cautiously round, a machine gun suddenly opened fire at him. He sprang back round the corner, took a hand grenade from his belt and flung it towards the machine-gun crew. After the explosion, he looked round the corner and saw that the Germans were dead. Now he pushed on through the pungent-smelling, smoke-filled gallery, past the battered bodies of the machine-gun crew towards a distant entrance shaft—which almost certainly connected to the German trench. Near the foot of the shaft he placed a charge, touched off the fuse and made his way back to the crater. An occasional flare bathed him in light and he had to freeze at once. Even inside the crater he could be seen by the Germans.

Meanwhile, a party of sappers had gone out into no-man's-land and were boring from the surface, probing for the tunnel from above. The rest of the incident is partly conjecture. Apparently Brisco joined the party which was soon afterwards seen by flare light. The Germans opened with rapid fire and the sappers began to dash for the poor protection of the crater cover. Brisco and one other were wounded either before they reached it, or just after. And, at a quarter to six in the evening of the 14th, the Germans fired their mine. It brought heavy loss of life to their enemies.

During most of that day, the British had been cruelly battered by very heavy shell-fire. For this reason, a whole platoon of Lancashire Fusiliers were sheltering in an old German tunnel when the mine exploded. The tunnel collapsed burying all but three of the fusiliers. Two more mines followed almost immediately—and then, as a final calamity, troops of the German 124th Regiment were seen running towards the Bluff. A furious and unexpected attack was coming.

The reason for such sudden activity was not understood by the British until later—when news came through of big German assaults further south at Vimy and Verdun. The Bluff operation was to be a useful diversion. It succeeded quickly. By six-thirty, the Bluff and all trenches near it were in enemy hands. So was the entire 172 Company mine system, and much of the lost ground was red with fresh blood. Total British casualties from German mines and assault fire were officially put at 67 officers and 1,227 men.

Among them were an officer and more than 40 men belonging to—or attached to—172 Company.

A series of desperate British counter-attacks begun that night failed. As the two sides struggled in close combat, the weather deteriorated further into watery sleet, slush and bitter winds. Men lying wounded on the ground began to freeze and died in a special degree of misery. By the morning of the 16th, the British effort had to be stopped. German soldiers held the Bluff.

But the position was not as final as it seemed. Better organized attacks were carried out by the British 76th Brigade on March 2nd, and the whole of the lost area was recovered. Four parties from 172 Company took part in the assault to help drive the Germans out of their mines and then occupy as much of the system as possible. They fought hard—and with the inevitable further losses.

The Company was by now seriously under strength and suffering from extreme weariness. To help it re-start the bitter war underground, a section from 250 Company was sent along the same day.

The party, led by Lieutenant Andy Holmes, debussed in blinding snow at six that evening and began trudging with the help of a guide to the front. Large troop movements were taking place in the area and the guide became confused. Soon the party was lost and Holmes had to take over responsibility for direction, map reading on the snow covered, dark and almost featureless countryside. They arrived at two o'clock in the morning, wet to the skin and chattering with cold. There they met the amazing Brisco, as full of life as ever (he was eventually killed in 1917) who had a hot meal ready and prodigious quantities of rum waiting for them.

Soon mining and counter-mining was blasting the churned-up sogginess of the Bluff with the same desperate vigour as before. And it was to turn out that mine fighting would be the only important form of combat to be seen there again. It ended in lasting defeat for the Germans.

One-seven-two Company had only a few more weeks to serve at the Bluff. In April they were relieved by Canadian tunnellers who took over the struggle—and went steadily ahead to win it by the following December. But by then, many important changes had come to tunnelling practice and organization.

Before 1915 ended, Norton Griffiths and Harvey had together won General Fowke over to the idea of the massive mining assault. The scheme still seemed unlikely to win approval, for even with the Engineer in Chief's backing the High Command were cool to it. But with Fowke's heavy driving power behind it, there was real hope for the scheme at last.

Two of the three men Norton Griffiths had asked for to carry the operation out were now not likely to be available. Hepburn—172 Company's C.O. had been sent home in November, 1915, suffering from the after-effects of an early gassing at Hill 60: he was never again fit enough for front-line duty. Hickling, in command of 183 Company, was occupied down near the Somme and was due to be attached to the British 4th Army when it came to be formed on March 1st, 1916.

In any case, the longer the delay in winning acceptance for it, the bigger the scheme was becoming in Norton Griffiths's mind. It could not now depend on individuals, so the loss of two capable men hardly mattered.

9

PREPARING FOR A BIGGER EFFORT

NINETEEN-FIFTEEN had been a year of growth and experiment for all fighting forces in the war—but for none as much as for the British.

Her professional army had almost vanished among the 375,000 Britons lost during the abysmal first 16 months of war. A vast new fighting force had had to be improvised and rushed—half trained—to the front. And there the men had had to be taught about gas, machine guns, the creeping barrage, deep mines and other new techniques that the generals themselves knew little about.

Britain had plenty of cause to feel pride in the endurance and fighting spirit of her soldiers—but in little else. By most tests, it had been 16 months of heavy humiliation.

Loos had proved that the Commander-in-Chief was using hopelessly out-dated generalship on the new mechanized, mud-ensnared, spread-out war of 1914. Then, French commanders had shown that they could dominate their British counterparts and drag them along as a half-willing supporting cast in an essentially French production.

There had been scandalous trouble over British-made armaments—which had been too few in number and of deplorable quality; hand grenades often failed to explode at all or fired too soon blowing off the arm of the thrower; shells burst in the gun barrels or lay as mute and motionless as a pig of iron; the front was becoming littered with what officials described as "blind shell" and the soldiers knew as duds; howitzer crews so often blew themselves to pieces with their own maniac charges that they nick-named themselves the "Suicide Clubs".

Bitter squabbles at the top had upset the unity of command which an army must have if it is to fight efficiently. Above all else, there was the flagging spirit of the Commander-in-Chief; since Loos Sir John French had been depressed—in startling contrast to his mood eleven months earlier when full of Irish charm and optimism he had pronounced that the Germans were "playing their last card". Now he was even openly doubting the Allies' chance of winning the war—a confession likely to have serious effects on morale. The general situation for Britain was blackly unpromising.

Month by month it grew clearer that changes must come, and finally—as the wet autumn gave way to an even wetter winter—they did. Field-Marshal Sir John French was retired to a home job, somewhat against his will, on Sunday, December 17th. General Sir Douglas Haig, Commander of the 1st Army, nine years younger and a calm, resolute and dedicated soldier, took his place.

There were many other changes, too, in a general shake-up that sent vibrations through the whole B.E.F. organization. Among the important appointments made were a new Chief of the Imperial General Staff, Lieutenant-General Sir William Robertson, and a new Chief of Staff in France—Lieutenant General Sir Launcelot Kiggell. Many military services were reshaped and strengthened to enable them to meet the fearful challenge ahead. Everyone knew by now that victory—if it could be achieved at all—would strain every muscle and sinew the Allies had. The days of muddling through were over.

The tunnellers were among the more obvious candidates for attention, and they were not overlooked. Hard and bravely though the tunnelling companies had worked, the discouraging truth was that they were not materially assisting the progress of the war. A whisper began among some infantry commanders that they positively impeded it: first, by absorbing men who could be better used on the surface, and second, by blowing huge craters which had to be held—and which also obstructed troops attempting to advance.

These were disputable points. What could not be contradicted was the heavy consumption of man-power compared with the results achieved. By the end of 1915, 20 tunnelling companies had been formed and each employed up to 1,000 men, and an ever increasing amount of equipment. Losses, too, were alarming; about 1,000 men a month were killed, wounded or sick, and had to be replaced. And, as General Harvey felt and later confessed, "There was little to show for it." He was right. There were a number of isolated mineshafts and, running from them, a tangled multitude of galleries. Enemy lives had been taken and German morale somewhat shaken. And that was about all.

There was no proper plan and little control over operations. The whole concept of mining was tactical rather than strategical. Yet the outlay in men and money entitled the army to something better.

Towards the end of the year a letter arrived from the War Office at G.H.Q. mentioning the anxiety being felt in London. It suggested that a high ranking officer should be given the title "Inspector of Mines" and put in general control of all tunnelling companies to co-ordinate their efforts.

But the General Staff at St. Omer was already arriving at similar conclusions. General Fowke had for long been worried about the tunnelling companies, and their contribution to the war. As far back as spring, 1915, he had told the General Staff that while he had no doubt they were doing good work, it had been very local in scope. Ever since then he had sat awkwardly on the fence supporting tunnelling companies and arguing the need for them—yet feeling full of anxious doubts about whether they were giving proper value for their keep. The General Staff now asked that an Inspector of Mines should be appointed with, under him, a Controller of Mines for each Army. The Inspector was to be responsible for giving out orders and information to tunnelling units, and for gathering properly detailed reports about their work. Fowke at once agreed to set up the organization.

He asked Harvey to work out the details. By now Harvey, although still only giving part of his time to tunnelling affairs, had become deeply interested. He had come to believe that mining should be—and would be—of vital importance in this extraordinary war which he now referred to as "the siege of Germany". With alacrity and care he settled down to the creation of the new tunnellers' hierarchy.

Probably Harvey already saw himself as the new Inspector, and he was certainly willing to take the job on if asked. He took the opportunity to provide the Inspector with adequate power and extreme freedom of movement. This freedom seemed to Harvey of the greatest importance—he wanted the Inspector to be able to turn up without warning anywhere on the tunnelling front. "I drew up a charter," he said later, "which would enable the Inspector of Mines to visit any mine, anywhere, and at any time, without any reference to the headquarters of the formation." Only one other officer had the right to roam the battle area like this, and that was the Commander-in-Chief himself. Privately Harvey doubted whether the General Staff would agree to his proposals. But they did, without complaint. He was delighted.

Then Fowke offered the appointment to another senior engineer, Brigadier-General H. F. Thuillier, and it looked as if Harvey's connexion with tunnelling was about to end abruptly. As it happened, Thuillier was hoping for an appointment as Director of Gas Services—which he was soon after awarded—and he turned the Inspectorate offer down. Harvey decided not to risk losing it a second time and promptly asked for nomination. Fowke willingly agreed. So Robert Napier Harvey, nicknamed "Ducky", now promoted to the temporary rank of brigadier-general, became the British army's chief tunneller with effect from January 1st, 1916. He was then 47 years old, a sturdily built, handsome man of square jaw, dark hair—receding now at the sides—and full, greying moustache. He was well known to the official war historian, Brigadier-General Sir James Edmonds, who once said of him that "there is no milder mannered man"—a curious and most misleading compliment. In fact, Harvey was a dryly spoken man, a disciplinarian, often irascible, always energetic and (perhaps more markedly than anything else) thorough in all that he did. These qualities were all that many officers serving under him saw. They were not the kind that make for popularity and he was not a popular commander. The C.O. of 250 Company, Major Cecil Cropper, once summed up his view of Harvey by remarking that he was "peremptory, short-tempered . . . disagreeable . . . and what I call a bounder." However, there was a soft side to Harvey's nature, and some officers—particularly those who worked very closely with him— saw it. He was generous in what he sought to do for people rather than in what he said to them; when he did pay compliments to subordinates, he did so with touching warmth and usually behind their backs. Harvey was contemptuous of outward displays, a formal, taciturn man who felt that good work was merely normal and proper—and not something to enthuse about.

After Norton Griffiths's death, in 1937, Harvey lavished the kind of public praise on him which lesser men might well have feared would tend to cut their own stature down. Such a calculation would never have occurred to Harvey's honest and objective mind.

In his office he had, at first, two Assistant Inspectors of Mines; a brilliant and conscientious medical officer in charge of rescue work; a mechanical engineer, three clerks and two draughtsmen. Later, he added an officer in charge of plans and records—and a geologist. A Controller of Mines, with lieutenant-colonel's rank, was stationed at the headquarters of each of the—at the time—three Armies. With this team, Harvey set about implementing an ambitious six-point overhaul of tunnelling procedure:

FIRST, *he decreed that there was to be no offensive mining unless it formed part of a thought-out military operation involving the use of surface troops also.*

SECOND, *mining defences were to be designed to a definite and approved plan.*

THIRD, *The General Staff was to be kept fully informed about all important mining works.*

FOURTH, *the results of mine-firing were to be reported to the General Staff.*

FIFTH, *the Inspector was to advise the General Staff about the transfer of tunnelling companies from one army to another.*

SIXTH, *the Inspector was to attend to all such matters as appointments, reinforcements, supplies of stores and equipment.*

It meant that there would be no more arguments with Brigade and other local commanders about who gave orders to the tunnelling companies, and no more casual blowings. From now on, each mine was to play a deadly part in the struggle for victory. And to achieve this, the tunnellers had become the nearest thing to a private army that serving officers had ever seen.

The new organization caused apprehension and discontent here and there among tunnelling officers who felt that the wrong men had been given control. Major Hunter Cowan, commanding 175 Company, was dismayed to find that the Controller appointed over him, Lieutenant-Colonel Alexander "Fatty" Stevenson, knew little—at least in his opinion—about mining practice. "I never did care much for mining," Cowan wrote in his private diary—"but now that I am chased by someone who knows less than I do and who in turn is hunted by someone still less informed; well, it's time for the war to stop!"

But Harvey, the newly emerged man of iron, fiercely determined to make the tunnelling effort achieve all that had been hoped for it, would have replied that his controllers were not appointed for their technical knowledge—and nor was he. What he wanted were energetic hustlers of the Norton Griffiths type.

Among the many tasks Harvey faced was the desperate need to end the muddle and delay that had beset the supply of equipment since tunnelling operations started. First it was necessary to standardize the types of mining gear to be used. With vigour, irritability and some success, Harvey strove to reconcile the often contradictory opinions of his officers on the question of what was best for use in battle-front conditions. Soon modern pumps, dynamo lighting sets and efficient surveying and digging tools and instruments began arriving at stores. So did scientific listening equipment which, at last, gave a good picture of the enemy's position and activities.

The development of a worthwhile listening aid had been a particularly baffling problem. Cambridge University had produced a device made up of a tuning fork and diaphragm electrically amplified. An employee of an instrument making firm had offered another, again electrically operated, and built on to a metal spike that was driven into the ground. But tests proved both instruments to be grossly over-sensitive: they recorded a constant barrage of sound. Here the greatest difficulty was brought out: how to amplify mining sounds without amplifying all others.

By the autumn of 1915, "biscuit tin" listening aids had, for the most part, been superseded. But only by devices that gave no more than marginally better results. Short sticks each with a single vibrating wire-type earphone attached—an instrument used by Water Board inspectors—had grown popular. So had an improvised arrangement using heavy French water-bottles; these were filled with water, laid flat on their sides in pairs and listened to through medical stethoscopes. Many tunnellers rated them the best idea that had emerged by that date.

Then shortly before the end of 1915 Norton Griffiths and Captain Ralph Stokes of 174 Company (who was about to be appointed Harvey's chief assistant) came across a new device by chance, while investigating other equipment in Paris. It consisted of two wooden discs filled with mercury, faced with mica and bearing nipples to which a stethoscope could be plugged. The aid—a development of the water-bottle technique—had been evolved at the Sorbonne. Norton Griffiths and Stokes were amazed at the results it gave, and made immediate arrangements to take a sample back to headquarters.

Harvey also was impressed by the instrument and had a number made up and distributed for testing by companies. Enthusiastic reports soon started coming in to headquarters. Major Hunter Cowan noted that "results obtained were very encouraging. It is the only sound magnifier that does not lose timbre and quality . . . attributes most important to us. It is not enough to know Fritz is somewhere there—we want to know what he is actually doing".

The geophone told them. And by moving each of the two discs on the tunnel floor until the sound of enemy work was equally balanced in both ears, a trained operator could lay off an exact bearing towards it.

Down in the chalk of the 3rd Army front, hearing the enemy had always been easy since picking and sometimes even blasting techniques had to be used. It was often not possible, however, to pinpoint the position from which the sounds were coming with much accuracy. The fact that accurate bearings could be laid off with the geophone was full of promise. Captain Thomas Richardson, a 30-year-old, quiet-mannered and earnest officer in command of 185 Company, decided to make thorough tests on his mine system at La Boisselle, five miles north of the Somme.

Richardson had a three-decker mine system, the deepest tunnel being down by the water level, about 100 feet under. He decided to go with another officer, Second-Lieutenant Arthur Latham, into the middle level tunnel with two geophone sets while a third officer, Lieutenant Edward Lyall, made deliberate noises in the deep one. Richardson and Latham planned to locate Lyall's precise position by geophone if they could.

At lunch-time Richardson was crouched right forward at the face of a listening gallery and the tests were going well when the Germans blew a most unexpected and heavy camouflet that damaged the galleries and sent a tornado of poison gas crashing through them all. Almost immediately afterwards the gas ignited in a secondary explosion which flung a vast jet of flame through the workings.

The first that two 185 Company subalterns, Robert Howland and Thomas Smith, knew of the disaster was when they arrived for duty in the early afternoon and were met by an anxious faced infantry officer asking if there was anything he could do. When they realized what he meant they dashed into the mine to help without pausing to put on safety equipment. At the entrance they found another officer who had been inside at the time, an experienced 56-year-old engineer, Lieutenant Stafford Hill. He had been gassed and badly burned, but was still alive.

Down in the tunnel they found Richardson and Latham. Richardson was already dead. Latham lived, but was breathing very badly, grunting and snorting and deeply unconscious. They loaded him on to a spoil trolley and began wheeling him up an incline towards the entrance. While they struggled with the effort in the cramped confines of the tunnel, Latham's tortured breathing suddenly stopped. He was dead. Wretchedly Smith and Howland decided it had been a mistake to move him. There were many other bodies lying in the galleries, and Smith went round gathering keepsakes and tying them in handkerchiefs to send to the victims' relatives.

That evening they lifted the bodies of Richardson and Latham on to a ration cart and sent them to the near-by town of Albert for burial. The other ranks were buried in a common grave near the mine. Total casualties came to twenty. It was not the serious reflection on geophones that it seemed. By the time listening started the Germans must have laid and tamped their mine and nothing remained to be done but to fire it. There would have been no noise for the geophones to detect.

The geophone was in fact adopted and quickly justified the faith that Harvey, Norton Griffiths and the others had shown in it.

Harvey believed that improved training was vital. Already some schooling—mainly in rescue work—was being given to selected men at Armèntieres. Now he pushed forward a more ambitious scheme that developed soon into highly organized Army Mining Schools. By June, one had been started in each Army where officers and men began attending for exhaustive 10-day courses in mine fighting, listening, digging, timbering and rescue work. Military mining was fast becoming an established and technical form of warfare.

But Harvey's mind was mainly occupied with the idea of the grand mining offensive against Messines Ridge; the idea that he and Norton Griffiths had discussed together so often. Fowke's decision to support the plan had not yet produced any apparent result.

Then, suddenly, word came for Fowke, Harvey and Norton

Griffiths to attend a high-level conference of Army commanders to be held on January 6th, 1916. The chance to state their case was coming.

As could have been predicted, it was Norton Griffiths who did the talking. He plunged into his subject with the same zest and forceful-ness and with the same lack of respect for the glittering array of red-tabbed, grey-haired generals that he would have shown if he had been addressing his own rough-cut constituents in Wednesbury.

He said that if the mining scheme could be completed in the man-ner now being proposed, 10,000 soldiers' lives would be saved in the big attack. Indeed, he added, they could walk to the top of the heavily fortified ridge smoking their pipes. To the generals, now accustomed to the idea that a frontal attack was hopeless because of the enemy's strength, it must have come as a startling proposal.

Norton Griffiths went on to say that the plan was not so much to blow out the top of the ridge as to "earthquake" it—a technique made possible by the fact that the ridge was "virtually one big hill of sand sitting on blue clay". He guaranteed that not a single Ger-man machine gun would "bark" on the day of the attack *if* opera-tions were preceded by "our little earthquake".

The generals heard him out, listened to further supporting re-marks by Fowke and Harvey and then summarily rejected the scheme. The three engineers returned to their quarters in de-jection.

But late that night Fowke came hurrying to Norton Griffiths with dramatic news. The generals had changed their minds. Permission to earthquake the Messines Ridge would be given after all.

Just a handful of high-ranking soldiers knew why. An all-out combined Anglo-French offensive that was to win the war out-right was being planned for July. The Commander-in-Chief wanted something dramatically big to hurl at the Germans as a diversion in the north. On reflection Norton Griffiths's scheme seemed about right. It might mean a second victory, and if it failed there was the comforting knowledge that it was not the main battle.

So the tunnellers *were* going to be given the chance to show what they could do.

Harvey knew now that he had a major operation to command. Years later he remarked of it that "this was the biggest thing I ever commanded in my life". It had a very good effect on him. Major Cowan observed that: "I think his promotion has cheered him up no end and he is a much more companionable man than he used to be some 10 or more months ago. He certainly looks fitter in every way . . ."

Cheerful though Harvey undoubtedly now was, he forced the pace as fiercely as ever. A young officer on his staff, Lieutenant H. R. Dixon had a warning device on his desk which Harvey buzzed when he wanted to speak to him. The arranged signal was supposed to be five rings. But Dixon calculated, to his alarm, that the usual number of stabs Harvey made at the bell-push was fourteen. He used to respond in what he has since described as "a state of terror".

10

THE LESSON OF HOHENZOLLERN REDOUBT

TWENTY-SEVEN miles south of Ypres, near the shattered village of Loos and in front of a coal mine and its bedrabbled slag heap, stood a dead position known as the Hohenzollern Redoubt. Here the Germans had dug and wired themselves into a forward-facing bulge in their front line. Their special orders were to protect the coal mine at whatever cost, mainly for its sprawling 20 feet high, flat-topped slag heap which gave fine views of the British lines. The garrison crouched crowded together in the intricate network of trenches that made up the redoubt, resolutely determined to obey.

Men of the British 1st Army soon found that Hohenzollern was about the fiercest of all the positions ahead of them. When they hurled themselves forward into the wasteful, inconclusive and bungled Battle of Loos in September, 1915, it was the Hohenzollern defence that brought them to a bloody crash-stop in the north. After charging wildly through a choking smoke screen—that failed to blow forward as had been hoped—and then through murderous, non-stop fire, four Scottish regiments did overrun some of the redoubt trenches on the opening day of the battle, the 25th. But the gain could barely be held for a week. On October 3rd the Germans came smashing back to reclaim most of their lost ground. The British were left holding only one part of an outer fringe trench of the redoubt known as Big Willie. And the whole offensive by the 1st Army was thrown now into confusion and soon halted.

The French, struggling with a two-prong offensive further south, were also in trouble. Their Commander-in-Chief, General

Joffre, had very early given orders for the effort to be slowed, and by September 29th it had virtually stopped. Hasty plans were made to regroup the depleted and weary forces of both countries for a second push. But, as the days passed, there were repeated postponements of the action and then, suddenly on October 8th the Germans opened a surprise four-hour bombardment and followed it by surging out of their trenches in a full-scale counter-attack.

Although by nightfall the battle died down leaving both sides roughly where they were, it forced the Allies to postpone their already badly delayed attack even further.

Eventually, on the 11th, the French made a half-hearted attack against Vimy Ridge, gained a little ground—at the cost of over 2,000 men—and settled down for second thoughts. On the 13th, the British tried once more to take the deadly Hohenzollern Redoubt and other nearby objectives. Despite the crippling ammunition shortage, a bombardment by heavy howitzers and field guns was maintained for two hours before the assault. Gas was also discharged in almost ideal wind conditions. But neither did as much harm as had been hoped and expected. Much of the gas sank into shell-holes and remained there. Then, in the early afternoon, the 46th Division attacked in the traditional, open country, running and whooping manner. At once they were struck by devastating machine-gun fire and as the men pitched forward, dozens at a time into the chalky mud of the area, some regiments all but disappeared.

For this sacrifice a little more of the outer part of the redoubt was captured and there were very small gains against other nearby targets. It was found when the fighting ended in the small hours of the morning of the 14th that for this, 4,000 further British soldiers—civilian soldiers for the most part—had been lost. It was the end of the unforgettable Battle of Loos. General Haig, then commanding the 1st Army, did make plans to attack again, but abandoned them a week or two later when winter weather arrived to fix the two sides where they stood.

Mines had not been used in the battle; but now it was clear that for months to come any further offensive action in the sector would

The entrance to an early British tunnel by the River Lys (Ypres sector) 100 yards from the German front line. Tunnel entrances were kept as secret as possible and often disguised. This is probably the only such photograph in existence.

(*Above*): Norton Griffiths (*right*) somewhere in Flanders with the ubiquitous 1911, $2\frac{1}{2}$-ton chocolate-and-black Rolls Royce that he took to France. The car was disbodied by a shell but survived the war and was known to be running in the thirties.

(*Below*): On May 5th, 1915, the British fired mines under German trenches in the Neuve Chapelle sector. The Germans promptly retaliated. This is an entrance to one of their tunnels.

(*Right*): The inside of a German counter-mine tunnel being driven at Neuve Chapelle. German sappers were noted for the neatness of their workmanship.

(*Left*): The end of the same German tunnel. Sides and roof have been smashed in by a British camouflet.

(*Above*): How Ypres looked to the British in 1915. "I do not suppose," wrote
tunnelling company commander on May 31st, "that there is one single house un
harmed." Here Norton Griffiths (*right*) looks at the rubble.

(*Below*): How Ypres looked to the Germans, at the same time. This amazingl
good picture was taken by the Germans from Hill 60, two-and-a-half miles awa
The two prominent buildings are, (*left*) the Belfry; (*right*) St. Martin's Cathedra

(Above): The Germans were extremely good at rushing and holding newly-blown craters. Here they have entrenched themselves in a Hohenzollern crater lip.

(Below): Bad soil and water conditions meant that this German tunnel in the Ypres bulge could not be sunk deeper than about 30 feet. Permission to fire a charge from it was refused on the grounds that four infantry dugouts would be destroyed.

(*Left*): A post-war picture of a late British entrance shaft near Hill 60—probably the vertical entrance to the Berlin Tunnel.

(*Below*): Captain (later Colonel) Arthur Eaton, of 184 Tunnelling Company, photographed in January, 1916, with the German flag he brought back after swimming alone to the German rear via the Somme river. He was reprimanded by the C.-in-C. then awarded an immediate D.S.O. in the field.

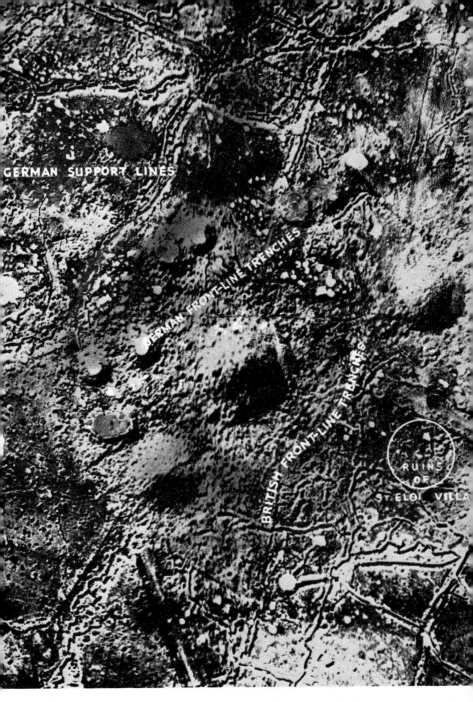

GERMAN SUPPORT LINES

GERMAN FRONT-LINE TRENCHES

BRITISH FRONT-LINE TRENCHES

RUINS OF ST. ELOI VILLA

An aerial view of the massive craters resulting from mines laid by Douglas and Birtle of 172 Company and fired on March 27, 1916.

(Above): One-eight-five Company officers. Major Euan Tulloch is seated at centre. H. W. Graham, then a second lieutenant, is sitting on the extreme right.

(Below): One-eight-five Company men. Under Tulloch the unit became efficient and confident. Most of these men would be ex-coal miners.

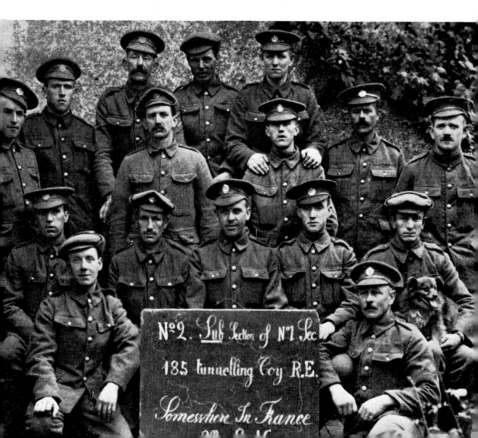

(*Above*): The Somme mine that was detonated too soon. Hawthorne Ridge Redoubt mine shown exploding ten minutes before the start of the Battle of the Somme. Three sections of the German 119th Reserve Regiment are dying in the debris, but the early firing revealed that an offensive was imminent.

(*Below*): The Somme mine at La Boisselle, 450 feet across, and the largest crater red during the war. It obliterated nine German dug-outs and the men inside them. T. H. Smith, a former 185 Company tunneller, is standing on the bottom.

(*Above*): A view from inside one of the giant Messines craters. This is Spanbroek-molen, 430 feet from rim to rim and one of the nineteen mines that staggered the German army on June 7th, 1917.

(*Below*): Spanbroekmolen crater after the war was a 40-feet deep lake, half of which can be seen in this photograph taken in 1960. Visitors are challenged to throw a stone from bank to bank and despite the encroachment of weeds, nobody can.

(*Above*): This German dug-out was half buried by debris from the Spanbroekmolen mine. Four German officers found inside were comfortably seated and outwardly unhurt, but dead from concussion.

(*Right*): The Spanbroekmolen crater was bought by Lord Wakefield and presented to Talbot House (Toc H) as a war memorial. It was named the Pool of Peace and this commemorative headstone erected.

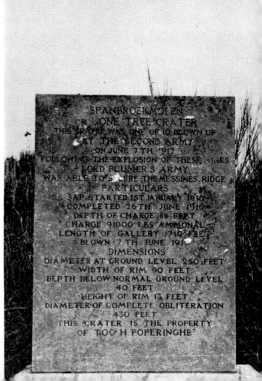

SPANBROEKMOLEN
OR LONE TREE CRATER
THIS CRATER WAS ONE OF 19 BLOWN UP
BY THE SECOND ARMY
ON JUNE 7TH 1917
FOLLOWING THE EXPLOSION OF THESE MINES
LORD PLUMER'S ARMY
WAS ABLE TO SECURE THE MESSINES RIDGE
PARTICULARS
SAP STARTED 1ST JANUARY 1916
COMPLETED 26TH JUNE 1916
DEPTH OF CHARGE 88 FEET
CHARGE 91000 LBS AMMONAL
LENGTH OF GALLERY 1710 FEET
BLOWN 7TH JUNE 1917
DIMENSIONS
DIAMETER AT GROUND LEVEL 250 FEET
WIDTH OF RIM 90 FEET
DEPTH BELOW NORMAL GROUND LEVEL
40 FEET
HEIGHT OF RIM 13 FEET
DIAMETER OF COMPLETE OBLITERATION
430 FEET
THIS CRATER IS THE PROPERTY
OF TOC H POPERINGHE

(*Above*): Hill 60, once a neat railway embankment, photographed in August, 191
An early (and small) mine crater is shown surrounded by shell-holes.

(*Below*): A mine chamber on the Albert front. For some charges the chambe
were as big as a large living-room. The officer is using a geophone listening a

have to go underground. Orders went to one of the most experienced of the tunnelling companies, 170, to take over.

The Company had already distinguished itself in some bitter mining contests just three miles to the north at Givenchy. Despite seven months of effort, many losses and the hard lessons that go with pioneering, morale in the Company was good. The Commander, a regular R.E., Captain Frank Preedy could take much credit for that. Though only 28 years old and a short, slight, physically unimpressive man, Preedy had given his company excellent leadership. He proved many times that he was—as one of his former subalterns, William Morgan* has recalled—a first-class soldier and "as brave as a lion". Norton Griffiths was greatly taken with him and had tried, unsuccessfully, to persuade Lieutenant-General Sir E. H. H. Allenby, Commander V Corps, to take him as mining adviser.

From the beginning, he showed a sensitive broadmindedness in dealing with tunnelling officers and men. He was another pure-bred soldier commissioned in the Royal Engineers at 19 and carefully reared at the Corps' Chatham base in the traditions of honour, valour, gentlemanliness and, in somewhat lesser degree, engineering.

At first, Preedy had worked strictly to the military handbook, ordering narrow tunnels of some three feet by two feet to be dug. It made movement a misery. The men were forced to crawl, or walk bent almost double and repeatedly whacking their heads on the roof; when two men wished to pass, one had to lie flat while the other crawled over him. Some of the experienced mining engineers on his strength were horrified by such conditions. Among these was Morgan who, as an underground railway engineer, had well-tried views on the subject. A number of officers pleaded with Preedy to forget the book and increase the size of the tunnels. The advantages, they pointed out, would be much easier working conditions and some chance of rescuing hurt or gassed miners. Preedy listened tolerantly and agreed. From then on 170 Company

---

* Later a tunnelling company commander himself—of 255.

tunnels were a more comfortable width and height—about five feet by four. It meant extra excavations and more dug chalk to dispose of but the new roominess proved very worthwhile.

An early visitor to Preedy at Hohenzollern was Norton Griffiths, who arrived on October 24th in his usual breathless flurry. This was the sixth tunnelling company he had called on that day, but he was still aggressively alert and hungry for information. He was excited to hear of the redoubt with the pit-head—known officially as Fosse 8—and its observation slag heap lying closely ahead. They were ideal immovable targets and he at once began urging an ambitious mining programme, reporting to Fowke and Harvey that here "a *big* offensive work should be started . . ."

Preedy, himself an eager and energetic personality, arranged at once for digging to begin, and while a shaft was sunk in the front line an awkward survey of the German position was made using compasses and periscopes from behind the protection of the trench parapet. At a depth of about 35 feet, work began on a system of tunnels and connecting galleries, intended to reach a hundred yards and more out through no-man's-land and under the redoubt. But within a day or so, before any real progress had been made, ominous sounds were heard that could only be German miners. Clearly they had started first and were well ahead. They were already below, and even behind, the British line.

It was an emergency situation and Preedy did the only thing he could. He ordered a heavy mine to be rush-laid and fired in the newly started tunnel, even though it would be unavoidably close to the shaft bottom. It made a massive explosion which ruined the shaft and a length of the line and left a gaping crater where it was least wanted. But it almost certainly destroyed some of the German tunnel and its occupants—which brought the priceless reward of a little time.

Now a bitter, all-out struggle began between the rival miners, with the British side already desperately pressed at the outset. But Preedy started fighting furiously back with a newly standardized tactic known as "offensive-defensive" mining—a method which

Harvey, when he became Inspector of Mines soon afterwards, made obligatory for such situations.

The subsoil at Hohenzollern was chalk overlaid with clay. Twenty feet down and still in the clay layer, a gallery was driven parallel to the front line and slightly ahead of it. From there a large number of tunnels were driven forward, side by side, some 60 feet apart. Whenever German work was heard close to one it was immediately charged and fired. The neighbouring tunnels—one on each side—were then spurted forward and turned slightly inwards to converge towards the German gallery which the enemy would now be repairing or redriving. As soon as more German sounds could be heard clearly in either of the converging tunnels, another mine would be fired.

A roughly similar manoeuvre was used when the Germans blew first. Either way, 170 tunnellers squeezed quickly towards the attacking German gallery behind its face. It was nerve-racking but exhilarating work for the British tunnellers. Most infantry commanders had used them as little more than a stationary underground buffer. Now these days were over by Harvey's orders, and whether the infantry generals liked it or not. The tunnellers had become assault troops fighting their way forward with superior skill, energy and courage. With exhausting speed mines were dug, charged and fired over and over again. And yard by yard the Germans were forced back the way they had come. Some three months and 50 mines after the start of operations it was the turn of Preedy's men to find themselves on the far side of no-man's-land ready to attack. It was specially pleasing to the dogged, gallant Preedy who always yearned for a real fighting role in the war.

Yet the German effort had by no means been a total failure. Many of their charges had cratered to the surface throwing up high lips round the rims and daring German infantrymen had flung themselves across to man them. In this way they edged their front line forward a short but important distance on the surface even though they were losing ground below it. The British line was forced not only back further out of the redoubt, but also down on to a lower level. The Germans began to overlook it and promptly put their snipers to work potting at unsuspecting British soldiers as casually as sportsmen.

But while the sweated battle in the clay was fought, Preedy had ordered three much deeper tunnels to be forced through the chalk using patent drills in place of the traditional picks. The noise of the electrically driven drills biting through the chalk was considerable—but different and less revealing.* With the help of the clamorous action overhead, Preedy hoped to keep the presence of the deeper tunnels secret. By February they had been pushed safely—and apparently undetected—to the German lines. Preedy had them loaded with massive 7,000-lbs., 8,000-lbs. and 10,055-lbs. charges of ammonal respectively, and stood ready to cause the biggest up-heaval that even the battered battlefield of Hohenzollern had yet seen. He can hardly have anticipated the cool reception the infantry commanders gave his announcement that all was ready.

The truth was that the Germans had shown themselves so adept at seizing and holding newly blown craters that Lieutenant-General H. de la P. Gough, commanding the 1st Corps then holding that part of the line, hesitated to compete for three more; especially for such large ones. For these would be giant craters with towering lips. Whichever side took and held then would dominate the other's front line. Past experience suggested that despite the advantage the British would have in knowing just when the mines would go off, and the disadvantage the Germans would suffer due to the shock and losses of the explosion, the day might still be lost. In some inexplicable way the Germans had shown a knack for this man-oeuvre that the British could not equal.

But the alternative was to waste the laboriously laid charges with

* Three former 170 Company officers could not remember these drills when this book was being researched. Two of them thought it unlikely that such aids were in fact used. However, it is known with certainty that the Company possessed at least one drill (made by Hardy Pick) as early as August, 1915 and that six further drills were ordered *before* December. Also, German soldiers in the area heard a buzzing which they believed to be the sound of drilling (see text). Significantly, it stopped before the mines were blown.

their enormous destructive power. The situation was discussed at
length. It was a time of great anxiety for Preedy. He feared that at
any moment the Germans might discover the mines lying mute and
menacing beneath them. In the end Gough decided that the issue
could not be dodged; the mines must be fired—and soon. Hasty
preparations were made for the kind of attack that was to need every
ounce of heart and muscle the British side could muster. The date
was fixed for March 2nd (1916), zero: 5.45 in the evening. Two
battalions of Royal Fusiliers were to make the assault. Preedy was
to have a party ready to go over the top right behind them to search
out enemy tunnels.

Usually a softening-up bombardment preceded such attacks.
This time it was dispensed with in the hope of greater surprise. So
the last minutes of waiting passed in curious silence. The Fusiliers
stood tense and ready by their ladders waiting for the word.

Ahead lay the 50 yards across a wet and glutinous no-man's-land
and the hellish uproar of the craters. Could they beat the Germans
at what seemed to have become their speciality? Soon the
answer would be known.

*   *   *

The Allies had long ago found that of all the enemy soldiers they
had to face, the Bavarians were the greatest menace. These men,
reared in the shadow of the towering Alps, were hardy, dogged
often ferocious fighters. When they took over a new part of the
line the bad news always travelled with special speed to the other
side of no-man's-land. There the French or British would curse
their luck and grimly prepare for trouble.

It was the Bavarians who had so persistently taken and held the
craters blown by German miners during the winter stalemate at
Hohenzollern. Two battalions of them—the 3rd Battalion the 18th
Bavarian Regiment and the 1st Battalion the 23rd—made up the
garrison of the redoubt. Still serving with the 23rd was Sergeant
Michael Schneider of the 10th Company. The regiment, now
rather weary and battle-worn, had been transferred from the bloody
mudholes of St. Eloi to the equally hideous front of Hohenzollern.

And there the advance of Preedy's tunnellers quickly took their toll of their nerves. The Bavarians were still most willing to fight an enemy they could see; but, like many other good soldiers, they dreaded the men who stalked invisibly from below.

Their ears soon noted the harsh, scouring buzz of 170 Tunnelling Company electric drills pushing slowly, inexorably towards them. Unlike the German engineers who were puzzled by the unfamiliar sounds, the infantry decided at once what they were: mines! To them the ceaseless thrum, the strange little tremors in the ground that came nearer and nearer their feet could only be that. Some of the men were terrified.

One morning while Schneider was walking with another N.C.O., Sergeant Weikel also of the 23rd Bavarians, a bearded private rushed out of a dug-out to speak to them. The man, an infantry-man, was most excited. He complained that even if the engineers could hear nothing suspicious from below, they—the infantry— could. They knew the English were underneath them and, for his part, he refused to stay there any longer.

Schneider and Weikel went down into the dug-out to investigate and there found five or six soldiers squeezed into the tiny space. They were all listening; and they all had frightened faces.

The two N.C.O.'s forced their way among the arms and legs and started to listen themselves. Schneider caught his breath at the sound he heard. Subsequently, he recalled that it had seemed much like the rasp of a dentist's drill. He, too, now reacted with alarm and dashed off to find an expert, returning soon with an N.C.O. of the Pioneers. But the Pioneer—a calm Prussian—decreed that this was not the sound of mining work. When Schneider pressed him to say what, in that case, it could be, the Prussian blamed it on the rats.

Then the bearded and still excited private urged that the British might be using hand drills. At this the Prussian laughed and replied that he was crazy to suggest it. To be effective, he added, the drill would have to be electrically driven and that would take a large amount of power. He ruled it out as a serious possibility.

But that afternoon the sappers did make special arrangements for a listening check, and for an hour the troops were ordered to remain absolutely quiet. Trained miners considered the sounds reaching them from the chalk bed. And the next morning the Prussian N.C.O. came round again to deliver the verdict. As he had thought, he said, the sounds—whatever else they might be—were *not* the sounds of mining.

The bearded private, still unconvinced and terrified, promptly moved out of the trench to the rear. Schneider, who knew he should stop him, allowed him to go.

The dreadful noise of drilling continued almost non-stop for day after day. Once Schneider relieved his own strained feelings by tossing a hand grenade down an empty listening shaft in reply; his orderly Adam Kirsch followed by throwing several. Sometimes the crash of these explosions brought a lull in the sound of drilling. But never for long.

Then, suddenly, the drills became ominously silent. Four days passed—and still they were silent. For the next four days, Schneider was to be out of the trenches, resting; he went with even more than the usual gladness. But when he returned, there was still no sound from the drills and still an oppressive feeling of danger in the air. Now Adam Kirsch, the orderly, had become very worried. This time, he assured Schneider, they would be blown up. He begged that they should move to the rear.

Schneider replied that that was impossible. But he was himself feeling worn out and jumpy, and he spoke again to the Pioneers. This time they took him down into their own shallow galleries to prove that the British could not have come through. But Schneider argued that the British might be much deeper and could have passed underneath long ago. He wanted to see a mine exploded that might catch and crush British tunnellers still at work on their charges. Apparently his words had some effect. That day the Pioneers suddenly altered their attitude of confidence and announced that a mine would be blown the same evening.

As it happened, Schneider was put in charge of the raiding party that would rush out to the rim of the new crater. The mine was fired and Schneider and his men went forward unopposed and dug in. When dawn came they found that they had a clear view into part of the British trench. Schneider and Weikel spent most of the day sniping at British soldiers who made the fatal mistake of still believing that they were hidden behind their parapet.

Eventually the British must have realized what was happening, and that night they sent a small party to assault the new crater. Schneider knew they were coming when he heard the defensive wire his men had put up being pulled away. He gave the warning by firing a flaming Very flare into the middle of the party. A short, vicious exchange of fire followed and then the assaulting party withdrew.

Time passed, and still the Bavarians awaited the great British blow that they feared. They liked to group together now for companionship, united by the dull terror in their hearts. Adam Kirsch had come to feel that they should be sleeping in the open trench, since in the dug-out their heads would be dashed against the roof when the mine went off; but in practice he remained inside. Another soldier—an old friend of Schneider's—remarked that the ground looked very hard to fall on. And later he became very bitter about the fact that they had to stay there, loudly questioning the whole point of trying to preserve the Hohenzollern Redoubt. Gently but firmly Schneider quietened him, knowing that the orders were quite emphatic: Hohenzollern had to be held. Argument did nothing to help.

Towards the end of February heavy rain and snow fell, filling the trenches and dug-outs with ice-cold water and greatly adding to the misery of the garrison. British fire power increased also, knocking giant holes in the Bavarians' defences. On March 1st, Schneider's unit was due for a very welcome rest period behind the lines and that night gratefully handed over to the 11th Company of the 18th Regiment.

It was the next evening, at 5.45, in deepening twilight that 170 Tunnelling Company officers fired the devastating mines they had laid with the help of the drills. Three terrible fountains of earth shot immediately into the sky. German witnesses noted that there was a moment almost of silence as the earth, trench materials and shattered human beings gyrated through space. Then came the screams of buried but conscious men to be drowned at once by the crash and shudder of a sudden British bombardment opened up in support of the charging Fusiliers. Thick smoke clouds drifted over the broken Hohenzollern Redoubt dimming the flares and gun flashes.

Underground in German tunnel No. 6, Private Ludwig Lange of the 19th Regiment of Pioneers was fighting to free his feet. He remembered a terrible moment of buffeting that ended with the discovery that he was trapped; a monstrous outside pressure had distorted the timbers of the roof and walls, clamping two butt-jointed frames against his feet like an outsize pair of pliers. He could see his electric torch lying on the ground where he had dropped it; it was still alight, casting a narrow beam on the scene of havoc. Near it lay his pipe.

Five men had been down at the face with Lange driving a lateral right and left, roughly parallel with the front line, 200 feet out under no-man's-land; three more had been in a chamber to the rear of the tunnel. It looked like nine men altogether, in a common grave.

But soon four of the face workers, all uninjured, came crawling to Lange's aid and managed to free his feet; he was not much hurt. With the help of the torch, the five looked round the wrecked tunnel. They found the remaining face worker lying trapped in the woodwork, by the look of it gravely injured about the head. They moved to the rear to see what chance there was of escape. The answer was numbingly clear: None. The entrance shaft had fallen in and countless tons of broken chalk mixed with mud barred the way. And near-by, the chamber had collapsed on the other three pioneers who were whimpering vainly for help.

Seconds later, Lange and his comrades realized that death was coming to all of them more quickly even than they thought: For the first time they noticed the water; it was splashing and swirling round their feet; the tunnel was flooding, quickly.

For twenty horrifying minutes they crouched, devoid of hope, waiting for the end, dully watching the cold, cloudy water creep inch by inch up their legs. Then—with the water at knee level— Lange had an idea: a few days before he had worked as helper to a surveyor in a neighbouring tunnel. He recollected that it ran parallel to this one and was not, he believed, a great many yards to the right. Already a start had been made on the lateral that was supposed to link the tunnels up and now Lange began to wonder if it might just be possible to dig the connexion through. With luck the other tunnel would be clear to the surface.

They began to work at the top of their strength doing short, ten-minute spells in turn. In only 25 minutes they made contact. The opening was narrow, barely wide enough for a cat to go through. But fresh air percolated through it. One after another they went forward to fill their lungs refreshingly. Then, with wild energy they clawed at the chalky soil until the hole was big enough to admit them. Lange wriggled through and shone his now dimming torch along the neighbouring tunnel. It seemed intact. Soon all five were up at the entrance, listening to the clamour of battle. A Bavarian lieutenant saw them and called them out to fight. They were suffering from shock and exhaustion and were unclothed, except for trousers; but they struggled out into the shattered trench, took tunics and rifles from bodies lying near and opened fire.

Among the worst hit infantry units was the 18th Regiment's 11th Company—Schneider's relief. Nearly half its strength was lying now in a crude grave beneath countless tons of debris. Some of these men were alive and a few lived on for over a week. Schneider himself, and his comrades, were at tea. They had missed the dreaded moment after all, though only by a matter of hours.

*   *   *

The two battalions of Fusiliers charged towards the reeling Bavarians as fast as they could cover the heavy ground. Speed, as they well knew, was their best guarantee of victory.

Even so, many of the Hohenzollern defenders were ready to meet them with ferocious fire. It was beginning to seem that mines and shells—however destructive—could not be conclusive against a stubborn enemy. The Bavarians recovered quickly from their shock and leapt at whatever fighting positions they could find. Even some who had been hurt by the blast and debris crawled forward to help.

A corporal, Friederich Noll, though severely wounded and losing blood, instantly began to draw himself to and fro along the front hurling hand grenades without pause at the attackers; two privates Hugo Jung and Josef Hollander, scrambled forward to stand with extraordinary courage almost fully exposed at the remains of their parapet firing and throwing bombs. They were soon joined by others. As the night grew cold and unusually dark a struggle developed that was bloody and most bitter.

The first victory went to the Fusiliers, who took the craters and a number of older ones near by. In one not previously known to the British—and now named Triangle Crater—a tunnel entrance was found. The 170 Company raiding party was told. Led, it is thought, by Lieutenant Thomas Brown, its two N.C.O.'s and eight men raced at once across the fire-swept no-man's-land to investigate.

Fifteen feet down, near the bottom of the crater, they found an opening which they promptly entered. Now they were in a small-bore, close-timbered tunnel—about four feet six inches by three feet—pointed towards the British line. Cautiously they followed the passageway along, noting that it sloped gently downwards all the way. It was soon clear that the German miners had had to work with poor supporting services: there was no electricity, no tramway and the only apparent ventilation came through a six-inch galvanized iron pipe. Yet the workmanship was good. The 170 Company experts shone their torches on it and were impressed.

About 50 feet down the tunnel a joining gallery came in from the left. It appeared to rake off towards the German trenches so Brown placed two men to guard it while he and the others crept on. But in a few more yards the tunnel ended as a tangle of debris; it had evidently been collapsed by an earlier British blow.

The party made its way back to the guard and turned down the tunnel leading towards the Germans. At about 40 feet a short, apparently uncompleted fork went off to the right. Twenty feet further on another rather mysterious short length, totally wrecked, came in from the left. Stealthily the raiders moved on until they found themselves emerging at the far end into a major tunnel where they had to turn left or right. To the left lay the German front-line trench, to the right, the British. They turned right first and there found the tamping and firing leads of an earlier German mine ahead of them, all still in place and effectively closing the tunnel. There remained only one exploration to make: the journey towards the Germans.

Step by step they advanced along the narrow gallery. Soon it began to incline upwards and they knew they were nearing the German line. Suddenly a draught of air began to blow freshly on their faces and before long it became very strong. Now they were close to the darkened entrance, right in the heart of hostile ground. It was a moment of extraordinary drama as they crouched like ancient conspirators deciding what to do. Their only arms were three revolvers, a few hatchets and eight portable charges; yet a whisper's distance overhead a bitter battle shook the ground.

The first danger was of discovery. At any moment the Germans might return to the tunnel and then one of the savage, hand-to-hand underground fights that both sides dreaded would follow. And if a cool-headed German threw just one well-placed hand grenade among the huddled raiders, its effect—in so confined a space—would be appalling. Brown ordered the entrance to be sandbagged off and a tedious, hurried labour began. The heavy bags were dragged in from Triangle Crater, then hauled the long and awkward journey to a point near the German entrance. There a barricade three bags thick was built.

Then, in the hope of closing the gallery permanently to the Germans, five of the mobile charges were stacked near the barricade. They were prepared for firing, quickly backed with five feet of chalk tamping and the fuses (two) were lit. The party withdrew.

The charge was a failure. When they looked back to inspect

results they found that although a good deal of soil had been shaken down, the tunnel was by no means closed. There was still a clear way through over the top of the debris. It was disappointing, but nothing more could be done for the moment. The raiders, now tired from their long labours, withdrew.

They found that at least on the surface events appeared to have been going well. Despite the darkness, the heavy going and the fierce German defence, the Fusiliers had taken their objectives and were holding on. A large piece of the Hohenzollern Redoubt was in British hands.

But, as it happened, the Germans counter-attacked at dawn—March 3rd. They maintained a terrific pressure towards Crater A, the southernmost of Preedy's giant new craters and the one that gave the best view of the redoubt. Local reserves—including Schneider's unit—had been rushed to the area. The men were attacking across such boggy fields that their boots and socks were sucked from their feet; but they struggled on barefoot on the wet winter ground. Next day—the 4th—they recaptured Triangle Crater, which lay close to Crater A and in the path of the attack.

Lieutenant Brown's raiding party had made a quick survey of the German mine system while down it two nights before; this showed a gallery leading straight from the Triangle Crater towards another known as Crater 1, a key point occupied by Fusiliers. The danger was obvious: it would now be a simple matter for German miners to charge the gallery and blow the garrison to pieces. Either a further withdrawal would be necessary (which would have been serious) or the German gallery must be lastingly blocked.

It was another job for 170 Company. Preedy detailed another officer, apparently Lieutenant Archebald, to enter the German mine to destroy it. He was to be accompanied by only one man, a sergeant.

A working party dug strenuously for hours from Crater 1 and finally forced a way in. Archebald and the N.C.O. entered the gallery. By means no longer known, the two men could tell that

Germans had very recently been there; but, for the moment, they were nowhere to be seen. The damp, tomb-like tunnel was deserted.

With great daring, Archebald and the sergeant crept stealthily the whole length of the gallery, back to Triangle Crater, and almost in the entrance placed a light guncotton charge, fused it and fired it without tamping. The ground here was clay already partly broken by other explosions. It fell in exactly to plan and formed a solid block in the tunnel.

But there was still the other gallery that branched away to the German trench. Archebald hurried to the spot where the previous attempt at sabotage had failed. He decided to try another untamped charge which would have the special merit of being quick. It was incredible that the Germans appeared unaware so far of the value of their galleries in this position; they had to be expected at any minute—the more so since the noisy stoppage of the Triangle Crater entrance took place. A 112-lb. charge of guncotton was laid and fired.

But this one, though relatively heavy, was a distressing failure. It actually enlarged the tunnel to about seven feet at the point of the explosion. The soil here was chalk. It seemed too strongly knit to collapse from any charge simply dumped in the void of the gallery. Eventually a special chamber was dug into the side of the tunnel-wall and a 300-lb., thoroughly tamped charge of ammonal pushed into it and fired. It squeezed outwards with great force and col-lapsed the communicating gallery at last. By some astounding oversight, the Germans kept clear while the work of destruction went on.

A day or so later, on March 7th, the weather grew colder than ever and heavy snow fell. The battle began to subside. But, un-expectedly, on the 18th, the Germans punched back with another whirlwind attack. First came a merciless bombardment; trench mortars lobbed shell after shell into the British-held craters. Then came the charge. It began badly. Five mines fired in support went off so short of target that many of the charging Bavarians were flung from their feet. By the time they were up again, the anger of battle had left them; the assault was losing its vigour.

One man saved the moment for the Germans. Lieutenant Muller, in command of a reserve company of the 18th Regiment, stood watching in dismay from the rear. Then, without orders, or a pause even for thought, he led his men out in a dashing charge all the way to the craters where they closed with the British defenders. Muller's action restarted the attack; and this time it succeeded.

The British moved out of their stinking craters, away from the hideous sludge of mud and blood in the bottoms, away from their pathetic pallisades that slithered down the sides at every quake, and retired to their old front line.

For them it had been a sad engagement: two thousand men killed, hurt and missing without gain. But it had also been an important one. It had shown that mine craters—large and tempting though they were—could not be held for ever. The question now arose: should they be held at all? Brigadier-General A. B. E. Cator, in command of the British force on the fateful 18th March, thought not. He gave his reasons in his report of the setback. The General Staff agreed.

From then on, the near lip alone was fought for and manned. The Germans saw the wisdom of the change and adopted it themselves.

Despite the disappointing outcome, Harvey and Norton Griffiths were pleased with 170 Tunnelling Company's work. The fault—if fault there was—belonged to others. Harvey took the trouble to drive over for a word of congratulation with Preedy.

It gave great pleasure to the lion-hearted little Commander who cared so deeply about the glory of his unit .

11

THE LESSON REPEATED

BACK in December, Norton Griffiths had called at the head-quarters of 172 Company at the hamlet of Reninghelst, near Ypres, for a word with Captain Gilbert Syme, the new Commander. It was the first meeting of any importance that the two men had had. Syme was among the oldest of the tunnelling officers (he was in his forties), a greying dark-haired man with a neat moustache and a tendency to chestiness. Like his predecessor, Clay Hepburn—now a gas victim in England—Syme was a quiet, cultivated man who liked to think for a moment before acting, often chewing absently at his pipe-stem while he did so. He was slimly built, fastidious, and probably more sensitive than many mining engineers. There were smiles and a few jeers when he hung some pictures on his H.Q. walls. Viewed several ways, there seemed a risk that Syme would fail the lightning test of a Norton Griffiths once-over. But Syme was also a resolute man, efficient and subtly ambitious. He had already distinguished himself by removing, with Hepburn, the German charge at St. Eloi, and been rewarded with the Military Cross. In the event, Norton Griffiths approved of him at once.

At that December meeting, the first of any importance that the two men had had. Syme hit out with a complaint. He had inherited three deep shafts from his predecessor, Hepburn, which he was most anxious to develop. But recent 5th Corps orders were making it impossible. The Company was already fighting it out with the Germans in the filthy mud bath of the Bluff. Now the Company was required to employ most of its strength digging a vast system of shallow, defensive galleries along much of the

Corps' five-miles-long front. In Syme's view this was a misuse of his unit's function.

Norton Griffiths must have had the greatest sympathy for the new Commander's feelings. He had himself campaigned repeatedly for a new mining policy on the Ypres front. Only a month before, he had reported to Harvey and Fowke that the Germans were becoming steadily more active before the 2nd Army, and predicted that there would be a sudden demand for more tunnelling companies—but "to defend, not attack". He said then (as he had often said before) that he was "very unhappy" about the mining situation on that front. Syme's news seemed to show that the policy was as firm and unchanging as ever. In fact it was not; although neither Norton Griffiths nor Syme at that moment knew it, the Army Commander, General Sir Herbert Plumer, *did* believe in aggressive mining and had once urged it on the Commander-in-Chief. It was the General Staff of his 5th Corps who did not; and it was from them that Syme took his operational orders. But they were soon to have to change their attitude.

Plumer was already planning a hard-hitting assault at St. Eloi, to take back the ground lost nine months before to Sergeant Michael Schneider's unit, the 23rd Bavarians. He remembered that German mines had played an important part in that defeat, and planned now to give British miners the chance to strike back. Meanwhile, there was nothing much Norton Griffiths could say. On the principle of the dripping tap wearing away stone, he proposed that a local deep mining scheme should be worked out and put in for approval; then, in the usual hurry, he left. This time it was for St. Omer, and a talk at headquarters. On the way, the back axle of his maltreated Rolls-Royce broke—the sort of frustrating delay that Norton Griffiths always found unbearably vexing. Next day he renewed his complaints about the mining policy of the Ypres front, and remarked that there was as yet no movement on the part of the 2nd Army to lay out a big, offensive scheme.

By this time, the idea that such a big offensive scheme would eventually be used in the Messines-Ypres sector had begun somehow to be accepted in the Engineer-in-Chief's office and elsewhere. A number of tunnelling company commanders were thinking their own schemes out, and even beginning them. And when Norton Griffiths next called on Syme—on December 16th—he found him keener than ever to go deep into the smooth clay near St. Eloi.

In Norton Griffiths's mind this was confirmation that a good man had been put into an important command; he was greatly pleased and reported that "this new O.C. is promising well". He must have wished he could give him a freer hand.

But Syme's chance was approaching. Less than three weeks later came the official approval for an all-out mines attack at Messines that Norton Griffiths with his eloquence and passion had done so much to win. And by then Plumer had worked out the details of his earlier attack at St. Eloi; it relied heavily on mines. Syme was ordered to produce exactly the type of earthquakers tunnelling officers liked.

The Company had been operating in two halves—one at the Bluff, the other at St. Eloi under the command of a 30-year-old Yorkshire-born Scot, James Douglas. It was Douglas who now took over responsibility for the new project. Men were diverted week by week to his detachment from the Bluff, until soon he had 600 men—most of the Company—under his command.

Douglas, a tall, athletic-looking and handsome Lieutenant, settled eagerly down to the task. It was a strange twist that had put him in charge of so large a programme. He lacked the qualifications of most tunnelling company officers. He was not a mining or civil engineer—as the majority were; he was a geologist. Nor was he a Royal Engineer—not even a temporary one. He was a Gordon Highlander from the 1st Battalion seconded—slightly against his will—for special duties with the R.E. Despite many invitations, he refused to be transferred. Whenever possible, he wore the kilt or tartan trews.

Douglas had orders to lay five mines from the three shafts and work went rapidly ahead. Sometimes the Germans turned very heavy fire on the zone causing casualties in the front and com-

munication trenches near the mineheads. One of Douglas's officers
—a Canadian, Second-Lieutenant Livingstone—went down with
17 wounds (a company record) and was returned to a hospital in
London. But the St. Eloi detachment knew that, on the whole, it
was lucky; there was less squalor and horror there than at the loathsome windswept Bluff, a mile or so to the north-east.

On February 14th came the terrible news of the German attack
there and the loss of the whole British network of mines. There
was the distressing loss of 42 of the company's men. Three had been
killed and an officer had been wounded. But most worrying of all
was that 38 men were missing, and many were undoubtedly
prisoners. Most would have known of the St. Eloi workings. The
question now was, would the Germans get it out of them? And if
so—what then? Anxious days passed, and with relief the St. Eloi
detachment heard and saw nothing suspicious.

To keep the pace at its fastest, Douglas organized footage races
between shifts. To the winners went a prize that they really valued:
a bottle of whisky. Number 5 tunnel showed the most promise.
With its chamber 410 feet away under two lines of German trenches,
it was ready by February 24th, the first to be finished. A few days
later, on March 4th, number two arrived on target—the famous
St. Eloi hump—the "poisonous ulcer" to the Germans and
"mound of death" to the British.

The remaining mines were also coming forward with gratifying
speed. And meanwhile ton after ton of ammonal was arriving a
mile away at the railhead. Carrying parties manhandled the 50-lb.
boxes to the shaft head each night. This was dangerous work. A
cheery Second-Lieutenant, "Paddy" Williamson, was usually in
charge. Each time before dawn he would shake the sleeping Douglas
by the arm to tell him all had gone well. It was a relief. Ammonal
could go off if hit. It was bad stuff to take risks with.

Douglas, assisted by his second-in-command, Lieutenant G. P. B.
(Jack) Birtles and a gallant corporal, prepared all the charges for
firing himself. For many hours a day he lay priming and inserting
detonators, putting them in 25-lb. water-proofed primer charges

of ammonal, wiring each charge up and, finally, testing by shooting a low power charge through the detonators too slight to ignite them but strong enough to give readings on test instruments.

It was done too soon in the opinion of Norton Griffiths. He blew in on March 3rd, and was horrified to hear that mines in so exposed a position were being charged weeks before they would be used. But the work went on.

Then, when Mine One—the western-most tunnel—was 330 feet out and more than half-way over no-man's-land, enemy mining was heard overhead. Douglas went down himself to investigate and there was no doubt about it. At nine o'clock one evening he ordered work to be stopped and sat in the long silent gallery a few yards back from the face, listening to the German footsteps overhead. They were extraordinarily clear. Immediately over Douglas's head they were always distinctively loud—louder at this one spot than anywhere else—and he discussed the phenomenon with Birtles, a tough, practical, middle-aged engineer who was by now a firm friend. Together they surmised that at that point the enemy gallery must change its level. What Douglas could hear was the thump of German boots coming carelessly down some sort of ladder and landing heavily on the new, lower level.

It was satisfactory to note that the Germans were above and not below them. But the position was critical none the less. Douglas ordered work to finish on that tunnel for fear of giving the whole project away. But the tunnel could not be vacated. Listeners had to be posted to keep watch on the German movements. Soon they reported that work overhead had apparently stopped. Nerve-racking days followed, while the lonely listeners huddled tense and silent, down near the tunnel face, watching the flickering candles and wondering if each minute was to be their last—that dreaded moment when the German shift officer reached for his exploder, checked the leads, then whacked the plunger down.

And at last, on March 10th, it happened. All the listeners—there were three—died at their posts, under countless tons of Flanders clay released by a heavy German camouflet.

Douglas and Birtles, armed with a canary in a tiny wooden cage, went down at once to investigate the damage. A full 20 feet of the tunnel had been crushed out of existence; there was no hope of survivors. As the two men struggled to manœuvre themselves in the cramped space, the canary's cage suddenly broke and the bird flew out.

Because it revealed to the Germans that an active mine was near, the loss of a canary was always regarded as serious. Some four months earlier there had been a major canary crisis down near the Somme: the 178 Company cook had accidently set fire to a wooden aviary placed close to his field kitchen and although he extinguished the flames quite promptly a few of the 100 or more birds in storage escaped through the damaged part; they flew at once to the wire defences in front of the trench and perched there. An order was given for their recapture at once whatever the risk. An officer and a party of men had to leave the cover of the trench in bright sunshine, crawl to the wire and there pop their hats over the birds one by one. It was a faintly ludicrous but intensely dangerous operation; mercifully the Germans were slow to react. Ten minutes or so passed before they saw the British soldiers behaving so strangely at the wire. By the time they opened fire, the party was slithering back into cover with most, or all, of the canaries.

Another day, a solitary bird flew out to the remains of a bush far out in no-man's-land and there began to twitter. It was too far out to retrieve so the infantry were asked to kill it with rifle fire; they tried to oblige but missed repeatedly and at last a mortar was ordered to range on the canary. One of its shells made a direct hit and the bird and bush were totally destroyed.

Douglas and Birtles were lucky. They recaptured their bird while still far down the tunnel, near the wrecked face. The next problem was how to make the long, hands-and-knees scramble to the entrance shaft without hurting or losing the little creature on the way. Of course they could kill it; there were plenty more canaries. But somehow, despite the cheapness of their own and all their comrades' lives, they shrank from throttling this tiny bird. Finally,

Douglas wrapped the canary in his handkerchief and suspended it from his mouth for the journey back. He could feel the feathers fluffing against his chin. It was a considerable sacrifice; Douglas suffered from a life-long dread of birds.

Listening had to be maintained along the remaining 310 feet of tunnel. Renewed noises soon implied that the Germans were planning to blow again. On March 12th an elaborate new detector by the Western Electric Company was put into the tunnel to aid the listeners. This battery-powered device picked up earth tremors and converted them into electrical impulses which were then fed to a telephone receiver. In theory, very precise readings of distance and direction should have been obtainable. The machine turned out to be less of a success than had been hoped. But it was good enough to confirm the listeners' suspicions. It began to look as if a retaliatory camouflet would have to be blown even at the risk of drawing attention to the deep level work.

Meanwhile, Douglas pushed ahead with the firing arrangements in the other tunnels. On the 15th, number two was completed; on the 18th, number four. Fifty-six thousand pounds of ammonal—exactly 25 tons of about the most powerful explosive known to man at the time—had been laid. Then an extraordinary misfortune befell the eager Lieutenant. While showing another officer how to use the small, automatic pistol issued for use in the tunnels, Douglas was accidentally shot through the right leg.

In great pain he limped to his quarters at the hamlet of Dickebusch without reporting to the doctor. By now he knew that the date of the big assault was to be the 27th. Today was the 20th. If he went sick now he would miss the sight of his massive mines going up. For 48 hours he endured the pain, deadening it with as much aspirin as he dared to take. Birtles, the good friend, was watching with growing unease. Then he went to tell the doctor.

As Douglas had feared he was shipped away at once to hospital. At least it meant a visit home. On the journey he asked if he could be wangled into a Bruton Street hospital, London, where he knew Livingstone had been sent to recover from his 17 wound battering.

It was arranged. The two 172 Company officers were put in beds side by side where they could whisper together about the important day—still top secret to the world outside—soon coming.

On the 28th, they asked eagerly for morning papers. There they read that the mines had gone up as planned. But it was small-type news and the implication seemed to be that the assault might not be the quick, conclusive success that had been hoped.

In fact, it turned into the same old story as before—a highly successful series of mines, an artillery barrage, a roaring assault by the infantry and in the end something which, if not a defeat, was at least very much less than victory. And, of course, at the usual heavy cost in lives.

Six mines had gone up in all, a small one having been hastily tacked on at the extreme right during the last few days as an extra. The total charge exploded came to 73,900 lbs. of ammonal—nearly 33 tons. Its explosive effect was more than 20 times greater than the mines blown at Hill 60 eleven months before.

Syme had come up from headquarters in Reninghelst to perform the ceremony of firing. He found that Birtles had run all the wiring back to a specially strengthened cellar in St. Eloi, all that was left of a shattered building. Side by side the two men fired the mines at 4.15 in the morning British time, 5.15 to the Germans. It is thought that twin exploders were used, one for each officer. They fired the two biggest mines, numbers two and three, together at exactly zero hour; the rest followed quickly. Within a few seconds the debris from the last of the great St. Eloi mines was belching towards the cold, dawn sky.

Syme went hurrying away at once, back to headquarters, his interest seemingly gone as soon as the plungers had been pressed. He saw little of the dumbfounding effect of the mines that ripped open the clay, sent sheets of flame driving upwards as if enveloping St. Eloi, killed between 300 and 400 Germans in the 18th Reserve Jaeger Battalion and rocked the trenches for far around. And he saw nothing at all of the bitter action that followed.

It was the Fusiliers again who went over. After a night of lying

out on the freezing ground without adequate clothing, they
attacked even before the mine debris had fallen.

The incredible Germans still managed to man their machine
guns in places—with deadly effect. Also, the mines had so changed
the landscape ahead that the assaulting British soldiers were confused and unsure of their positions. In cold wet weather the struggle
waxed and waned for days. Conditions were so bad and the battle
so furious that constant reliefs had to be arranged for the exhausted
troops.

On the 30th, the Germans took two of the craters. On April 4th
the entire Canadian Corps moved in to the, by now, crumbling and
watery trenches. But the position simply could not be held. By
the 5th, the Germans were holding four of the craters and after two
more weeks of muddled, wearisome fighting, they took one more,
plus an old crater near by. There the battle of St. Eloi ended.
Casualties were much the same as at Hohenzollern—about 2,000
killed, wounded and missing. And for much the same result.

Douglas heard all about it from Birtles who came home shortly
afterwards on leave. They felt greatly pleased with their own part
of the operation, for it at least had been a success. "Two medals
will be coming to the company for this," Birtles predicted. "A
D.S.O. for you and an M.C. for me." And soon two medals were
awarded—but to other officers.

For Douglas and Birtles there was nothing. Not even a mention
in dispatches.

*   *   *

Norton Griffiths missed the great eruption at St. Eloi. He was 40
miles away on March 27th, down on the 3rd Army front and
deeply involved in an old, familiar argument. The six-shilling rate
—the tedious issue that had been a blight on tunnelling company
organization ever since the start—was causing trouble once again.
He must often have looked back to that cold, wet day at Westminster when Dave Evans, Garfield Morgan and the ten other
miners from the 8th South Wales Borderers had refused to sign
their transfer papers for a two-and-twopenny rate. There had just

been a second or two to decide what to do; then, pressed by the urgency of the need for miners, he had raced downstairs to the street, called the men back and signed them indiscriminately at the higher rate. From that moment there had been trouble. The men, after years of fighting for what they regarded as their rights at home against the pit bosses, had refused to be restrained either by army regulations or pleas to patriotism; they had clamoured unceasingly for the higher rate for almost everyone. And by now the Miners' Federation of Great Britain had joined in the rumpus and was pressing the War Office for a clear understanding about pay. Officials were working up to a demand finally made in mid-April for the six-shilling rate to be paid to four-sevenths of all tunnelling company sappers—a demand that the War Office decided it must allow.

Yet tunnelling company commanders were still supposed to be distinguishing between the skilled face worker digging, guiding and timbering the tunnel, and the various sappers who assisted him. The position had been chaotic.

Not that Norton Griffiths worried about it very deeply. He knew that the quickest way to obtain volunteers was to offer high pay and he felt that that was what mattered most; if some unfairness resulted, it would just have to be put up with. Once a two-and-twopenny miner complained that Norton Griffiths had promised him six shillings and had actually made an entry in his paybook to that effect. He showed the book to Norton Griffiths angrily in support of his story. Norton Griffiths studied the entry for a moment. "Ah," he said, "it's in pencil. That doesn't count."

But on March 22nd he confessed to Harvey that "all O.C.'s appear to be frightened of six-shilling men from England". And so they were. They felt strongly that the right procedure was to promote men in the field; besides making surer that only genuinely skilled men were upgraded, this method gave the men an incentive to good work. Acceptance of newly drafted or transferred men with the skilled grading, on the other hand, was a *dis*incentive. It meant that commanders often had to hold back miners who had proved themselves worthy of promotion. Otherwise they would finish up with surplus "tunnellers" and no "mates".

The O.C.'s had also been shocked to discover that once a man had been rated at six shillings he could not be down-graded again. Each month this dilemma grew more serious. Many of the first tunnellers were old men already tired from years of labour when they joined up, and had since been stressed to the point of physical breakdown by front-line conditions. Norton Griffiths referred to them with characteristic bluntness as "worn out crocks" and "broken reeds". They hung about the bases often doing little or no work but still drawing the higher pay of skilled men. Norton Griffiths's solution was to have a purge; he urged Harvey to go round with a doctor to have all these lags formally checked over and discharged; but Harvey, faced with the desperate need for more and more men, does not appear to have taken the advice.

Norton Griffiths believed that sewer drivers—the real clay kickers—would still be welcome by O.C.'s as imports from England even at the higher rate so long as they were first-class men. He mentioned the fact while down on the 3rd Army front on March 27th—and was soon disillusioned. The commanders of 174, 182 and 185 Companies were all most emphatic that they wanted no more six-shilling men, whoever they were. And their Controller of Mines, Lieutenant-Colonel Bertram Danford—a forceful, cheery man whom Norton Griffiths liked—backed them up. Since a further batch of 900 six-shilling miners were right then being signed up in England, it looked as if a minor crisis was in the making.

Norton Griffiths ducked out of the argument and left for head-quarters. Next day he hurried to Ypres for words with General Petrie—Chief Engineer of the 5th Corps and a mining sceptic; and to Reninghelst, headquarters of 172 Company. He was eager for news of the St. Eloi affair. Petrie was clearly delighted with the result of the mines and willingly conceded that they had been a real success.

And at Reninghelst there was jubilation. Proof of the destructive effect of the mines was still coming in; that afternoon a batch of German prisoners were dug out of the ragged debris. They brought the number taken alive to exactly 200 so far, and there was now no doubt that the enemy's casualty rate had been very high.

Syme had arranged a special dinner of fat turkey to celebrate, and asked Norton Griffiths to join him and other officers at the mess table. He accepted. So, as the weary, suffering infantry settled down to a desperate struggle they were doomed to lose, the officers of 172 Company toasted what for them had been a triumph at St. Eloi.

Harvey took the good news more calmly at St. Omer, where he began an analysis of the operation to see what lesson could be learned. It is uncertain whether he saw the explosion himself or not. If he did not, he somewhere obtained a detailed description of the spectacle. He recorded that a mushroom-shaped cloud had appeared over each charge rising to a height of 60 feet which, as it began to fall, had spread widely ejecting a fantastic geyser of gas, flame and cloud some 300 feet into the air. The earth had been violently shaken but, oddly, there had been no roar; debris had been flung up to 200 yards.

Harvey also noted, as the dismal result of the St. Eloi struggle became apparent, that without communication trenches across no-man's-land, it was very difficult for assaulting troops to hold any gains.

This was certainly true. The Germans were adept with their machine guns—and they had plenty of them. They cut the assault parties to pieces as they raced exposed and defenceless across the open. It occurred to him—and to others—that shallow tunnels should be dug most of the way to the German line. This did become a further task for tunnelling companies on various future occasions.

Generally, the result of the mines had to be faced up to as disappointing. There was not only the quick recovery of the Germans to worry about: there was also the confusion that the very existence of the huge new craters had caused among the attacking infantry-men. They had been in doubt at times about where they were—due to the changed topography; and they had been forced to bunch together as they went round the crater rims. Both points were matters for concern.

A murmur that mines did more harm than good began among some of the infantry commanders; it was a point of view the C.-in-C. did not share. Haig was increasingly impressed by the work of the tunnelling companies, and by the value of the massive mine. Less than two weeks later—on April 10th, 1916—he gave orders for the assault against the Messines-Wytschate ridge, to be prepared. It was to begin, as Norton Griffiths and Harvey had suggested, with the firing of about 20 colossal mines.

In German eyes, too, the St. Eloi mines were nothing but a success. They were staggered at the power of the blow.

A week or two before the mines were fired, they had intercepted a British field telephone call that gave a hint of what was about to happen. An immediate investigation was made by tunnelling experts and a special air reconnaissance flown over the British lines, spotting for signs of the rich blue clay brought up from the depths. The result of the inquiries was reassuring. Nothing suspicious had been detected; and, in any case, announced the experts, the ground was too waterlogged for deep tunnelling.

Then had come the blinding shock of the March 27th eruption.

A brilliant geologist, Professor Passarge, was rushed to the front to investigate. The dreadful suspicion that they were being left behind in tunnelling technique was beginning to haunt the German commanders.

Passarge confirmed that this was so. As a result of his report a major reorganization of the German tunnelling service began. Instead of being work simply given to Pioneer units under the control of local infantry commanders, a special mining corps of seven companies was started. On September 1st that year an Inspector of Mines, Lieutenant-Colonel Füsslein, was appointed and took control.

The new system aped the British one. But instead of being 32 companies as the British tunnelling service had by that time become, it was seven. And instead of having a General at the head, it had a Lieutenant-Colonel.

Looking back on it all in later years, Harvey saw the turning point for Britain's underground effort as coming with the appointment of himself and his extensive staff in January, 1916.

From that moment the British tunnellers began taking the lead. Nothing underlined the fact more than the rather muddled German imitation of their methods.

12

MINING VIMY RIDGE

TWENTY-SIX-YEAR-OLD Frederick (nicknamed "Timber") Mulqueen, recently appointed Commander of 182 Tunnelling Company, stood in a battered communications trench and gazed in astonishment around him. It was March, 1916. He was on the west slope of the bloodstained Vimy Ridge. Back in September —at the Battle of Loos—the French had stormed the north tip of the ridge and taken it. Their great—and costly—feat had been loudly publicized at the time. The outside world assumed they were still there, on top in the north. Now the British 3rd Army was about to take over the sector and Mulqueen, part of an advance party, was among the first to discover that the situation had changed. The French had been dislodged by a surprise attack 18 days earlier and not a word had been said.

A nearby nameboard showed that Mulqueen was standing in "Ersatz" Trench. The board was German, dating back to the time when the enemy held this position; the French had left it there and continued to use the name.

They had also left the bodies of many soldiers—particularly of coloured Algerian Zouaves—unburied and unpleasantly close to the trenches. Looking back down Ersatz, Mulqueen could see them lying in a depression, named Zouave Valley in their honour, to the west of the ridge. Six months had passed since these men fell in the first bitter struggle for Vimy. They were rotting now, but still dressed in the scarlet pantaloons for which Zouave units were famous. It was not a pretty sight.

Nor was most of the line in this sector, now being hastily inherited by the 3rd Army. According to the maps, the ridge should have been held by a three-line defence system. In fact it was a hope-lessly flimsy, makeshift affair of shell and shallow mine craters linked by mean, straight-line trenches. In places it was less even than that—nothing more than a few sandbags laid on the ground. And everywhere there was a thick, bubbling quagmire of mud. Much of the front line was almost impossible to reach.

Mulqueen was directed to the dug-out of the local French engineering officer, a subaltern, who was to show him round. The dug-out turned out to be dry and comfortable and the subaltern obliging.

The Frenchman knew a few words of English and Mulqueen a very few of French. With the help of gestures and maps they under-stood each other well enough and were soon on cordial terms. It was apparent that there had been a good deal going on underground. German miners were very active and the French had fought back with spirit. The subaltern spoke freely about it all, backing up his words with clear, air-reconnaissance photographs; afterwards he showed his visitor round the mines. But they, too, were not quite what the British were used to.

The ground near Vimy consisted of about eight feet of watery clay resting on chalk. At a depth of 30 feet the chalk became so hard that it had long ago been dug out in places for use as a building material. Many rambling tunnels had been left as a result. The subaltern told how they had used them to blow up the German lines twice within the last five weeks. He was sure, he said, that the enemy had been badly hurt.

But Mulqueen's main reaction was an acute unease. It occurred to him at once that the Germans might find their way into these strange, uncharted, ready-made tunnels just as the French had done; then, he knew, he would have to watch out for trouble. An examination of the system did nothing to ease his mind.

The mines were not easy to enter. Two in particular—F3 and G5—both positioned well forward, were specially difficult. The entrances, which had been badly damaged and narrowed by shell-fire, reminded Mulqueen more of rabbit holes than anything else.

When he did manage to climb through, he found himself in a dark, oppressive, down-sloping passageway that was disturbingly eerie. He shone his torch on the roughly cut walls and weird-shaped shadows flickered and danced before him. Moving further into the mine he passed through a number of large chambers where the air was heavy and foul-smelling; everything ran or dripped with water. Mulqueen found it all most unpleasant. And before the two men parted, the Frenchman revealed that German miners were probably well forward in this sector. It was not what he said so much as his tense, strained attitude that told Mulqueen the truth. He returned to his unit with much to think about. And that day the Germans fired a heavy camouflet which wrecked the whole of one of the galleries to be taken over. It looked like an omen for the future.

The 3rd Army take-over had come when it did because of a massive assault launched by Lieutenant-General von Falkenhayn against Verdun, a fortified township held by the French some 200 miles south-east of Ypres. It began on February 21st, 1916. At first General Joffre, the fatherly, jolly-looking French C.-in-C. had remained calm; he saw no reason to change certain plans he was laying.

For months Joffre and his stiff-faced, untalkative opposite number for Britain, Sir Douglas Haig, had been trying to agree about their intentions for 1916. This was to be the year of the pulverizing, world-rocking assault to end the war. But the two C.-in-C.'s had differed about how and where it should be made. Sir Douglas had his mind set on a big push away up on the 2nd Army front at Ypres; but Joffre wanted a smashing blow 50 miles further south, along the banks of the river Somme. Haig, as usual, had felt obliged to give way in the end. An outline plan had been agreed: the attack *would* be astride the Somme; it would start in early July; and it would be a mainly French affair with strong British support—40 French divisions to 25 British. Then came the whirlwind German assault on Verdun.

As the dismal February days dragged by, it became clear that the Germans also had a knock-out blow in mind; and this was it.

Falkenhayn meant it to be the most venomous, furious battle the world had ever seen. First, two-million shells were sent crashing into the French defences. Then, in the gloom of early evening, came nearly a quarter of a million men hurled against a narrow front like a vast, expendable battering ram.

Suddenly Joffre saw that he had an emergency—possibly even a calamity—on his hands. There was no time now to think about the Somme offensive; only about help for the bleeding garrison at Verdun.

His 10th Army was still jammed in among the British. With desperate urgency he asked Haig to release it and fill the line with his own men. In an almost overnight rush, Haig formed the 4th Army and carried out a major reshuffle of his front-line troops to comply. The struggle for Vimy Ridge had become a British worry with startling speed.

What Mulqueen needed most was time. There was much to do before 182 Company could begin serious mine fighting in the new sector. Headquarter and billetting arrangements had to be made, the French tunnels required study, and future plans would have to be thought out. Also the men badly needed instruction in the science of chalk mining; their previous work had been in clay, near Armentières.

The likelihood was that while all this went on, the Germans would thrust ahead. But in the event, they for some reason did not. An unexpected lull in the underground war set in, for which Mulqueen was grateful. He made good use of the time.

Because tunnelling companies by now were better off for transport than almost any other type of unit, they were increasingly inclined to go well to the rear to establish their H.Q. and billets. The men appreciated the comfort and safety of their off-duty hours and worked the better for it. Mulqueen installed his company in Mingoval, several miles behind the line. He took over a number of sturdy houses as offices, an officers' mess and officers' quarters. The men were comfortably settled in large huts.

There had been a little grumbling in recent months. It was over a year since the men had been granted leave and Mulqueen felt some sympathy for them. It was not the easiest position for a new civilian-soldier commander to be in. But Mulqueen was a man of resource and energy, as Norton Griffiths had spotted months before. Only the previous October, Norton Griffiths had urged his appointment to the 2nd Army as a one-man ginger group on mining matters; but Harvey had said No, for fear of upsetting the Chief Engineer.

Mulqueen was relieved to find that he had an ex-Guards sergeant on the strength; he promptly put him to work drilling the men when they were out of the line to improve smartness and discipline; it seemed to do both.

At eleven o'clock each morning, he presided at Orderly Room. Defaulters, requests and complaints were brought before him. As a temporary soldier he found many of the matters that had to be settled quite baffling. A regular corporal applied one morning to be "married on the strength". Mulqueen had no idea what this meant but tried to appear as if he did and promised to look into it. At the first opportunity, he scurried round to see the Controller of Mines, Lieutenant-Colonel Guy Williams, for advice. Williams explained that there were two kinds of wives in the regular army: those married "on the strength", who were officially recognized and cared for in various ways by the army; and those married "off the strength" who were not. Mulqueen hastily cleared the request with R.E. headquarters at Chatham and was soon able to pass on the good news to the corporal that permission would be given. Like many other tunnelling company commanders, he was learning his job by doing it.

Punishment was another frequent worry. Mulqueen's natural sympathy with his miners' uncomfortable, dangerous life, made him incline towards lenience. One of the company's best men was a massive, hard-drinking Lance-Corporal Bannon. In the front line Bannon was unbeatable. But when resting at base he was continually being arrested by Military Police for brawling when drunk. Time after time he appeared before Mulqueen at Orderly Room.

After listening gravely to the evidence, Mulqueen's standard punishment was demotion to sapper. Both men knew it would be a temporary disgrace only. Bannon would go cheerfully back to the front line to resume his usual amazing output underground; Mulqueen would respond by re-awarding the stripe as soon as he dared.

He did not bring the spirit of lenience to more serious misdemeanours—particularly the kind he thought likely to damage morale. Mulqueen was faced once with two deserters who had been picked up by redcaps at Boulogne. After much thought he decided to put them forward for court martial. His own powers were limited to an award of 28 days Field Punishment Number One* which he felt was not enough. He was staggered by the court martial's sentence which was in due course announced as seven days F.P. Number One. What he had hoped would be an exemplary sentence and a deterrent had turned into almost the opposite. But, as bitter fighting about to break out was to prove, no harm had been done to the Company's discipline or ardour.

The real struggle began on April 7th. Listeners in a tunnel known as G4 announced that the Germans were mining towards them at speed. Mulqueen ordered a camouflet to be blown at once. It was the start of a frenzied contest that lasted for six weeks almost without a break and left indelible memories. Looking back on it in later life, Mulqueen described the period as one full of "rude shocks . . . Our men were buried and our nights made sleepless. We were striving to rectify a situation that threatened to overwhelm us."

The situation in fact did overwhelm them, at least for a while. Listeners' reports began to pour in showing that German miners were intensely active. They seemed to be advancing all over the front. In a frantic effort to contain them, Mulqueen ordered camouflets to be blown on April 7th, 11th and 12th. It was old-fashioned defensive fighting, there being no time to organize

* Field Punishment Number One consisted of putting a defaulter in irons and securing him for up to two hours a day to any suitable fixed object (in the old days a guncarriage wheel). The prisoner was also usually made to do work equivalent to hard labour in a prison.

anything better. But on the 19th, he fired two mines close together, one being a heavy four-ton charge.

The big mine seemed to do extensive damage and it threw up fine lips—the kind that the infantry could occupy—close to the German front. The rejoicing, however, was brief. Next day the Germans began a long series of punishing explosions.

First came a huge mine under the British forward trench. On the 24th they fired again, and the following day four separate mines rocked the British, causing casualties above and below ground. There were more explosions on the 28th, May 2nd, 10th and 13th. A shift officer, Lieutenant Frederick Aspinall, heard one of them being tamped close to his own gallery. The moment seemed to be one of great danger. He called his men out immediately and advised the local infantry commander to remove all but one sentry from the line at the danger point. Half an hour later the Germans fired, slashing open a large length of the front trench and burying the lonely sentry somewhere deep in the side of the crater. The man's battalion commander was furious, and when Mulqueen arrived in the line soon afterwards turned sharply on him for an explanation. Acidly, Mulqueen pointed out that there were limits to a tunnelling officer's foresight. And it was true that if the line had been cleared whenever there was danger, almost none of it on Vimy Ridge at that time would have been held. But the tunnellers began to come in for much criticism from the infantry they were trying to protect. It added to the heavy strain they were already under. Mulqueen began to notice changes in the appearance of his face when shaving: it had lost the roundness it used to have.

Very late one night he was sent for by Lieutenant-General the Hon. Sir Julian Byng (later Lord Byng of Vimy), Commander of the 17th Corps. The message instructed him to go at once to the General's H.Q., a fine château in Aubigny. Mulqueen hurried over to be confronted by Sir Julian and his Chief of Staff, Brigadier-General James Charles. Both men were obviously worried, Sir Julian especially so.

It was not a pleasant interview. Sir Julian said that he could not understand why the German miners were achieving so much success. He obviously regarded the situation as extremely serious and paced agitatedly up and down while questioning Mulqueen. They went over and over the position. Sir Julian asked repeatedly why 182 Company was not giving greater protection, and each time Mulqueen tried to convince him that with the men and time available nothing better could be done than they were doing. The meeting went on until the small hours of the morning, and then broke up with the Generals still not convinced. Soon afterwards, the Company was relieved of the part of the line held by 17th Corps men—the Neuville St. Vaast sector. Major Gilbert Syme's 175 Company took over.

Meanwhile, Mulqueen had had a hurried conference with Colonel Williams, the Controller, and helped by his advice had plotted a way to check the German onslaught. A tunnel was to be dug from a position known as B1 to a point slightly right of the British crater blown on April 19th; the Germans had converted this crater into a strongly manned and fortified point and had even connected it by a trench to an older crater 30 yards or so to the right. The B1 mine was intended to go off midway beneath this daringly constructed system, blasting the German occupants of both craters to pieces, and making a new rim that British infantry-men could rush and hold.

One acute danger had to be overcome: an enemy trench well to the right overlooked the target zone, and the British were likely to be cut down by heavy fire from there the moment they assaulted. To prevent this, Williams suggested that two mines should be fired simultaneously over to the right, near the German line, from a gallery known as C3; these would throw up high lips to screen off the German view of the attack.

Mulqueen liked the idea and adopted it. He added a third mine to go off in C3, and designed the B1 mine as two charges lying near each other. The total charge used in the operation came to 22,300 lbs. of ammonal. By May 15th all arrangements were complete.

At eight-thirty that evening Mulqueen fired the mines from just outside B1 entrance. The ground gave the, by now, well-known tremble of a deep eruption and a mass of broken chalk gushed upwards. Perfect craters with well-shaped rims were formed. Moments later, men of the Lancashire Fusiliers and Royal North Lancashire Regiment raced across protected by heavy shell-fire whirling over their heads. But the only Germans to be seen when they arrived were dead. It had all gone exactly to plan.

Next morning Mulqueen went over to study the new position. He stood proudly among the craters—soon to be named the Crosbie Craters, after the commander of the assault party, Lieutenant-Colonel J. D. Crosbie—and gazed around. It was dawn. Much of the German line could be seen in the dim light. The Germans themselves were strangely quiet and Mulqueen concluded that they must still be dazed. It seemed a reasonable supposition, for this was the second such shock they had suffered: twelve days earlier another tunnelling company, 176 under Major Edward Momber*, had fired four mines to form three mammoth craters only a few hundred yards to the north; and they also had been held and fortified.

Mulqueen was right in thinking that the Germans had been badly shaken. But their silence had a more sinister meaning than he supposed. Their commander, General Freiherr von Freytag-Loringhoven, had become so worried by the way the British miners were turning the tables on his own that he decided drastic action must be taken. Behind the quiet of the German lines, a plan was being prepared at furious speed.

*   *   *

Another tunnelling company, 185, had been fighting on the Ridge as hard and almost as long as Mulqueen's 182. It took over a sector two miles to the south on April 1st, 1916. And, like Mulqueen's Company, it found it had walked into a desperate situation. The report of the trained officer-listener, who was sent down all

---

* Momber, Love and Kennedy craters, blown on May 3rd, 1916 and promptly rushed and held by 21st Battalion London Regiment and the 3rd London Field Company, R.E.

the galleries as a preliminary, could hardly have been more grave. German miners were forcing their way through the chalk with relentless vigour everywhere. One-Eight-Five Company was not even to be allowed the week or two to sort out its affairs that 182 had enjoyed.

The unit's commander was Major Euan Tulloch, 26 years old, a handsome young man with sharp, well-balanced features and a faintly quizzical expression; he was the youngest but one of the Company's officers and had held his command just two and a half weeks.

Tulloch was soon to become a distinguished commander, much liked and respected by his comrades above and beneath him; but at this early stage he was not exuding more than limited confidence. He had been delivered to the Officers' Mess on March 14th by the 3rd Army Controller of Mines, Lieutenant-Colonel Bertram Danford, dumped and left, without announcement or ceremony just before lunchtime. Officers strolling into the mess were surprised to see the stranger at their table, and there was some awkwardness at first.

One-Eight-Five Company had never quite recovered from the loss of its original C.O., Captain Richardson, killed in the geophone-testing incident of February 4th, 1916, at La Boisselle. The senior lieutenant at the time had been an officer from the Canadian Veterinary Corps, William Wilson. Wilson, a French-Canadian, had earlier been transferred from veterinary to tunnelling duties, on the grounds that he had trained in civilian life as a sanitary engineer and had run sewer laying contracts in Quebec. But he was not popular. The fact that he put up captain's badges after Richardson's death and took charge, made him less popular still.

The meeting between Tulloch and Wilson was particularly unhappy. Tulloch said that on relinquishing his temporary command Wilson would have to take his third pip down. Wilson, who spoke with a Canadian drawl and had a Canadian irreverence for authority, refused. Controller Danford resolved the deadlock by transferring Wilson to base at Rouen, to await a command of his own;

he was eventually given 256 Company—the last of the tunnelling companies to be formed—in July that year.

Tulloch kept very quiet during his first weeks with the Company. The officers under him speculated on whether this was his nature or whether, perhaps, he was hoping to learn from his older, more experienced subordinates. Whichever it was, it soon became clear that the new C.O. was no mere figurehead. Under him the tensions that had threatened the efficiency and harmony of the unit began to disappear; and this change came quickly.

Tulloch had just been settling in when the orders to take over a sector on Vimy Ridge came in. He had had 18 days of comparative quiet on a front due east of Arras—18 days to get to know the officers, N.C.O.'s, the Company machinery he had inherited and the complex duties of a commander. It was not long. Then came the quick switch four miles northwards to the Ridge, and a rapidly mounting crisis.

As soon as Tulloch realized the great danger the infantry were in from German mines, he urged that they should be withdrawn—at least from the most critical positions. But Sir Douglas Haig had already made it clear to the infantry commanders that he not only wanted the line held, but for the Germans to be fiercely harried from it to take their minds off the Somme, and his preparations for an offensive there. Tulloch's suggestion was promptly and a trifle coldly rejected; and orders were issued via Hyland, the Controller, that no infantryman below the rank of brigade commander might be told of the fearful danger they stood in.

But many of the junior ranks already knew. One brigade commander told Hyland a story of a conversation he had had with one of his battalion commanders. "I suppose you know we've been mined," the battalion commander had said. The Brigadier had rounded on him at once and asked, "How the hell do *you* know?"

"The men say so," the battalion commander had replied casually. And there the subject had been dropped.

One-Eight-Five Company went to work with all the energy it could muster. New galleries were started, directed towards the

German sounds and driven ahead at speed. The officers felt that their reputation was at stake, and hated the unfairness of the test. And they hated the deception that had to be kept up with the infantry. One day Lieutenant Harry Graham met a Scottish infantry major who asked if "things" were "quiet down below". The two men were standing in the front line at a known danger-point. "Yes, sir." Graham replied as convincingly as he could. "Not a pick heard during the night."

But he had gone a shade too far. The Major knew well that picking had been heard very near, and that same night, at a post known as M33; the men there had reported the fact to him. He told Graham about it.

Graham gave the only reply he could. "That's our miners working. The Hun is still some way off . . ." But in his heart he felt wretchedly sure that the Major and his men were right. The Germans were squarely underneath them.

A few of the older tunnels taken over by the Company had entrances far out across no-man's-land and these were pressed into use in the emergency—mostly as listening posts but occasionally for mine firing. The journey out to them, along a trench hardly more than inches deep, was a tense and dangerous operation. It was an all but impossible undertaking during daylight; and at night there was a grave risk of scrambling straight into the arms of a German patrol.

Once a high-lipped crater had to be blown from one of these marooned tunnels to cut off the view from a German observation point. Lieutenant Benjamin Plummer, of 185, with a sergeant and sapper, went out at nightfall to do the job. Three men from the 9th Battalion the Royal Scots went with them, to mount guard at the tunnel mouth while the charge was laid, wired and tamped.

For Plummer and the other two the night passed uneventfully, apart from the hard work that had to be so quickly accomplished, and the ceaseless rumbling of shell and machine-gun fire from the surface. Sometime before dawn they emerged and were astonished to find no trace of the guard. Plummer assumed they had walked out on him, and was furious. He returned safely across no-man's-land and went to complain to the Royal Scots' Battalion Commander. There he was informed that all three men were believed to be prisoners of war, captured in a sudden swoop by a German night patrol. The Battalion Commander was angry also, and inclined to blame Plummer for the loss. Plummer retired ruefully from the argument. Not a sound of the incident had reached him underground. He was lucky not to have been taken himself and knew it. And next evening, the mine was successfully blown.

On April 28th, German miners struck their hardest blow on this front. At half-past one in the morning, 185 Company's front erupted in a huge, spread-out explosion that crushed dug-outs, obliterated trenches and caused numerous casualties. First reports showed that the Germans had fired about five mines. The figure was later corrected to thirteen. German infantrymen followed with a limited attack, but were driven out when British reserves came up and closed with them.

Graham arrived on the scene the next morning and was shocked by the grisly desolation to be seen. One buried Highlander was still living. The debris had piled up to his shoulders and stopped there, leaving him helpless but able to breathe. Two of the German raiders had started to dig him out to make him their prisoner, but had been forced to withdraw too soon. They had struck him viciously on the head with a shovel before leaving; and the sturdy Highlander had survived it all; he was being extracted when Graham passed.

The tunnellers toiled first to dig out buried men, and then surveyed the damage. It proved not as great as it looked. Little harm had been done to the Company's system of mines.

And now that the Germans had actually blown their mines, the two sides met on roughly equal terms. A general sense of relief spread through the Company. It increased when careful checking showed that the German mines had exploded exactly where listeners' reports had said they might, and although the infantry—who felt they had been let down—were very critical, a feeling of competence actually grew among 185's officers and men. Work began on a new and efficient network of galleries which plunged to the water level, 70 feet down in places.

In the early hours of May 22nd (1916) news came through of serious trouble further north, involving 182 Company's sector. Almost the whole of Mulqueen's mining system was reported lost.

It was true. Freytag-Loringhoven had put his anti-mining plan into action. After a monstrous bombardment, more concentrated and deadly than anything yet experienced, he had attacked at seven forty-six on the evening of May 21st. It was then that the assaulting troops had first been dimly seen ploughing through a thick pall of smoke and dust towards what was left of the British. They took the position almost unresisted; and with it all but one of 182 Company's mines.

Most of the duty shift had been sheltering from the shell-fire in dug-outs a short distance to the rear, and casualties were few. Mulqueen heard of the mêlée in Mingoval from Tulloch and at nine o'clock sent a message recalling the men to headquarters, there to await developments; a strong counter-attack was expected. But repeated attempts to set it up failed—due mainly to the remorseless German fire. On May 23rd Mulqueen had gone forward to assess the situation when one of these devastating bombardments began and he took shelter in a dug-out. There were ten of them packed in there, and as the ground rocked and trembled Mulqueen played "cut throat" Bridge with two subalterns. Seventeen times the candles were blown out by the stunning concussion of nearby shells.

The Germans held their gain. The fact was finally accepted by the British at about the end of May. On June 5th, Mulqueen gave orders for seven new galleries to be started from the new front line.

Freytag-Loringhoven's very local attack did not reach south to Tulloch's Company, which was having a relatively quiet time. Both sides were digging industriously but few mines were fired; and when they were, their intention was more cautionary than offensive.

Scare reports still came in but were seldom of much consequence.

At midnight one night, Lieutenant Harry Graham was handed a message from the duty shift reporting definite sounds of German work close to their gallery. The weather made it particularly unwelcome news; for days it had been wet, and when Graham put his nose out of the dug-out rain was still whipping out of a black sky. In depression he set off with a geophone under his arm, along the mud-swamped duckboards towards the gallery entrance to investigate. On the way he slipped and fell flat in the filthy quag and dropped the geophone out of its box. He stood up cursing with rage in the knee-deep mud and dredged about with his hands for missing parts of the instrument. When at last he arrived at the gallery he found the sappers greatly agitated and all discussing the danger. Brusquely Graham entered the gallery and for an hour moved the geophone patiently from point to point, listening. There was nothing to be heard. He knew now that the men had been frightened by some quite innocent local sound. What had it been? Near by was an infantry dug-out, and Graham went to it first as an obvious suspect. It proved a good guess. The men said they had been smashing firewood with a pick a short while before. Graham was able to tell his shift to get back to work and to use their heads next time they had a fright; he did it loudly, with much raw feeling.

The mining stalemate lasted month after month and was, in fact, to continue until the big British-initiated Battle of Arras was fought in April, 1917, when the whole of Vimy Ridge was captured and firmly (and permanently) held. There was time for some good living during off-duty hours. One-Seven-Two and 175 Companies were by now also at Vimy Ridge, and the officers of all the companies entertained each other in their messes and in an officers' club opened at Arras.

Most tunnelling officers were hard drinkers—a habit they picked up in the tropics and brought with them to the war. A 185 officer, Thomas Smith, once confessed that he used to swallow three quarters of a bottle of whisky a day at the front and that this was not exceptional. There were many parties; they were gay and noisy affairs and some were rough. After a bout in the mess of 176 Company it was found that windows, crockery and chairs had been broken and even the doors damaged.

The horseplay one night turned into a practical joke against a nervous medical officer temporarily attached to the Company. Two lieutenants, Robert Howland and the adjutant, Percy Shute, put on gas masks late one evening after the M.O. had retired and banged suddenly on his bedroom door shouting, "Gas, gas! For God's sake warn the camp!" The M.O. sprang in alarm out of bed and began to look for his gas mask. It was lost. After a few moments of frantic searching he ran next door to another officer to borrow his. But the other officer, who had been out to dinner, was furious at the commotion and hit the M.O. on the ear with his fist. By this time the doctor was sure he could smell the gas and was in a frenzy of excitement. Tulloch now joined in the joke by calling, "Get a move on or you'll have all my men and officers gassed." The doctor was eventually calmed down and advised to send air samples away for analysis at the Corps laboratories. Writing of the event in later years, Harry Graham said, "But the only gas the analyst could detect was alcohol."

Tulloch, Mulqueen and Syme (172 Company) became particularly friendly and often met for a quiet chat and a drink. Mulqueen was much impressed with Tulloch for his dry humour and imperturbability. Tulloch puffed a narrow-stemmed pipe and Mulqueen observed, as he has since said, that "at embarrassing moments he speeded up the rhythm and that was all".

This calm of Tulloch's was severely tested in early June (1916), when 185 Company suddenly found itself in serious-sounding trouble with the authorities. The Provost Marshal had been investigating looting charges said to involve it.

The story went back to early February, during the temporary command of Captain Wilson and while the Company was based in Albert. The officers' quarters there had been uncomfortable due, mainly, to a lack of carpets. Yet a nearby shop, abandoned by its owner who had fled, had many carpets visible through the windows.

It had been a tantalizing situation for long enough. Soon after Wilson took command, he sent five subalterns out late one night with a service wagon and wire cutters on what he described as a salvaging job.

They cut their way in through a fanlight and almost cleared the store of everything useful. The haul transformed the mess and sleeping quarters and within a day or so there was cosy comfort in all the rooms while outside it snowed. Then, maddeningly soon, came orders to move to Arras.

Wilson went ahead of the unit and found that 185 Company was to be about the first British unit to move in. He had a free choice of billets, and chose two rows of good houses for his officers and men. All were very well furnished. By now the company had so many home comforts in its hands that off-duty hours were passed in extraordinary luxury. Even the dug-out up in the line was furnished and carpeted. The officers were living "like eastern potentates"— as one of them later confessed.

Then, towards the end of May, came another address change. Arras, now under heavy German fire, had become an unnecessarily dangerous H.Q. zone and the Company moved to a hamlet further back, known as Haute Avesnes. It took with it its amazing and always growing cornucopia of comforts. But this time, while the long labour of loading up the wagons went on, a group of French civilians watched, braving a bombardment to do so.

A few weeks later, two gendarmes and some un-uniformed Frenchmen called unexpectedly at the camp and looked round. Some officers noticed with unease that they showed a most unusual interest in all the furnishings on view.

Next came a party from the Provost Marshal's office to interrogate Tulloch (about the least guilty officer of all) and the adjutant, a cheery, knock-about, practical-joking lieutenant, Percy Shute. Asked about a piano in the N.C.O.'s mess, Shute explained that it had been loaded in place of a canary cage by accident; he blamed the stress of the bombardment. To explain a night commode found in an officer's hut, Shute told a rambling story about the officer

having come from the Gold Coast with a bad dose of dysentery—
and the commode. The explanations grew less and less likely.
Then, before the Provost Marshal's men left, a chilling development took place: Tulloch, as C.O., was put under open arrest,
pending the setting up of a Court of Inquiry.

Frantic efforts now began to dispose of everything that could
possibly be claimed by civilians as theirs. When the excitement
was at its peak, Wilson telephoned Tulloch. In his unflurried
Canadian drawl he offered to take away all the evidence to his own
newly formed Company H.Q. for storing until the trouble blew
over. Gratefully Tulloch accepted and the 185 Company's luxuries
soon after disappeared—temporarily, it was understood—in
Wilson's lorries.

The Court of Inquiry sat and acquitted the Company on all
charges. But the victory had its price. When Wilson was asked to
return the furniture he regretted he was unable to; being such dangerous material to have, he explained, he had had it all burned.

It was many months until 185 Company was able to recreate an
atmosphere of comfort in its quarters. And when it finally did,
everything was promptly lost again in a disastrous fire.

Long after the event one of the officers involved argued that the
fate of Arras, Albert and all their houses and furnishings had been
obvious, anyway, and added, "It was simply a case of putting to
practical use what would have undoubtedly been destroyed." In
other words, Wilson's word for it had been right: it *had* been
more a case of salvaging than looting.

Most tunnellers, uncomplicated extroverts that they were, would
have agreed.

Before 185 Company left Vimy Ridge (in April 1917), it had dug
seven miles of fighting and communications galleries through the
chalk. It was proud of its record.

13

MESSINES RIDGE:
THE "BIG IDEA" IS STARTED

MINING in the watery clay of the Ypres salient was never allowed to stop, despite the many rival demands made on tunnelling companies' time. As far back as mid-summer 1915, 175 Company had started a long, wearisome, fantastically optimistic, underground plod from a point more than 200 yards behind the British front line to the German garrison on Hill 60. The ground was already so broken by earlier craters that C.O. Major Hunter Cowan had decided to go deep—and under it—if possible.

The new tunnel was driven horizontally into the side of the Hill 60 railway embankment then, a few yards along, given a downhill slope. It was here that serious trouble started. The subsoil grew almost impossible to handle. An unstable clayey-sand fell in shapelessly at the face and squirted through chinks in the timbers; it got into the eyes, hair and clothing of the miners and clogged the water pumps being used in a futile attempt to keep the tunnel dry. Some shifts, after struggling gamely for a full eight hours, came off without measurable progress having been made. News of the struggle spread to other companies and brought a virtual end to inclined shafts in loose ground; it became standard practice instead to sink a vertical shaft—which could be more easily boarded or tubbed—with a level tunnel breaking away at the foot.

But the 175 miners persevered. By November they were well down into firm blue clay and pushing a narrow gallery levelly towards the hill. They began to talk of it as the Berlin Tunnel, joking that Berlin was where it would end.

That month a newly formed company, 250, was settling down to a most ambitious programme under the command of Captain Cecil Cropper, a metal mining engineer from Northumberland. Cropper was a handsome man of good physique and commanding manner; his experience of active service tunnelling had been brief but intensive. He had come from 173 Company and some sordid fighting at Aubers Ridge, a black spot in the British line about half way between Ypres and Vimy.

He was an able but temperamentally somewhat difficult commander. He resented interference from Harvey, and regarded Norton Griffiths as hardly more than a showman-adventurer who "threw his weight about". But he kept these thoughts to himself, and Norton Griffiths responded with feelings for Cropper that were approving and even cordial; his satisfaction increased when he heard that Cropper was planning a scheme that lined up very well with his own ambitious plans for a major shake-up of Messines Ridge.

Cropper's headquarters were at La Clytte in the Canadian Corps' area, centrally facing the ridge and about three miles back. The Canadian Chief Engineer, Brigadier-General Charles Armstrong, worried about the mining situation on his front, had been pressing for tunnelling companies for the Corps' own to be formed as hurriedly as possible. He had a large number of former miners already available, and authority was given for the formation of one company on the spot the next month, December. Two more were also authorized, but to Armstrong's disappointment were to be formed in Canada and shipped out during the spring. Meanwhile the main underground defence had to fall on 250 Company. Armstrong ordered Cropper to lay out an aggressive scheme.

For a while Cropper scraped about at some shallow waterlogged tunnels in poor sandy soil, dug originally by Hepburn's 172 Company and abandoned months before. It soon seemed clear to him that nothing could be achieved from these starting points.

He moved further towards the rear one day, testing the ground for changes in its geology, and found places where the clay came to within 15 feet or so of the surface. This was promising and he ordered trial shafts to be sunk; but even here the clay proved too deep to reach. At about 10 feet, terrific hydraulic pressures were set up that forced sand through the timbering faster than it could be dug out, and eventually each shaft began to tilt out of plumb, a preliminary to collapsing. So Cropper went further back still, until, in the beds of streams and elsewhere, he found the fine, smooth, stiff, blue clay coming up almost to ground level. He decided to start the scheme back there. Soon he walked round to see Armstrong, to explain his plans and to hand in a report setting them down in formal terms. Armstrong listened in surprise at the ambitiousness of the proposals, then gave the word to go ahead, adding that he would see that the report was sent on at once to 2nd Army headquarters. "And if you can do it, Cropper," he said doubtfully, as they parted, "you're a darned good man." Cropper was quite confident that he could.

On December 18th, Norton Griffiths came bustling round. By then, Cropper had four shaft sites marked out and was already well down into the clay at three of them. Matter-of-factly he explained that he was aiming a four-gallery attack at the ridge. There were a number of strongly fortified German posts up there, opposite his two-miles-long front, and he was already planning to attack five of them—marked on British maps as Hollandscheschuur, Petit Bois, Peckham, Spanbroekmolen and Kruisstraat—from underground. It was amazingly audacious, and even Norton Griffiths must have been somewhat taken aback for a moment. The distance to go was an unprecedented 2,000 to 3,000 feet in most cases.

Cropper's four tunnels were to be of quite exceptional importance—were, in fact, to win a permanent place in the history of war. Norton Griffiths saw that what he had grown accustomed to describing as "the big idea" had been grasped and acted on by somebody at last. With great satisfaction he reported the facts to Harvey, and added a reminder that 175 Company's Berlin Tunnel had been driven about 600 feet towards Hill 60, and was at that moment passing under the British front line. It meant that a major shake-up of the ridge might soon come about of its own accord, without the need for top-level permission and elaborate co-ordinating machinery. The main fear was of a local order being given to blow one of the mines prematurely, and by itself. Norton Griffiths begged Harvey to guard against this possibility and suggested that there should be no thought of fitting any of these mines before April. If some time *after* that date they were all fired simultaneously, he pointed out laconically, "good can be done". But even the mention of April was wildly optimistic. He had probably taken the current estimate for clay kicking, which was about 25 feet per day, and divided it into the average distance of 2,500 feet, so reckoning on 100 days' work. In practice, a very long tunnel brought many new problems of soil disposal and ventilation, which would inevitably—and drastically—slow down the digging rate; and there was the likelihood of German interference to allow for. But Norton Griffiths may have over-simplified the figuring deliberately, in the hope that April would sound reasonable to any senior officers who might lose patience with too long a delay; he could always ask for an extension of time later.

Then came the tense meeting of January 6th (1916) with the generals—and the calamitous rejection of the Messines Ridge "earthquake" idea—followed, dramatically, a few hours later, by its acceptance. It was almost a personal victory for Norton Griffiths, and a great one. Three days later, on Thursday, January 9th, he was outwardly rewarded when the promotion he had himself asked for the previous September came through. But Norton Griffiths, now a (temporary) Lieutenant-Colonel, knew that in the highly organized tunnelling service of 1916 there was less and less room for him. He began to confide the fact to tunnelling officers with whom he felt on good terms, saying that General Harvey could evidently now "spare him". And although from 2nd January he was considered assistant to the Inspector of Mines, the appointment was never gazetted, due—it was officially admitted—to uncertainty about how long he would be "available for permanent service".

Now, as his time with the tunnelling companies drew towards its end, Norton Griffiths had another major inspiration: in certain collieries, mechanical borers were used to drive mine headings and roads through coal seams. Could these not be adapted to bore through clay? It seemed very probable; larger models of broadly similar design had already been used on the London underground railway tunnels in clay.

Norton Griffiths put the idea forward with predictable zeal. He asked Harvey for immediate action, and urged that several machines should be obtained. As usual he was utterly confident. To order just one, for trial, he argued, would simply waste time; four or six should be brought out at once, and he listed what appeared to be six reasons why Harvey should agree. But behind the outflow of words only two valid points were being made—though both were important: that mechanical diggers would speed the work; and that speed was vital. In particular, he wanted a borer provided for Cropper, and another for the unit immediately on Cropper's right, the new 3rd Canadian Tunnelling Company. Two machines would be the minimum.

Harvey stood firm against all the eloquence and pressure Norton Griffiths put on him, and permitted one only to be ordered for the present;* it was to be used by Cropper. Plans to obtain it, the Stanley Heading Machine, manufactured in Nuneaton, went forward with a rush. A special cutting head designed for the hard, Ypresian clay had to be made, but was promised by the makers for delivery in six weeks.

Norton Griffiths and Harvey together called on Cropper to tell him about the decision. Evidently Norton Griffiths had it in mind that a gallery should be driven all the way to Wytschaete village, a full 3,000 feet further than the present plan. Inwardly Cropper was affronted at the way they seemed to have taken over his scheme, which they now discussed as if it had been all their own idea. The situation was full of irony. Undoubtedly, Norton Griffiths and Harvey *did* feel it was theirs; and certainly it bore a strong resemblance

---

* At least one more was shipped out later. It was used by Canadian tunnellers at the Bluff but was a failure.

to the plans they had been pushing for months. But Cropper had known nothing about this behind-the-scenes campaign and was amazed at their attitude. But he was keen enough to try out the machine and agreed to go forward with arrangements to receive it. He undertook to have a chamber dug at the foot of what had been named Petit Bois★ shaft, into which the borer could be lowered and assembled.

On February 10th (1916) Norton Griffiths called again, and was seemingly a shade displeased to find that Cropper was pushing hard ahead with clay kicking work on the tunnels, but had not made much progress with the arrangements necessary above and below ground for the borer. However, he extracted a promise that these works would now be speeded up, and assured Cropper that "Kitchener is personally interested in this". He dropped off a crate of port to engender good will, not knowing that Cropper was an almost total abstainer, then hurried away.

On Wednesday, February 12th, he left to meet up with the machine in London and speed it in his own irresistible manner to the front. He reckoned to have it at Boulogne in five days' time, and just before leaving arranged for two lorries to be on the quayside as from two o'clock in the afternoon of Monday, the 17th.

At midnight on the 12th he went aboard the ferry for Folkestone at Boulogne, expecting to be in England before dawn. But inshore mines delayed the boat's sailing all night. Norton Griffiths, who could flare into impatience if kept waiting a few unnecessary seconds was trapped in the quietness of the harbour for seven exasperating hours.

He arrived in his Westminster office eventually on the 14th, and by ten-thirty that morning was in energetic discussion with two representatives from the boring machine's makers who had called. From them he learned that the shipment problem was no small one. There were 24 packets altogether, with a combined weight of seven-and-half tons, to be carried from Marylebone Station (where they were presently lying) across south-east England, the sea,

★ Also known as SP. 13.

western France and finally down Cropper's shaft for re-assembly underground. Despite the unexpected size of the job and the delay he had already suffered, he was determined to keep to the original schedule; there were only three days left.

He hurried to the War Office to make arrangements and was referred to an R.E. Colonel, Daniel Brady. Brady had more disturbing news: the shipment was too bulky to travel on the light mail boat Norton Griffiths had had in mind. Then Brady saved the situation by promising to hold space on an ammunition boat leaving Newhaven the next night. To catch it, the packets would have to be at Victoria Station by four o'clock on the day of sailing. A group of lorries were immediately ordered, and instructions sent out to the station officials at Marylebone to release the shipment when they arrived.

Norton Griffiths spent the rest of the day arranging for a skilled engineer to be sent out to instal the machine and train Cropper's men in its proper use. A suitable man surnamed Carter was found, and Brady made quick arrangements to have him temporarily commissioned, ready to leave with Norton Griffiths for the front. This was very fine co-operation, and Norton Griffiths reacted by showing his capacity for unstinted (if unpredictable) generosity of feeling. In the midst of so much rush, he took time to write warmly to Harvey in Brady's praise. "Brady is a splendid man," he wrote, "and has done lots to unblock. I want you to . . . thank him."

Next day confusion broke out. After spending the morning at the War Office, Norton Griffiths discovered at about noon that the instructions to the Marylebone Station officials had not arrived and the boring machine was still there; further, and worse, the lorries had failed to turn up. Now a profusion of lorries were ordered—some through the War Office and some (the cost of which Norton Griffiths said was to be charged up to his personal account) through the Great Central Railway Company. At one o'clock the boring machine in its many bulky packages was still lying at Marylebone untouched; at that moment the chances of getting it aboard the munition ship seemed slim. But in the end, it was heaved aboard the last train to Newhaven and next morning Norton Griffiths heard that the machine—for which he hoped so much—was safely at sea on its way to France.

Soon after hearing the good news, he went aboard the ferry at Folkestone. By now he had signed up a second expert, R. D. Talbot, an experienced foreman, who was to travel out as a temporary sergeant to run the machine; and he had made arrangements for a specially designed wooden lining to be sent to support the tunnel and keep the wet air out of contact with the clay, a detail which was said to be important. The great experiment was about to begin.

Norton Griffiths's crossing was again delayed—this time for about 25 hours. But at last, on the morning of the 17th at eleven-fifteen, in very rough weather, the boat sailed. And at Boulogne he was pleased to see three lorries already loading up the machine, which had evidently arrived intact. Norton Griffiths hurried on to G.H.Q., arriving at four-thirty that afternoon.

Urgent matters in other parts of the line kept him away from Petit Bois shaft throughout the next two days. But on February 20th, he called on Cropper to find that the reception arrangements had gone ahead well, as promised. The hand-driven gallery had been driven forward about 300 feet. Cropper had had another shaft dug near by for the machine. His plan was to let it dig its own tunnel parallel to the present one and then, if it succeeded, it could go ahead on its own. Much of the machine had already arrived on the site and Carter, the expert, had been busy testing components.

The machine consisted of a chassis on wheels carrying a pair of rotating cutters at the front. These cutters were powered by a two-cylinder compressed air engine, which was in turn driven by a miniature generating station installed on the surface. As the compressed air blasted into the cutters they screwed themselves forward tearing out the face ahead and feeding the spoil back. While cutting went on, the machine was stabilized by top and bottom jacks. It was a massive and complex-looking affair. But Carter said he could have it working 48 hours after all the components had been lowered down the shaft—a drop of 80 feet. Privately Norton Griffiths doubted this, and warned Harvey that it was more likely to take about 72.

The handling difficulties, bringing the machine up to and down the shaft, were appalling. A light railway for hand trolleys had been laid but, because it was in view of the German lines, could only be used at night. Also, the loads carried were much heavier than the rails were able to support, and derailments were frequent. Each time this happened the exhausting burden would have to be groped for in the dark and lifted by hand up onto the track again. It strained the men's nerves as much as their backs. One night a tremendous clamour broke out, and an officer who raced to the spot found a vicious free-for-all fight raging between members of a carrying party; beside them stood a derailed trolley. It was obvious what had happened: there had been the accident, followed by angry recriminations. Then someone had struck a blow . . .

Sometimes daylight came before a heavy component had reached the shaft; hasty attempts at camouflage would then have to be made and the load left all day; the boring machine was officially supposed to be most secret. But the extraordinary goings-on at Petit Bois shaft were impossible to conceal and, although there was a delay of several weeks before it started, the Germans turned a high concentration of fire on the area. Wild rumours began to circulate about the new mystery weapon. Cropper and his men did little to contradict them, since they seemed more likely to do good than harm to his side.

About this time new urgency was given to the mining programme. On February 14th, the Commander-in-Chief had (joylessly) accepted the French plan for a great mid-summer battle along the Somme. But he still believed it was in Flanders that something like a decisive victory could be won; so he reserved the right to make a push of his own near Ypres, a week or two before the Somme joint operation began. The Messines Ridge mines were to be an important part of it; orders went out to be ready for action by mid-June.

The main worry was Cropper's Petit Bois tunnel. It had been aimed at a little salient overlooking the German lines. Probably it was the most important tunnel of them all; but it was also the longest and the least likely to be ready in time if hand and foot digging had to be relied upon. And Cropper already had doubts about the machine.

At a consultation with the Controller of Mines, Stevenson, Cropper was asked if he could double the rate of advance at Petit Bois. The tunnel was still 1,000 feet short of even the British line and some such dramatic speed-up was clearly needed. How this could be achieved remained obscure. The men were already under pressure. By now two of the 250 tunnels—Spanbroekmolen and Kruisstraat—had been taken over by the 3rd Canadian Company. But there were still three major ones to drive, Hollandscheschuur and Peckham, besides Petit Bois. The men were working as fast as they could.

On about February 23rd, a grave faced Cropper arrived at the Petit Bois site and asked for the officer in charge, Second-Lieutenant Henry Tatham. He described a new method of working he wanted tried out. Instead of timbering close up behind the advancing face, he said, the face gang was to work seven feet ahead of a tidying up gang which, in turn, was to work ahead of a timbering gang.

Tatham protested. He said the face gang would be in great danger from a collapse so far ahead of the timbering, and pointed out that they had already had what he called "slickensides" with a mere nine inches of unsupported clay. Tatham added that he was afraid there would be loss of life. But the order stood.

Next shift, Tatham went down with the men and told them of the new procedure. He was quite aware, he said, of the risk involved; but orders had to be obeyed. He arranged for a niche to be dug for his own occupation near the face and for work to be stopped for a minute each hour while he went fully forward into the face to listen.

The rate of progress leapt up. For three days Tatham lived in his niche, having food sent down, straining at all times to catch the slightest sign of soil slippage, and going forward each hour for the official check. While carrying out the last of these face checks—just prior to being relieved—Tatham detected a faint groan from the soil. Immediately he gave the miners' warning cry of "Hist!" and shouted for them all to run for their lives. As he and the men scrambled in startled confusion towards the rear, 40 feet of the tunnel collapsed; about two weeks' work to put right. But no one had been killed, or even hurt.

After this, the new method of digging was abandoned and hope had to centre once more on the machine. On the evening of March 4th, it was switched on for the first time and ran well. For several hours it moved steadily forward at about two feet per hour, boring a luxurious six-foot diameter tunnel. The first sign of trouble came after it had been stopped for a routine check-over. When the power was switched on again, the machine seemed unable to move forward. Examination showed it was gripped fast in the clay around it, which had been affected by the humid air after all and was swelling grossly. With great difficulty the machine had to be dug free. And from then on there was nothing but hitch after hitch. The power output continued to be too low, and every time the machine stopped it had to be dug out. Attempts to keep it going continuously were thwarted by failures in the electric motor driving the compressor: it blew its fuses so often that the supply of fusewire gave out, and when an exasperated sapper used barbed wire instead, worse damage was promptly done and the machine stopped again. At once the clay began to swell, and by the time repairs were completed the machine was locked in its embrace again; the wearisome digging routine restarted.

But by far the worst difficulty was the machine's baffling tendency to dive. "We never discovered why," wrote an eye-witness, anonymously, in an Old Comrades Association Bulletin, "but this machine showed a complete disinclination to proceed towards Germany, but preferred to head to Australia by the most direct route." Prolific advice was offered to the sweating Carter and Talbot, and prominent among the givers of it was Norton Griffiths. During a visit on March 12th, he decided that almost everything was wrong with the equipment and reported in the gloomiest of terms to Harvey. He blamed the "scratch motor engine and dynamo" which, he said, was a hastily gathered together outfit never intended to work with the cutter; also, the adjustment of the cutter tools in the face, he thought, "was not quite right"; he felt there was something wrong, too, with the position of the arm of the cutting tool; lastly, he gave a complex, lengthy and improbable explanation for the machine's tendency to dive, blaming wings extending sideways into the clay and designed to check a tendency for the whole contraption to rotate. Oddly, he had still not lost faith, and two days later was urging Harvey to set up a special six or eight man team to instal future cutters.

But others were beginning to feel differently. By the time the machine had dug its faltering way through 200 feet towards the Germans, the experts lost heart and went home. Harvey apparently shared their feelings, and issued orders for the machine to be abandoned where it was. Its rusting remains lie there still, 80 feet under Belgian soil. For months after hope had been abandoned, rumours trickled through to Cropper and his men that the mystery weapon was far beyond the Messines Ridge and still going. They shrugged their shoulders non-committally, reluctant to admit the truth.

So, rather ignominiously, Norton Griffiths's last contribution to the tunnelling force ended. On March 21st he asked to be relieved of his duties, and put forward an application for two months' leave effective from April 1st. It was necessary, he explained, that he should attend to his private affairs "which involved personal obligations of considerable importance". His old friend Fowke, "the Chief", had recently moved up to become Adjutant General, and the application was referred to him. He granted it at once.

On the 29th of March, Norton Griffiths performed his last liaison duties for Harvey. In the battered but still smooth-running Rolls-Royce, he visited 171 Company five miles south of Cropper's shafts, at a sector known as Ploegsteert Wood. Here another group of deep mines were being laid, at the southern tail of the Ridge. He arrived early in the morning at the sleeping quarters of the acting O.C., Captain Henry Hudspeth, a stocky, energetic north-country-man and coal mining engineer. In some embarrassment, Hudspeth scrambled into his clothes and aboard the huge car.

As they drove towards the front, Hudspeth gave an account of the Company's activities. There was plenty to tell. A mining pro-gramme hardly less ambitious than Cropper's was well under way. Four major galleries were already out deep in the blue clay. At one, dug from Trench 127, there had been a frightening moment when running sand had come spurting through the face, like water under pressure, and had had to be held back by a massive concrete and sandbag dam. At another, from Trench 121, German counter-mining had come so close that work had had to be stopped for weeks.

Norton Griffiths was affable and relaxed; he seemed less in-terested in probing the work than usual, and to Hudspeth's surprise spent much time taking photographs—in defiance of stringent regulations. He promised to send a print of a picture of Hudspeth to his mother, and to write her a line describing their meeting. On April 12th he was to keep the promise and write a characteristic letter:

My dear Mrs. Hudspeth.

I promised your most excellent brave boy I would send you the accompanying picture of him.

It is a small token to one who is doing *invaluable* work—great work, and if you only knew you would indeed be proud of him.

I left him in the best of health, jolly and looking very fit. Believe me.

Sincerely Yours,
Norton Griffiths.

Hudspeth smiled when he saw the letter later. Fit, he might have been. But jolly?

In the afternoon Norton Griffiths went up to Hill 60 for his last wartime visit to that blood-soaked corner. There had been trouble there during the last few days in the shallow level tunnels. On March 17th, 175 Company had blown a camouflet after hearing the Germans very close. On the 19th, the Germans had replied with a blast that collapsed the roof of the British tunnel without, as it happened, causing casualties, but only ten minutes after 175's O.C., Major Cowan, had been standing beneath it on an inspection. Then both sides set about preparing to fire again, and one of the nightmarish races began, with death the almost certain price of running second.

On the afternoon of the 19th the British were ready. At top speed the electrician handed the firing leads to the shift officer who snapped them on the exploder and immediately fired. The boom of a charge going off followed—but from the wrong place. With numb disbelief the officer discovered that the wires given him had been the wrong ones. He had fired an emergency charge in the entrance shaft for use only to destroy the Company's own tunnel if the Germans seemed likely to take it. Worse, three infantry-men had been killed. Two of their bodies had been blasted into the air and now swung, shattered and grotesque, from the stubby branches of a tree. The stricken officer sent an S.O.S. to headquarters, then pulling himself together with an effort, fired the proper charge. The Germans had still been beaten.

For days the two dead soldiers hung in the tree, coated with the last sleets of winter. A 175 Company sapper, Hubert Leather, working in a different part of the mine, had the ugly sight pointed out to him. The officer responsible, somebody told him, was drunk at the time—too drunk to tell one set of leads from another. The story spread widely, but was totally untrue. Cowan had taken a full report of the incident to the Controller of Mines, Stevenson, and apart from a few routine inquiries no further action was taken.

More trouble had followed swiftly. A captured German told of a countermine being driven hard towards the Berlin Tunnel. As a result, Stevenson was rumoured to be considering whether a camouflet should be blown to check it. The great tunnel was obviously in danger, but Norton Griffiths believed a decision to fire a camouflet would be a disastrous mistake. He sent an urgent request to Harvey to prohibit the firing. Harvey replied calmly that he did not think this was contemplated. But in that he was wrong. Stevenson did fire a charge, and events were to prove that on the whole it was the right decision after all.

On the 30th, Norton Griffiths left for England with the pleasing knowledge that the great shake-up of the Ridge was rapidly taking shape. He had achieved all that could have been hoped for and was probably glad enough to go.

Harvey missed him.

14

THE COMMONWEALTH JOINS IN

THE first of the Commonwealth tunnelling companies was formed in New Zealand. Four hundred bronzed, strong, hard-living miners and prospectors paraded for training in September, 1915—and shook up the near by city of Auckland as it had never been shaken before. With candid relief the Aucklanders watched them sail three months later for the front. On March 15th, 1916, they moved to the line near Arras, a sector held on the surface by the 51st Division Highland Territorials. The New Zealanders and the Scots quickly made friends.

Lieutenant J. C. Neill of the tunnellers has recorded an early encounter between one of his men and a Highlander who had stripped to the waist and was studying his shirt intently. The newly arrived New Zealander asked why. "What?" retorted the Scotsman. "Have ye nae wee beaties yet? Ah weel, here's twa to make a stairt with." And smilingly he seemed to pass them across, pinched between his finger and thumb.

Tough though they were, the New Zealanders were shocked at first by the filthy and verminous conditions they had come to; but they settled down to work without delay. They were big men and dug big tunnels—mostly a whopping six feet three inches high by three feet six inches wide. And because they liked to see the ground they were working in—arguing that it talks to miners who know the language—the tunnels were unlined and only supported here and there by rough props.

The brawny New Zealanders showed very early that they could dig.* Within a month or so they were hacking through the chalk

* The New Zealand Tunnelling Company fired a successful series of mines on May 3rd, 1916 near Arras. Although these were the only major mines the

at nearly 600 feet a week, and before long they were claiming (though such matters were not easily proved or disproved) record footages.

Two Canadian tunnelling companies arrived at almost the same moment as the New Zealanders. They were named the 1st and 2nd Companies and joined the already experienced 3rd Canadian Tunnelling Company in the Ypres area.

At that time also, 1,600 Australian miners were fretting in temporary camp at Fremantle, *en route* for France. Their troopship had struck an uncharted rock, and was undergoing repairs which added a three week delay to an already tediously lengthy journey. The men were bored and irritable. They had renamed their ship, the former S.S. *Ulysses*, the "Useless"; their O.C., a prim and demanding Regular, Lieutenant-Colonel Cecil Fewtrell, had become "Colonel Futile". And as morale sagged, Fewtrell clamped ever sterner measures on what had all along been a petty and often harsh discipline. An Australian subaltern, Second-Lieutenant Oliver Woodward, who had himself been threatened with a return home in irons, has said of those days that, "This was when we developed whatever fighting spirit we later showed; the memory of all those carpetings made a man long to spring at someone's throat."

One officer with the contingent retained his good humour through it all. He was Major Edgeworth David, a grey-haired, wiry man of 58. In private life David was a world-famous geologist, a professor at Sydney University and a grandfather, now slightly bent at the shoulders. Despite his uniform and military title, it was still as "The Professor" that he was most often known.

David had done more than anyone to raise the so-called Mining

---

New Zealanders fired, camouflets and flanking manoeuvres continued until September. Then the Company was transferred to work on an amazing chain of underground caves found to run from Arras towards the front line. The caves were converted into a safe assembly centre which accommodated troops (up to 20,000) and also allowed a heavy flow of traffic to move through. The New Zealanders were warmly regarded for their work on this immense project which saved many allied lives.

Battalion. He had been first to suggest the idea to the Minister for Defence, and then, when approval had been given, was the first officer signed on the strength. For weeks after that he campaigned for recruits with an energy that amazed and often worried those who loved him; and David was one of the most loved of men—loved by his family, by his students and by colleagues. News that he had enlisted was printed as far afield as in the *Scotsman*, where it was seen by one of David's two daughters, then living in Edinburgh. She wrote at once to her mother: "I did a little weep and a little laugh, and my heart swelled with pride in him and sorrow for you ... If it was not for his dear white hair one would believe him to be twenty-one years old ... God bless and keep safe our 'perfect gentle knight'." David's efforts to straighten his shoulders, his decision to throw aside his old umbrella as unmilitary, brought smiles to the faces of his family that—as his other daughter has recalled—"were akin to tears".

Throughout the long and broken journey to France, David kept himself busy studying, giving lectures to the troops and writing lucid and often moving letters to his wife. In early May the battalion reached France. "Here we are at last within sound of the guns ..." wrote David. "The last few days have been some of the most memorable in our lives." He went on to describe how touched he had been by the courage of the black-clothed women of France, and "the sweetest little dears of children" struggling on without their men.

By then he had grown a regulation moustache which he described as the "worn-out toothbrush type", and which, to his surprise, came out as dark brown, and which he was playfully accused of dying. "Anyhow," he wrote, "one consolation is that Colonel Fewtrell's is not much, if at all, bigger ..."

On May 8th, 1916, the Australians arrived at their headquarters in Hazebrouck, three and a half miles due west of Ypres, in the 2nd Army area. The first night there was cold and wet; the men lay in their billet beds listening to the rain and chilling reverberations of artillery fire from the east, and wondered about the future.

David's original idea had been that the force should act as a largely self-running mining battalion fighting with the Australian infantry. But Harvey said a firm No to this, and on the 10th, the 2nd Army Controller of Mines, Colonel Stevenson, broke the news at an assembly of the officers. Australian tunnellers, like the other Commonwealth and British tunnellers, were to come under the Inspector and Controllers in the ordinary way. The force was divided into three tunnelling companies—the 1st, 2nd and 3rd—plus one special unit named the Australian Electrical Mechanical Boring and Mining Company. This last soon became known as the Alphabetical Company, for brevity. It took over a large workshop in Hazebrouck village where it built and repaired equipment. The other units went off at once for a short training period to work with experienced companies at the front. The 1st Company, with Oliver Woodward, and the 2nd, remained in the 2nd Army area; Woodward felt humbled by their lack of fighting experience and somehow worried by the ranks he and other officers held, feeling that they had not yet earned them. But their chance—and in particular Woodward's—was soon coming.

The 3rd Company, commanded by Major Leslie Coulter, (a gallant young officer whom David used to descibe as "the Flower of Chivalry") went south to La Bassée, in the 1st Army, area for training with 251 and 254 Companies. The men attached to 251 found they had been flung into a specially fierce and uncomfortable mining battle. Some were put in the care of Coporal Sidney Johnson, a veteran with eight hard months' experience behind him. They found the mine dripping and often awash with ice-cold water that rose and fell unpredictably; Johnson had crawled through about two feet of it often and stood all night with water to his waist; he had become toughened and almost indifferent to conditions that sorely tried the newcomers. And near the face there was a tremendous atmosphere of danger; here silence was insisted upon and digging had to be done with three-foot long "push prongs"—tiny, narrow spades almost like arrows.

Once one of the first of the night shifts stumbled suddenly out in alarm shouting that "the Gerries have broken through!" Johnson rushed to the entrance and studied a burning candle. The flame was steady. He knew that a hole into German galleries would allow a current of air to blow through; the steady flame made it unlikely that any such thing had happened. After a pause of a few minutes, Johnson posted some men with rifles at the shaft top, then glanced round the party. "Come on, Australia," he said. "We'll have a go now." As he started into the mine, two of the men jumped forward at once and went with him. Johnson soon saw what had happened; at the face a large pothole in the chalk had been entered; it had nothing to do with the Germans. The men resumed work, a slightly sheepish look on their faces; but Johnson held nothing against them; the first days in this cold tomb of a mine could strain anyone's nerve.

A number of officers had become supernumary as a result of the new set-up of the Australian miners. Among them was Fewtrell—who was posted soon to a pioneer battalion. Even David's role was slightly obscure at first. Harvey—as he candidly admitted later—had not at this stage realized the value of an able geologist; though nominally attached to G.H.Q., the Professor's early weeks were spent wandering almost as a free-lance from company to company along the British front offering help where it was wanted.

During the early days, he came down to the La Bassée-Loos area to study the unpredictable rising and falling water that made most of the mines there so miserable. He walked round with the chivalrous Coulter and another officer one night, close to the German lines.

Suddenly a flare spluttered into the sky illuminating the three men brilliantly. In the same instant they heard the whistle and crack of bullets coming from the right and one whipped between Coulter and David. David wrote home to say what happened next: "Coulter immediately moved up on my right, which somewhat irritated me at the time, and although no words were spoken we executed a kind of waltz or schottische around one another in the moonlight until at last I succeeded in re-establishing our original marching order . . ." He had earlier complained that the other officers seemed to regard his life as more important than theirs, a point of view that he described as "tommy-rot".

In June, Oliver Woodward, still a second-lieutenant, now on the strength of the 1st Company, won the Australian mining force's first decoration—the Military Cross. His unit was down on the Armentières front, about two miles south of the southernmost part of Messines Ridge. The 1st Canadian Company had been holding that sector and lingered a while to show the Australians around; but only for days. On May 21st, the Canadians marched out—headed for St. Eloi where they were due to start another deep mine aimed at the ridge. Just before they left, a German gallery was unexpectedly broached; there was a moment of high excitement, until it turned out to be blocked at the other end and apparently disused.

Woodward, feeling tense with the responsibility, took charge of the first all-Australian shifts that afternoon. Two days later, when his relief came up, much of the tension had gone; already he knew they were on top of the job. But very soon after, on June 9th (1916), Woodward learned that he was to be tested again, and in a way that sent a sinking sensation through his heart and stomach. The C.O., Major James Henry, announced that he had chosen him to cross no-man's-land to a ruined house in German hands; he was to blow it up with a portable charge and return to the lines.

For 16 hours, Woodward wondered if he had it in him to do the job. He made no attempt to blind himself to the fact that he felt fear, hoping for strength enough to conceal the fact from others. Two other ranks were to go with him Sergeant Fraser and Sapper Morris. They all busied themselves preparing a 100-lb. charge, attaching firing leads and, in case they failed, a burner type fuse.

When zero hour came, Woodward found the strength he needed. At midnight he went over the top with Fraser, Morris and a four-man infantry escort, dragging the bulky charge through the grass and around the shell-holes to the house. They were right beside the German trench now, close enough to hear voices with startling clarity. It seemed amazing that they had not yet been seen. Then Woodward decided that to demolish the house properly, he must enter it to lay the charge in the basement.

With the greatest coolness, he and the other two climbed up over a pile of tumbled bricks lying in their path and entered the dark ruins. Frequent blinding flares lit up the scene but still they went about their work undetected.

As they left the house, the charge in place, Woodward decided to fire by means of the fuse. This was quicker; but, of course, also markedly more dangerous. They huddled in a group out in the unprotected loneliness of no-man's-land and Woodward struck a match, shielding it as best he could from German eyes. The fuse failed; somewhere along its length it had evidently parted.

Now Woodward led his men back to the house to check the electric leads and soon found a break which they mended. Next they paid 150 yards of wire out, crawling back towards their own line as they did so, checking for further breaks. They found another five. Then somehow (though there ought to have been a surplus) the end of the leads was reached while they were still well short of the trench and even outside the British barbed wire. So Woodward, standing alone, fired from there, then ran wildly for the trench, thrilled by the noise of the charge going off behind him.

A week or two later, Company Orders carried the announcement that Woodward had been awarded the M.C. David was delighted and described the event in a letter home. "Young Woodward," he wrote, "the quiet little officer in our No. 1 Company who . . . blew up the building where the Germans had placed machine guns, is to get the Military Cross. We are all delighted, and very proud . . . I was some miles away . . . when this was happening, but heard all about it—not from Woodward who considers any reference to it almost indelicate—but from others."

In fact, Woodward's main reaction had been one of embarrassment, made sharper by the fact that no awards of any kind went to Fraser and Morris. And when these two came over to congratulate him, his feelings reached a peak of wretchedness and he begged them to realize that he was the victim of what he called "Over enthusiasm and lack of discretion on the part of senior officers".

However, in one way at least, the position must have pleased him more than he admitted. For months before Woodward joined up, unknown women had sent him white feathers by almost every mail.

It was a good reply to them.

*   *   *

For the whole of the spring of 1916, Sir Douglas Haig continued to plan for a double summer attack—first the lone British move through Flanders and, second, the joint assault at the Somme. So month after month the tunnelling effort was kept up along the Messines Ridge.

It was a wearisome time for the tunnelling companies involved. Patches of bad ground and persistent countermining by the Germans harrassed and distressed the men as, sweating and swearing, they struggled to advance at speed.

Up at Hill 60, the 3rd Canadian Company felt that nothing else could quite match the hellishness of the Berlin Tunnel. The soil around it was bad—much of the area by now had become a bog from the combined effects of water, mining, shelling, trenching and the hauling of heavy loads. Rotted corpses still lay in vast numbers on—and just below—the surface, a gross and hideous affront to the sensibilities of the living. Jaundice and boils were commonplace. A scratched hand had come to require (by orders) an immediate injection against tetanus. Generations of lice laid their eggs, hatched and thrived to old age in the hair and clothing of officers and men. And all the while the Germans were known to be near, probing and listening; so stealth and caution had somehow to be combined with speed.

Part of the Canadian inheritance had been 200 feet of collapsed main gallery—destroyed by 175 Company just before they left. This was one result of the camouflet Norton Griffiths had begged Harvey to prevent, on his last active day with the force. But it had also ruined a German countermine—and had done the job so thoroughly that it was never reclaimed. The reconstruction of a wrecked tunnel was a task all miners loathed; crumbling ground and shattered timber hampered the work and there was the ever present risk of meeting gas trapped in pockets. But the first 800 feet of the Berlin Tunnel still stood intact and the C.O., a burly, eminent, mining engineer from Western Canada, Major Angus Davis, ordered the remaining 200 feet to be won back. With gloomy vigour, digging was started. It went quickly ahead.

To the right, 250 Company was having almost as hard a time of it. By early June, Hollandscheschuur Tunnel had been forced 800 feet across no-man's-land in the face of persistent flooding, accurate German mortar fire (aimed deliberately, it seemed, at the mine entrance) and heavy German countermines. At Peckham, a mile and a half further south even worse trouble had been met. Here a short, quiet spoken, former coal-mining Welshman, Second-Lieutenant Haydn Rees, had been exhorting the men to conquer what, at times, seemed impossible odds: the clay alone was a serious hindrance; it swelled uncontrollably. Timbers, that proved strong enough in other tunnels, snapped like cheese sticks and had to be replaced with massive seven-inch balks. The floor wracked so badly that a wooden tramway laid for spoil-removal trolleys had to be ripped up and replaced. As elsewhere, mortar fire had had a devastating effect on progress; and on April 29th an unexpected raid, that looked as if it might succeed, had sent the tunnellers rushing to the firestep, to fumble with unfamiliar rifles. But, when morale was low, Haydn Rees pointed out that they were really fortunate to be where they were; for Peckham was the only tunnel site along the Ridge where German countermining was wholly absent. This was curiously true. German miners were fighting back with spirit to the north and south, but at Peckham they never came close enough to be heard—though geophones were constantly manned in case.

The most dramatic spring and early-summer advance of all was made at Petit Bois, in the long, fateful tunnel where Norton Griffiths's machine and the controversial new digging method had both failed. By early June, Cropper's men had kicked their way through 1,600 feet, despite more of the mortar fire and endless trouble with the maddeningly swollen clay. Electric lighting and compressed air ventilation plants had both been installed. At 1,600 feet the tunnel was to divide into a two pronged fork to allow twin charges to be fired. Early on the morning of June 10th, twelve men were down at the fork when surface workers felt the ground give the, by now, unmistakeable quiver of a major mine shock. Two spouts of clay erupted from just in front of the German line and fell back to form ominously blue crater rims, easily seen from the British side. That blueness meant the mines had been deep as well as powerful. The Petit Bois workers had been heard by Germans standing on the bottom of an old crater overhead. This was their reply. With one charge in particular they had aimed well: it was almost directly over the tunnel.

A rescue squad in Proto anti-gas equipment was rushed to the scene. They reported a grave situation: a blockage had been found 1,250 feet in from the entrance shaft; it looked as if 300 or more feet of tangled debris might have to be cleared to reach the men. Their chances of survival were now rated poor. Probably they had already been crushed or, if they escaped that, gassed. In any case, it would take many hours—maybe several days—to reach them and there was little likelihood that the air trapped near the face would last out. But Cropper ordered an all-out rescue attempt to be made on the assumption that there might be survivors.

After a hurried consultation of officers, it was decided that instead of clearing the debris, a new bypass tunnel would be driven alongside. Periodic probes would be put out to see where—if anywhere—the old tunnel could be re-entered.

Haydn Rees, knowledgeable about rescue work from his days in the collieries of Wales, was called from Peckham tunnel to join with other officers in running the operations. The men sprang at the clay and tore their way through it at incredible speed. Normally, 15 feet a day was considered good. But the Petit Bois rescue teams held an average of 40.

In fact the trapped men had all survived the concussion of the mines. It had come with fearful suddenness—the crash of the explosion, the slow rumbling and splintering of wood as the walls and roof closed in behind them, and the sudden total darkness. But no one had been hurt. They had picked themselves up and crawled towards the broken end of the narrow tunnel to inspect the damage. There, when they found they were trapped, an argument had begun. Some had thought that they should try to dig their way out. One rock of a man in particular, Sapper Bedson from Cumberland, had said No. Bedson was an experienced miner from the White Haven collieries; his advice was to lie still, so conserving energy and air for a long wait; in time, help would come.

It was too much to ask of trapped men. They clawed in turns at the wreckage, gripped now by an animal instinct for freedom that reason could not, for the moment, reach. But the foetid atmosphere soon stopped them, and brought them down, fighting painfully for air.

They gathered eventually by the fallen end of the tunnel where a little air still seeped through a break in the ventilation pipe. It was no more than a trickle and next to useless. But they breathed it deeply and in hope. Then, shortly after three in the afternoon, the trickle calamitously stopped. Death was coming very close.

At five o'clock, Bedson advised the others to spread out and made his own way slowly to the face end of the tunnel. There he made himself a bed of sandbags, lay down, removed the glass from his watch so that he could feel the time, and placed his water bottle beside him. The face end was slighty elevated and the air a trifle less foul.

The others remained where they were for a while, gasping together at the opposite end of the tunnel. Bedson half dozed. At about three o'clock in the morning, a Sunday, he heard them spreading themselves out at last. Soon there was silence but for a cough, an occasional moan and the jerky, exaggerated breathing of eleven men slowly suffocating to death. The first died that Sunday afternoon. The others followed. By eight o'clock on Monday evening, all but Bedson were gone.

On the Tuesday, the rescuers uncovered a damaged length of ventilation pipe which they repaired in the hope that some air might find its way through. A little did, enough for Bedson to detect a slight improvement in the atmosphere quite quickly. Each day he made a slow, painful journey to the fallen end. There he listened for sounds of help coming. Day followed day and none could be heard. As he crawled past his comrades he paused by each one to make sure he was dead. Every 24 hours he wound up his watch. Thirst was a worry. He had about a pint of water to keep him going. Often he took some into his mouth and swilled it round but always put it back in the bottle. With massive resignation, he waited.

On about the fourth day, though work went on at top speed, hope was abandoned by Rees and the other rescuers. Twelve graves were prepared in a village churchyard and left ready. Then at last, after six and a half days, contact was made. An officer peered in on the Friday morning, saw the row of dead men and withdrew from the appalling smell to let clean air drift through. He carried the news to the surface: All dead.

Bedson neither saw nor heard them; but he was slowly aware of a pressure drop and crept off to investigate the reason. He was standing at the hole when the rescuers returned in the afternoon. They gaped for a moment, wordless with surprise. "It's been a long shift," Bedson murmured. "For God's sake give me a drink."

Harvey heard of the incident with amazement, and at once sent word that he wanted to question the indestructible Bedson, whose mind, even when he first emerged, had been described by a doctor as "clear and rational". But he was too late. The medical corps had rushed him home to recuperate. And one of the graves in the churchyard went unused.

Work on Petit Bois tunnel was resumed at once. It was taken on to 1,800 feet where, once more, it split right and left to allow two immense charges to be placed.

But by now, mid-June 1916, 250 Company had lost its place as principal miners of the Messines Ridge. The distinction had gone to

171 Company, holding the southernmost three and a half miles underground. Its present commander was the able, energetic, regular R.E., Major Gordon Hyland. He was soon—on July 30th— to be appointed Controller of Mines to the 3rd Army on the Arras front. Meanwhile he had been pushing his unit—the old hard hitting and already famous 171 Company that had blown up Hill 60 14 months before—to the limit; and indeed, beyond it. Hyland had undertaken to drive six major tunnels, some to contain two or even three charges. Two tunnels were to be at the lower tip of the Ridge, started from Ploegsteert Wood. One of these had been completed in February (1916), promptly loaded with 30,000 lbs. of ammonal and wired—by the second in command, Henry Hudspeth; it was the first of all the Messines deep mines to be ready for firing. But at the other tunnel, close by, work had struggled to a premature stop during January from lack of man-power. Although a charge— again 30,000 lbs. of ammonal—was eventually placed, Hyland had been forced to abandon the position for a while.

Elsewhere, progress was good. The same rush to be ready for the pre-Somme push through Flanders was on. On April 20th, the laying and wiring of another charge in an unnamed tunnel driven from Trench 127 was completed; it was bigger—36,000 lbs of ammonal. And 50,000 lbs. of the same stupendous explosive was simultaneously being carried to a second chamber in the tunnel, 75 feet under.

By mid-June, five mines were ready and Hudspeth was preparing to wire up a sixth, Spanbroekmolen. This was to be a single ex-plosion, but of stunning power, by far the biggest charge ever fired by man at that time. Ninety-one thousand pounds of ammonal, packed in 1,820 sealed tins (they had flowed towards the mine en-trance in a seemingly endless stream) had to be arranged to explode at the touch of a switch. The responsibility on Hudspeth was heavy. He had given in much thought.

Wiring the comparatively small Ploegsteert Wood mine had been extremely difficult. It seemed to him that the main trouble was that the chamber had been already packed tight with ammonal tins when he started work; there was no room for him to move or to manipulate the detonators which he had to insert into the charge and connect to two independent circuits. It had been a 48-hour struggle, exhausting and exasperating. And also dangerous. The fulminate of mercury detonators were sensitive; shock, or even friction, might have set them off, and then the entire charge could have followed suit—with Hudspeth on top of it.

For Spanbroekmolen, he evolved a new method which Hyland approved. The charge boxes were to be stacked right and left in the great chamber, leaving a centre gangway free. Here Hudspeth would be able to crouch in comfort to make his connexions. In practice it worked well, and in two or three hours the job was done.

Next, Hudspeth planned to fill up the gangway with more ammonal tins as he left. But before that stage had quite been reached, Hyland and Harvey arrived to see him and came right down into the gangway. They had four bottles of champagne and drinking glasses with them. One of the Company's N.C.O.'s, Sergeant Robert Leonard, was looking on. Somebody smashed the end off one of the bottles and Leonard heard a voice shout, "Confusion to our enemies!" They all drank to the toast and afterwards refilled their glasses several times. When the party ended, the last tins of ammonal were put in place along the gangway and the mighty charge was sealed off. It was June 28th, 1916. Still no date had been fixed for the Flanders attack. And by now it was beginning to seem less and less likely to happen as the French moved ever more troops to the bloodiness of Verdun. The Somme was evidently becoming a mainly British affair and, as such, would be as much as she could likely handle. The mines—seven now were ready—might have to wait.

So it turned out to be. On July 1st, news flashed up the line that the Somme battle had begun. And from what little was known it sounded like the worst catastrophe of the war so far for the British. Sir Herbert Plumer, commanding the 2nd Army, and Harvey soon saw that with both sides so occupied further south, there would be time to carry out even more extensive undermining of Messines Ridge than had been planned. Orders went out for mine laying to contine.

But both generals knew that there was a breathtaking gamble involved. The mines were going to have to wait indefinitely, perhaps for many months, until the right strategical moment came. Could they be preserved? The tunnelling officer experts were frank about their doubts. It was not only the unpredictable danger of German countermining they feared, but also the effect of damp on the charges and wiring. Ammonal fired unreliably when it contained more than a mere 4 per cent of water, and it was highly absorbent. Who could say how long the sealed tins would remain totally moisture-tight? And there was the effect on the hemp and rubber covered firing wires of prolonged contact with damp ground. What would it be? No one was sure. Daily circuit-resistance tests were introduced at all mines, and anxiety increased when the first signs of deterioration soon began to show.

Mid-summer 1916 proved a fiercely active time on most parts of the British-German mining front. When the figures for June were analysed in Harvey's office, it was seen that a record number of charges had been fired. That month, 126 German mines had gone up, compared with 101 British.* And during July, the last new British tunnelling company was formed—256. Month by month the number of companies in the field had been increasing. Now the final total of twenty-five British, three Canadian, three Australian and one New Zealand had been reached.

Harvey—who had moved with the rest of the G.H.Q. staff from St. Omer to more central offices in Montreuil—continued to control the force with gruff impatience. He took a census to find just what size his command had become. The figure worked out at an average of 21,000 men, varying between a low of 18,000 and a high of 24,000. Harvey was taken aback to learn it. The thought occurred to him that this was two whole divisions of infantry, and he

* These figures were never exceeded.

began to fear that "no modern army can stand this drain on its strength". Losses also were phenomenal—over 1,200 new men a month were having to be found and fed into the system to keep it going.

Harvey did more travelling round the front now that Norton Griffiths had gone, using the same Rolls-Royce, which he had taken over. His visits were not much welcomed—for two main reasons: his uncertain temper, and his quaint behaviour under shell-fire. Harvey believed in the theory that shells never land in the same place twice. When a bombardment caught him walking near the front, he was inclined to ignore real cover and trot into a shell-hole, preferably a recent one. There he would stand, at evident ease, while shells crashed round him in thunderous profusion. Escorting O.C.'s felt obliged to stand with him, but did so with a knottiness of stomach and dryness of throat that took some concealing.

Though he seems not to have revealed it, Harvey had cause by now to be pleased with the force he commanded. More surely than anyone else he knew that the British were winning the war underground. It was not just a matter of the number of mines fired, but of accuracy, size and the speed at which they could be laid. On all these points Harvey's men were drawing ahead. That truth was soon to be obvious to all.

* * *

At seven-twenty-nine on the morning of July 1st, 1916, Captain Hugh Kerr of 179 Company stood in a dug-out beside the Albert-Bapaume road, six miles north of the river Somme, and waited. He was stooped over an exploder box, a hand on the plunger, his attention riveted on his watch.

Outside, a dazzling summer sun blazed upon a scene of contrasts—upon apple trees, quiet copses, still fresh fields, and 140,000 confident British soldiers ready to advance; upon the crude iron posts and thick belts of wire, coiled and inhumanly barbed, protecting the German lines; and upon acrid clouds of smoke and dust raised by seven days of British shelling, mixed in places with an early morning mist and hanging, almost static, in the air.

One minute later, on the dot of seven-thirty, the battle of the Somme began.

Kerr slammed the plunger home; simultaneously, a brother officer who had been standing beside him, Lieutenant John Allan, dashed outside to watch results. He reached the top of the dug-out in time to see the great cone-shaped eruption of chalk soaring darkly against the light blue sky. The sight was exhilarating. Allan was still rooted there, gazing upwards, when Kerr's voice came through to his consciousness. In anguish he was shouting that the mine—40,000 lbs. of ammonal—had failed to fire. "But it has, it has!" Allan called back. "Come and look!"

Kerr bounded up beside him in time to see the last half-second of the display, and the heavy pall of smoke it left behind. He was vastly relieved. After pressing the plunger he had heard no roar of the charge bursting out, nothing but the non-stop thunder of shell-fire, and had feared the worst. But the mine—known as "Y" sap—placed almost centrally on the Somme attack front, had done its job. A crater 165 feet across and 70 feet deep had been formed; in its massive rim, the shattered remains of 52 German soldiers lay buried.

And only half a mile to the south, another mine had been blown that overshadowed "Y" sap by both its size and achievement. Twin charges, 36,000 and 24,000 lbs. of ammonal, had been placed about 60 feet apart. Captain James Young pressed the plunger and observed that the firing had been successful. Just how successful emerged later. Young had blown the crater of La Boisselle, the biggest of the war—a single, vast, smooth-sided, flat-bottom chasm measuring some 450 feet across the rim. It had obliterated between 300 and 400 feet of the German line and with it nine dug-outs, all said to have been full of sheltering men. German casualties here were numbered in hundreds.

Altogether, seven* large and eleven small mines were fired by the British as a starter to the Somme. One of the largest—a 40,000-lb.

* There should have been eight. But one, at Tambour, placed by 178 Company, became damp and failed to explode.

charge of ammonal—had been quietly placed by 252 Company beneath Hawthorn Ridge Redoubt, a strongly defended high spot in the German line. This mine seemed likely to be of the greatest help to the northern part of the British attack.

But about two weeks before the battle was due to begin, Harvey learned that the Corps Commander responsible for that sector, Lieutenant-General Sir Aylmer Hunter-Weston, was planning to have the mine fired four hours before zero. Harvey was dumbfounded by the news. And when he heard the Corps Commander's reasoning, he was in no way reassured.

Hunter-Weston's plan was to rush the crater immediately it was blown, so that from its commanding position on the ridge covering fire could be given to help the main assault when it followed four hours later. The long pause was to lull the Germans into a mistaken sense of security—to make them feel, as the hours passed and nothing further happened, that the crater operation had been a local matter and not part of a coming battle.

To most infantry commanders involved, the plan evidently seemed good. To Harvey it sounded mad beyond belief. For if the British were by now more efficient at blowing craters than the Germans, it was equally sure they were slower at rushing them: as Harvey had sorrowfully noted, not one major mine-crater had been effectively held by the British.* As he saw it, the soldiers most likely to end up on the rim would be German. What effect would that have on the vital assault? With passionate conviction Harvey urged that the mine be fired at zero, and asked the Commander-in-Chief to intervene.

In the end an extraordinary compromise was agreed. Orders were issued for the mine to be fired ten minutes before the battle hour. The Lancashire Fusiliers were to rush the crater and hold it. Still Harvey was distressed; the reasoning, he argued, was "obscure".

But duly at seven-twenty the charge was blown; many tons of

* Even the Hooge crater had quickly proved—in the words of the Official Historian—"untenable owing to constant trench-mortaring and strafing".

chalk and the whole of three sections of a company of the 119th Reserve Regiment were blasted into space. Within 20 seconds the debris had landed—covering the surrounding ground in what looked like snow—and the Fusiliers were tearing across to the rim as fast as their legs would take them. But already they were late. With unbelievable speed the German survivors had scrambled from the chalk dust back on to their feet and were seizing the nearer part of the rim, which they held. And the firing of the mine had alerted units far up and down the line; they were pouring out of dug-outs now to man the parapets, correctly anticipating what was going to happen next. Harvey's fears had been well founded.

Grimly Kerr and Allan perched for the whole morning on top of their dug-out, listening to, and observing what they could of the start of the bloodiest, most frightful single battle Britain has ever fought. The brave young men of "Kitchener's Army"—every one a volunteer—advanced in the usual toy-soldier formations towards about 1,000 manned machine guns that cut them down in droves. As Kerr recollected it, "They kept attacking, attacking, attacking, and crumpled and lay like stooks of corn, still in extended order. They were England's best. The most terrible sight I ever saw." By the end of the day nearly 60,000 had been lost. Frantically, the Commander-in-Chief rephased his plans for a long, lower-geared campaign that only ended with the coming of winter weather in November. By then 410,000 British casualties had been recorded. The French, on their short front to the south, had lost another 190,000.

For this, a few square miles of territory had been won. The Allies considered it a victory. But strategically it had been a battle of blunders.

Nor had the mines done much to help. As the official historian later wrote, ". . . they were too much scattered up and down the front to produce a noticeable effect . . ."

Kerr and his comrades felt that this had not been their fault. No more than five companies* had been put on the work, and they had

* 174, 178, 179, 183 and 252.

been given only three months to do it. And besides digging the mines, they had had to provide an elaborate system of very shallow tunnels required for use as communication trenches across no-man's-land. In the event, these were hardly used, for the incredible reason that no one had thought to tell the infantrymen where they were.

Kerr's sappers had worked heroically hard; he had been truly proud of them. And it had been the same with the other companies.

All that had been lacking had been time. Given half as long as the Messines Ridge companies were having for their campaign in the north, the miners might have altered the whole pattern of the Somme. Or so they certainly believed.

15

FACE TO FACE UNDERGROUND

IT was mid-summer 1916. The listener crouched by the face of a shallow tunnel at Mount Sorrel, near Hill 60, checked his geophones and decided that the noises he could hear were definitely from German miners. They sounded close. Swiftly a runner took the news to the officer in charge of the section, Lieutenant John Westacott, of the 2nd Canadian Tunnelling Company.

Westacott, a 25-year-old peace time civil engineer, hurried to the face to listen for himself. The diagnosis had been right; the Germans were only a yard or two away and at about the same level. If left unchecked, they would break into the listening post within the next few hours. There was an efficient weapon for such occasions, the so-called "Torpedo", and the Canadians had become specially skilled in its use. Torpedoes were eight feet long pipes, eight inches in diameter and packed with 100 lbs. of ammonal; they were designed for insertion into a hole previously bored with a hand auger. Among a dozen or so that were kept in an underground store, conveniently close to the fighting tunnels, one was always loaded, primed and even fitted with its detonator, ready for instant firing. Westacott gave orders for it to be brought at once, and braced himself for yet more action . . .

He had already seen a great deal of it during his thirteen months in France. As an infantryman with the 19th Canadian Battalion, he had been gassed at Ypres, had fought in the battle of Loos and—with conspicuous courage—among the great St. Eloi mine craters of March 27th, 1916. This performance at St. Eloi had won him a commission in the field, and transfer to the tunnelling company at Mount Sorrel. While he was still new there, he met the Prince of

Wales* wandering unaccompanied along the front line, and invited him below to the section's forward H.Q. dug-out for a drink. The floor was paved with 24 tons of highly explosive ammonal in tins, but heedlessly the two men lit up cigarettes, poured themselves a glass of rum and talked. The Prince was interested in the tunnelling company's role—and impressed. He grew earnest before he left: "You have a great responsibility, Canada," he said—and privately Westacott agreed. They had the front-line garrison of Canadian troops to protect, *and* the hard-dug Berlin Tunnel with its deep mines about to be placed at Hill 60—the northernmost of the Messines Ridge charges. And the Germans were extremely active in the area.

Some days later, Westacott's men reported that contact had been made with the close-boarding of a German gallery. Westacott ordered the timbers to be silently removed and then, with a sergeant and two sappers, crawled through the hole. Twenty yards down the tunnel they came to a junction where a main gallery passed across their path, and in a few minutes saw the lights of a party of Germans coming along it towards them. It was impossible to make out the size of the party, but Westacott indicated that he planned to stun as many as possible with his revolver butt. He wanted them alive. "I'll take the first, sergeant," he whispered. "You take the next and you two men"—indicating the sappers— "take one each."

The Germans strode past the corner unaware of danger and were instantly felled from behind. As it happened, there were only three of them. There was no sound but for the dull whump of revolver butts on bone, and a minor skuffling as they sprawled on the wooden floor. Still silently, Westacott's men dragged them back through the hole, replaced the timbering to put investigators off the scent and dispatched the three senseless prisoners down the line for questioning. It was all very quickly over.

Then, on May 29th (1916), Westacott was sent on a four-day course on the handling of Proto breathing apparatus. At the time

* Later the Duke of Windsor.

it seemed just a welcome respite from front-line service, but in fact it undoubtedly saved his life. For next day, the Germans made a surprise assault on the mile and a half long front between Hill 60 and Hooge. Three mines were fired as a preliminary at Mount Sorrel, and it was there, too, that some of the most bitter fighting took place. All the 2nd Canadian Company's front-line officers were killed except one other, Lieutenant S. D. "Bill" Robinson, who, like Westacott, was away on a course. Both officers were immediately recalled—to find that the Germans now occupied the Company's entire mining system.

Next morning, a confused but bitter local counter-attack began. Westacott, briefly back in the role of infantryman, was at the front of it, advancing through a non-stop whirlwind of fire to savage hand-to-hand fighting with bayonets. He came through it un-scratched. His luck—by now becoming proverbial—was still holding. A little lost land had been regained.

On June 6th, the Germans fired four mines under the trenches at Hooge and made another small advance in that area. But the Canadians were now preparing a counter-attack of crushing pro-portions. Westacott's C.O., Major Robert Coulthard, mentioned it at dinner in the mess on about the evening of June 6th. He said that a party from the 2nd Canadian Tunnelling Company would have to go with the first attack wave to reclaim the mine system. Twenty-six volunteers would be required—one officer and 25 other ranks. Westacott suddenly became aware that it was in his direction that Coulthard was looking as he spoke. It was easy to see the sense of it. Apart from Robinson, the officers seated round the table were new, replacements ignorant of how the tunnels ran. And Robinson happened to be sick. Ruefully, Westacott looked up to meet the C.O.'s gaze and then rose to his feet. Coulthard was delighted and accepted the offer at once.

But after dinner, Westacott asked for a return favour: the right to marry a Kentish girl he loved. Canadian military policy was sternly set against marriage at this time. But, in the exceptional cir-cumstances, Coulthard agreed. As soon as the counter-attack had been concluded, Westacott would be given a short leave to go to England for a special-licence marriage, with the army's blessing. Delightedly, Westacott wrote his bride-to-be, Laura Hogben of Elham, with the news, the hazards and uncertainties of the future for the moment forgotten.

Wet weather caused a series of trying postponements of the action but, at last, on June 13th (1916) after a pulverizing bombardment by Canadian guns, the assault went forward. Westacott was with it, and again his luck held. He arrived at the mine entrances intact and entered the system.

It was in a state of indescribable chaos, battered by the German mines and subsequent annihilating shell-fire. The recent heavy rains had completed the disorder, filling parts with water and reducing many of the once neatly cut clay shapes to the formlessness of melting sugar-lumps. Some of the entrances were choked with soldiers all dead. In a mined surface dug-out Westacott found the body of a brother officer, Lieutenant George May, pinned to the floor by a beam and already partly eaten by rats. He tried to pull the body out and, in a moment of exceptional ugliness, the legs and trunk carried away. Outwardly calm, Westacott ordered the pieces to be buried with the other corpses and set about the work of restoration. But inwardly, he was saddened and deeply shocked. Twenty-five-year-old May, a darkly handsome engineer from British Columbia, had been a very close friend.

The mine system was fully back in service, and Westacott eagerly awaited his marriage leave on that midsummer's day when the listener reported Germans approaching his post square on. He was entitled to hope for no more crises until the important wedding arrangements had been kept. But now, as he sent for the emergency torpedo, it was with resignation that he did so. On this front, he knew a man was lucky if he had even a day or two of quiet between actions.

With feverish but silent speed and afraid, as usual, that the Germans were busy at similar work, the men bored a hole, pushed the torpedo down it, placed a few shock-absorbing sandbags, and ran the firing wires back a safe distance to an exploder. Then, just before Westacott was ready to fire, an alarm came down from the next listening post to the right: the Germans had been heard there, too, and again they were close. Tensely, Westacott discussed the new situation in whispers with his N.C.O.'s. It was most unusual for two points so close together to be threatened simultaneously. After anxious speculation on what it could mean, they decided that the advancing German gallery had suddenly sprouted a Y as it neared the Canadian workings. It was impossible to say why. But clearly the new attack would also have to be checked. Westacott ordered a second torpedo to be brought up and readied at once for firing.

By now, the German sounds first heard had stopped, an almost certain sign that a charge would soon be fired. But the Canadians won the race. In a few moments Westacott connected the exploder, called the men out of the workings, sent a rush warning to the infantry in the line to stand-by—and fired. With hardly more than a glance at results—which seemed satisfactory—he disconnected the exploder and scrambled with it to the listening post on the right, where the men were labouring to prepare the second charge. In just ten minutes, he was whacking the plunger down again for another successful blow. But tons of debris fell this time to form a formidable barrier between the Canadian and German mines.

Westacott had decided that it was his duty to explore the German system if he could get through. So now he hurried back to the post on the left for a closer look at the situation there. It was better. He ordered the debris to be dug clear with all speed, and while this was being done called for volunteers to go with him on the raid. Three sappers and an N.C.O., Sergeant Brown, at once came forward. All were handed revolvers and grenades and climbed into the cumbersome Proto sets in case of trouble from gas. On Westacott's orders they also took their boots off, to make the raid in the quiet of stockinged feet.

It took the sweating diggers 20 minutes to open up the German tunnel. As soon as the way was clear, Westacott switched on his torch and, with racing heart, crawled through. He was conscious of tremendous strain at this moment—of a consuming nervous tension that exceeded anything he had ever felt in hand-to-hand fighting on the surface. He forced himself on into the darkness, Brown and the others following close behind.

They found themselves in an extravagantly well-built, close-boarded tunnel, slightly larger than their own; the extra few inches in height allowed them to walk roughly upright, though with head and shoulders greatly stooped.

First, they studied the floor and walls for bloodstains and human fragments, hoping for signs that the torpedo had caught some workers at the face; none were to be seen. Soon they began to shuffle on silently and slowly down the long, dark gallery. After 40 yards they came to the centre point of the Y. As they had suspected, they had been advancing along one arm; now they could bear left down the stem of the Y towards the German lines, or turn sharp right along the other arm towards their own lines and the point where the second torpedo had been blown. They turned right.

After about another 40 yards of shuffling, they arrived at the mass of debris the torpedo had brought down. Lying among it were the dismembered bodies of two Germans who seemed to have been savagely flailed against the timber by the blast. While Westacott and his men stood examining the find, noises from the Canadian side of the barrier showed that a digging party was coming through and had made amazing progress. Westacott decided to wait, and in a few minutes was talking to another of his N.C.O.'s. He said he was about to go as far as possible down the German main gallery— the stem of the Y—to blow it up. Two mobile charges would be necessary. He instructed the N.C.O. to pick them up from stores and to bring them down the tunnel with all speed. Meanwhile, he and his party were going ahead.

As they prepared to set off back along the arm towards the main gallery, it occurred to Westacott that the risk of meeting German miners was now acute. They must have heard the torpedoes going off and would surely be sending a rescue party to look into the fate of their two face workers. The marriage he had so much been looking forward to in Elham's rural peacefulness began to seem exceedingly remote. He had a high regard for the German's skill and courage in hand-to-hand fighting, and was far from certain he could win the encounter he suspected was about to happen. With his torch (which he used sparingly) in his left hand and revolver in his right, he led his party forward.

They reached the junction safely, bore right and crept onward along the main gallery. Several more yards were covered uneventfully, then Westacott saw an ominous flash of torchlight ahead. His mind moved quickly. The Germans would undoubtedly head for the arm where their face workers had been, so he whispered to the men to about turn and go a few paces down the other arm and then to stop, to await developments. As Westacott's party watched, the Germans came rapidly to the junction and for a chilling moment seemed about to turn right. But the reasoning had been sound. They turned left. There were seven of them, an N.C.O. at the head followed by five men with a junior officer bringing up the rear. They all seemed very relaxed, with torches blazing ahead of them and heavy footwear clumping on the wood floor.

Westacott was thinking rapidly ahead. At any moment the Germans would meet his N.C.O. and sapper coming towards them, carrying the two mobile charges. The Canadians would almost certainly be shot if he mistimed anything now. Stealthily he crept round the corner behind the Germans, following in their steps and gaining on them quickly. Glancing over his shoulder, he saw that Brown and the others were keeping close up in single file. Westacott was just four yards behind the rearmost German when the lights of the mobile charge carriers first showed.

The Germans paused, then called out a greeting, evidently supposing the two men to be their own. There was no reply—and the advancing torches stopped. Excitedly the Germans chattered for a moment and then the N.C.O. at the front fired a shot. An answering shot came cracking back up the tunnel immediately.

At this moment, Westacott switched on his torch and the rest of the party promptly followed suit. The Germans turned in alarm, trapped now between two unknown forces. Westacott, face to face with the officer, shone his torch full in the other man's eyes. The dazzled officer shone his torch back and levelled a gun. For a fractional moment, Westacott feared the German was going to shoot first, but then he seemed to hesitate, shocked—as Westacott later decided—by the grotesquely hooded outline of the enemy facing him. At that second, Westacott felt his own gun lashing back with the kick of the recoil, and the German was clutching himself about the stomach. He fell. Relief swept Westacott's whole being. He had fired first after all—and aimed well. Next instant he threw himself down to allow Brown a clear field of fire over his body from behind.

Somewhere up at the front a Canadian voice was calling "For God's sake, shoot straight!" Then there was a crash of bullets, painfully loud, and the German N.C.O. was down, wounded—but still firing. Brown closed on him, kicked his gun out of his hand and shot him again—dead. The remaining Germans surrendered, calling the traditional "kamerad!" Westacott scrambled to his feet. A quick casualty count showed, on the German side, one officer, one N.C.O. and two men dead and one badly wounded; the Canadian figure was three sappers wounded—among them the two rearmost men who had never had a chance to fire themselves.

Westacott knew that the noisy fighting could not have gone unnoticed, and that a strong German support party would probably appear at any moment. He and Brown picked up the mobile charges and, accompanied by two sappers, hurried off again along the main German gallery. Fifty yards up beyond the junction, they dropped a charge and lit the fuse, then turned and stumbled as fast as conditions would allow back to the junction where they lit and dropped the second charge.

Westacott shouted at the others now to run for their lives, and they came blundering down the arm to the right—the one they had first entered by—arriving at the exit just as the charges fired. The concussion shock knocked them violently to the ground face first, and the last sapper was trapped by the legs in falling debris. Panting and exhausted they hauled him out to find one of his legs had broken. So the Canadian casualty count for the operation rose to four.

Some time afterwards, Westacott climbed back into the German tunnel to place and fire two more charges—as he said, "to make a proper job of it." He knew, then, that there would be no danger for at least some weeks from that part of the German system. The engagement was at an end.

Next evening, a note arrived by the ration wagon from the C.O. saying, simply, "You boys did a good job yesterday." With it came six bottles of whisky, and there were drinks all round.

Now Westacott felt he could allow himself to think again about his wedding and Coulthard's promise of leave. On July 18th, he came off shift to find the pass waiting. Within minutes he left the battlefield for England, and on the 22nd was married quietly in Elham's ancient parish church.

A 48-hour honeymoon followed, then he was due on a troopship at Folkestone for return to France. Laura Westacott went down to wave good-bye from the quayside; she wondered it it was the last time she would see her husband. It was not; but it was the last time she would see him whole-bodied.

Westacott found himself back near Hill 60 at ten o'clock the same night. He had two bottles of whisky, half the wedding cake, a cooked chicken, and a bag of assorted wedding gifts in his arms. His batman, a good soldier and servant, came forward to help carry the load to an advanced dug-out at Mount Sorrel. Westacott gave him the bag. The two men were walking down an exposed slope known as Observatory Ridge when the batman gasped suddenly at Westacott's side and fell. He had been shot dead. Sadly Westacott helped to bury him that night. The reality of the war, all its ugliness and pain, had come back with a rush. Already it was hard to believe he had been on honeymoon just a few hours before.

But in fact this front had become relatively quiet now, while the rival armies battered each other on the Somme. Westacott settled down to the wearisome, hazardous, unspectacular routine of defensive mining again, doing a theoretical four days on front-line duty and four days at rest, which often became six days on to two off as the casualties multiplied. On August 1st, charging was completed in the first of two deep chambers at Hill 60, and it became more than ever important to protect the system there from attack.

In mid-September, the Germans mined very close to the 2nd Canadian Company's workings, and during the night of the 15th Westacott hit back with two torpedoes. They brought the total of torpedoes fired by the Mount Sorrel section to about forty. With the help of these last two, a length of German gallery was captured.

Just before daylight, he left the tunnel by the main entrance in the front trench and set off along the line with a sergant. While below they had heard heavy shells exploding on the surface, and Westacott feared that some of the entrances might have been damaged. He was on his way to look them over.

The two Canadians turned a corner in the trench to find themselves walking into a group of infantry. In that same moment they realized who these men they were about to squeeze past were: Germans! The truth dawned with a shock like a kick in the stomach. Unknown to the 80-man shift at work below, the trench had been captured during the night—and with it all the entry points to the mine. Westacott turned and made what he later described as the longest jump of his life. Frantically, he and the N.C.O. crashed back through the main entrance and slithered down the first, short slope into the mine. Lightweight charges were kept at this point for emergenices; they snatched them down, lit the fuses and heaved them towards the entrance, then grabbed handbells—also stored conveniently for this kind of situation—and began to ring and shout a warning to the others.

It was some minutes until the Germans, after groping along the dark trench, found the damaged entrance and began blundering through. By then, Westacott had rallied a small group of men who were already finishing off a sandbag barricade about 30 feet down the tunnel, just ahead of a point where it took a ninety degree turn to the right (looking inwards).

The Canadians, awkwardly huddled together behind the sand-bags, began to fire their revolvers and throw hand grenades. Soon the tunnel was a frightful inferno of noise, smoke and confusion. For the first few minutes, all the invading Germans were killed at a distance. But with blind heroism they kept coming, and began to pour through the entrance faster as they comprehended the situation. Some rushed through the choking smoke and dust, stumbling over the bodies of their dead comrades, and actually reached the barricades. There they were killed—in most cases with a brass dagger, specially designed for tunnel fighting, which strapped to the wearer's wrist. The fighting settled down to a pattern of five to ten minute rushes followed by lulls of up to twenty minutes while the Germans counted their losses and prepared new attacks.

By a strange coincidence, Lieutenant Robinson, the only other long service officer on front-line duty in the company, was also in the Mount Sorrel tunnel with Westacott. He had come up out of turn to assist with a complex piece of surveying, and now, while Westacott controlled the first barricade, had been posting men at key points throughout the warren of tunnels in case of attack at any other of the system's entrances. An extraordinary spirit of no-surrender had gripped the entire shift.

After four hours of fighting, Westacott and his men were coming close to collapse from exhaustion, noise and the poisonous fumes that burned their throats and lungs. By now, as they shone their torches through the swirling smoke at the end of each attack wave, a horrifying scene of carnage could be dimly made out. Dozens of German bodies littered the narrow tunnel in grotesque disorder. There had been Canadian casualties, too, and these were being carried to the H.Q. dug-out near the rear of the system.

Westacott conferred briefly with Robinson to say that the front barricade could not be held much longer. He proposed firing a charge that would destroy the whole of the front section of the tunnel and entrance, withdrawing his men into the interior of the system. A suitable charge was kept permanently in position for such a crisis. Minutes later, it roared out, rocking the whole system like a ship at sea. A mass of debris blocked the way exactly to plan; there would be no more danger here for some time. But desperately needed fresh air had been cut off as well. The situation was still most critical.

Westacott and his party went below for a rest, leaving Robinson in charge. A lull had set in now that looked as if it might last. There was nothing much that could be done, except to await the next move.

At three o'clock that afternoon, the Germans discovered a small rear entrance into the mine, normally used for clearing out spoil to be dumped. They sprang in and shot the entrance guard dead. Sappers covering the guard from further in, returned fire immediately; the battle was on again.

Westacott rushed out from the dug-out to direct it as before. He soon saw that another retreat would be needed. The Canadians were very exposed and, fighting back, were going down one after the other where they stood with calm and orderly heroism.

In feverish haste, Robinson was having a barricade built round the first right-angle corner, backed by a second one further in still and round another such bend. As soon as possible, Westacott withdrew to the first position and the Germans surged forward in pursuit. The atmosphere, still poisoned from the morning's affray, grew very bad. Gas from the grenades was causing serious casualites, in addition to the men who were killed or disabled by wounds. The nightmarish battle raged on. As each tunneller fell, he was dragged into the interior and another man sprang immediately into his place. Westacott's astounding luck seemed to be holding as firmly as ever; he was still unscratched. But he began to wonder how much longer their lungs and bodies would stand the demands he and the others were making of them. He decided on a further retreat to behind the inner barricade, hoping for a chance to fire the destruction charge that would collapse the tunnel as in the morning's operation.

Urgently he called out to the rearmost of the fighting party to withdraw, and they did so. Westacott and a few sappers were about to follow when part of the forward barricade was blown out. They were almost fully exposed now to the advancing Germans; grenades promptly came arcing through.

By torchlight, Westacott saw one land beside him, just a foot or two away. He threw up his left arm to protect his face at the moment the grenade went off. The blast hurled him to the ground and unconsciousness followed. A vague comprehension returned in a few minutes. By then, he was lying on the floor behind the inner barricade where his men had dragged him. The clamour of battle was as loud as ever; he was aware of struggling terribly for breath in the dense smoke and gas that had gathered at floor level; it was some time before he realized that most of his left arm had gone. He was no more than on the verge of consciousness, and soon after again slipped away.

The Germans did not take the tunnel. They could not have known how near they were to victory. When they called the battle off, 60 of the 80 Canadian tunnellers had been lost, and the survivors were acutely distressed. Then, 24 hours after the siege of the mine had begun, the lost trench—only about 400 yards in length—was recaptured by British troops. The trapped tunnellers staggered gratefully out into the sweet fresh air.

It had been a day of glory for the tunnelling force and the Royal Canadian Engineers. But it passed unrecognized and even unknown —apparently—to all but those who had been directly involved. No word of it appears to have reached the ears of Harvey or the Controller, Stevenson. Mention of the event was even overlooked in the unit's own war diary, and came close to being forgotten for ever.

Westacott went back to England and a hospital bed. Helped by his bride-wife, he made a slow though good recovery, and twelve months later returned to the front line. But for many years he was haunted by memories. With sleep came nightmares; with the noise of a train, a resurgence in his mind of the horrifying clamour of the

underground battle at Mount Sorrel, September 16th, 1916.
Forty years were to pass before John Westacott—who survived the
war to become an eminent civil engineer—could bear to talk of
that 24 hours again.

The great Hill 60 mine, still in the hands of the 3rd Canadian
Company, had not been harmed by the raid—though the Germans
for a while had seemed to threaten its entrance. There, a bloodless
but still desperate battle was being waged against slippages and
water. A branch mine reaching out towards the Caterpillar spoil
heap 200 yards south-west of Hill 60 had struck bad ground and
serious falls at the face had followed. The Canadians had gone
deeper, to more than 100 feet down, passing successfully under the
patch, to form their second chamber on target. Then a new, more
serious disaster had occurred. The system—the whole of the Berlin
Tunnel—had filled suddenly with water. September, 1916 saw the
3rd Canadian Company striving to pump it clear, with machines
that had to be driven so hard that they constantly broke down. For
weeks it seemed hopeless.

And that month there was bad news for the British and Commonwealth tunnellers about their gentle geologist, David. On
September 25th, David was walking through a communication
trench near Vimy when he passed a deep well which he was told
had gone dry. He was currently engrossed in a study of changing
water levels in the chalk, so this came as interesting news to him.
Just a few days previously his findings on water levels in the Loos-
Vimy area had been issued as simple tables for the guidance of
tunnelling officers. They showed startling rise and fall differences
of up to 30 feet. David walked over to the well which turned out
to be a useful 100 feet deep. He decided to go down on the
bucket himself to examine the strata at the bottom.

Three officers with him lowered him slowly by the windlass. He
was sitting calmly on a wooden board set across the rim of the
bucket, his feet tucked under him. Then, at 20 feet, the windlass
collapsed without warning and David began to fall.

It took him one and a half seconds to reach the bottom. He had time for thought as the crude brickwork of the well flashed past, and he was sure he was going to die. There was time even to regret that it should be this kind of death. With tremendous violence the ageing professor and his bucket struck the foot of the well.

David recovered consciousness quite soon, to hear the other officers calling down to him anxiously. He called back saying, in his first sentence, that he wished them to note he had gone down the well on his own responsibility. At first there was no reply so he called out again, "Have you got that?" "Yes," they shouted back.

"Well, please send down a bandage for my head," David retorted. He was bleeding heavily.

Soon, a doctor was lowered to him to bandage his head. Then, his legs through two loops in a rope, David was hauled up. "Pull up slowly," he called, "and give me time to observe the water level in the shaft."

But, as he later confessed, this was bravado to "buck them up a bit on top". He had suffered severe internal injuries, a deep scalp wound and a pair of broken ribs. He was very seriously hurt.

Harvey was horrified when he heard the news and went down to La Pugnoy, where David was lying in hospital, to see him. He knew now that a top-ranking geologist was of great importance to the tunnelling effort—a view shared by the Germans who had many. David was very bright, explaining in mathematical terms how the board and the angle of the bucket had saved him. He was evidently going to live.

Six weeks after the accident, David was back at work, but in Harvey's office. Harvey told him that he would henceforth be attached to the H.Q. staff, and insisted that he must never go within 1,000 yards of the front line without first obtaining permission. The relationship between the two men was peculiar. Harvey spoke as sharply to David as to anyone—yet protested when David replied by standing primly to attention and throwing salutes at every opportunity.

Acting Captain H. R. Dixon, the young surveying officer on Harvey's staff, a profound admirer of both men, watched their association with delight. David would come out of the inner office with twinkling eyes to say, "It didn't hurt so much that time, Dixon." It became a standing joke that David the professor and scholar would put on the attitude of a boy going before the head when the General called him in. Once he came ruefully out with a report written in his own hand which he said Harvey had ordered him to write again.

But behind the semi-humourous by-play, unremitting hard work was going on. David's geological discoveries were making it possible for British tunnellers to use every natural advantage the sub-soil offered. Harvey, stabbing at his bell-push and snapping out orders as long as he could stay awake, made sure no such opportunities were missed.

By the end of 1916, the Germans were slacking off their mining effort, in the hope that their opponents would follow suit. But at least 15 mammoth mines had been lodged beneath Messines Ridge by then.

The war's biggest eruption was nearly ready for firing. There could be no letting up.

16

THE RIDGE GOES UP

LIEUTENANT-COLONEL FÜSSLEIN, in command of all German (4th Army) pioneer-miners at work along the Messines Ridge, knew by the end of 1916 that the British tunnelling companies were planning something big along his front. There had been various signs for him to read.

The first came in late summer. Füsslein's men were probing forward deep under a house and outbuildings, known as Petit Douve Farm, when they struck timber. They were about 80 feet down. At such a level, an obstruction was almost certain to be a British gallery, so an officer and eight men went down to investigate.

They removed some of the timber and found themselves staring into a huge mine chamber. It was packed tight with 35 tons of ammonal in tins. The officer gave orders for work on hauling out the charge to begin at once and remained in the tunnel to supervise. As the heavy tins went out, the firing wires became exposed. In his last seconds of life, the officer went forward to cut them. At that moment, Lieutenant Peter King, of 171 Company, excitedly rammed down an exploder handle and blew a second charge, a heavy camouflet. The German officer and all eight men were killed.

It was August 24th, 1916. One-seven-one Company, now under Hudspeth (recently promoted to command and the rank of major), had finished installing the main mine in July, and was advancing with an extension tunnel aimed at an adjacent German strong point. Almost as soon as work on this subsidiary drive began, rival minework had been heard. To shift officers King and Lieutenant Percy Ellis, it was soon apparent that the Germans were about to enter the main tunnel. They asked for permission to fire the charge at once. It was refused. In the view of 2nd Army Controller of Mines, Lieutenant-Colonel Alexander Stevenson, the result would be to give the secret of the mine away. All he could permit was a smaller (1,000-lb.) charge to be placed, strictly as a last resort remedy, in the off-shoot tunnel. It was this that King had blown when geophone listening convinced him, correctly, that the Germans were coming in behind the heavy tamping to the main charge.

But when the news reached Harvey at G.H.Q. that even the smaller charge had been fired, he was most concerned. He signalled Stevenson that he regarded the situation as very serious, and added that the blowing of the camouflet would involve the company in mining warfare.

He was right. On August 28th, Füsslein's men fired back with a heavy camouflet that Hudspeth estimated at no less than the equivalent of 6,000 lbs. of ammonal. It wrecked the whole of the main tunnel, buried four men and tore the firing circuit to pieces. The devastation was so complete that Hudspeth and Stevenson decided to abandon the mine. Somebody had the idea of diverting the near-by River Douve into the entry shaft in the hope that it would flood through to the German workings, and this was done.

The encounter had at once suggested to Füsslein—as the British feared it might—that something special was happening under the ridge. A few weeks later he had unexpected confirmation. An officer's batman with the 3rd Canadian Company defected while under open arrest for drunkenness, sprinted over no-man's-land and revealed all that he knew about the mining scheme. He included precise information about the location of a mineshaft near a point known as Factory Farm. The Germans promptly began a saturation shelling of the area and followed up with a raid.

The attack was watched by a 3rd Canadian Company shift officer, Captain Harry Urie, who was supposed to be resting. He raced up the line expecting to find the whole of the duty shift dead. Instead he found the men huddled together in the shaft house "scared to death", as Urie recollected it, "but safe". By then the

Germans had withdrawn. They had come to within ten feet of the shaft, but in some extraordinary way had failed to see it. The British side hoped this fact would discredit the deserter's story. But on December 25th (1916), Füsslein shrewdly reported to the German General Staff that British deep mining operations in the area were probably intended to support a surface attack. He asked for additional mining companies to help him fight back, and was granted three. But in most respects, German commanders were not yet disposed to take the mining threat seriously. Füsslein privately regarded them as "arrogant and ignorant".

In mid-February, 1917, Füsslein's men had another success. They heard tunnelling works under way at Spanbroekmolen, and at top speed began to prepare a camouflet. Again it was Hudspeth's 171 Company they had caught up with—and in circumstances that almost exactly duplicated the Petit Douve encounter.

A branch had been broken out from the main tunnel and aimed half right at a secondary target far back in the German lines. It was from this new work—and not from the great Spanbroekmolen mine that Hudspeth had wired with his own hands the previous June 28th, and which had lain silent and ready ever since—that the sounds were coming.

The first German camouflet went off when the branch, starting from a point about 650 feet along the main tunnel, had been pushed more than 1,000 feet forward. It did no damage, but struck a chill into the miners' hearts. With the Petit Douve disaster fresh in their minds, Hudspeth and Stevenson knew that they dared not retaliate. Progress, which until now had been so rapid, began to falter. A few days later a second camouflet did considerable damage, and Hudspeth now put a stop to further work.

But Füsslein's men were still not finished. On March 3rd (1917), they fired another camouflet close to the main 171 Company tunnel, and did massive damage. Hudspeth put on the anti-gas Proto set and with another officer, a highly trained Proto expert, hurried into the tunnel to see the situation for himself. He was still observing with dismay how extensive the damage looked when his companion suddenly collapsed. Hudspeth raced back to the entry shaft for assistance. But by the time help came, the Proto expert was dead—ironically from a leak in his equipment.

Hudspeth, inured by now to shocks, continued with the examination and was soon forced to face the fact that the vast, 40-ton mine had been lost, at least for the present. Tests showed a total wiring failure and a full 400 feet of the tunnel was too badly battered to repair. The utterly disheartening task of driving a new gallery alongside the worst hit part of the old began. It took more than usual courage to start; not only were there the gravest risks of further German camouflets that would crush, gas or bury alive the men at the face, but doubts were also growing about whether the work could possibly be completed in time. Opinion was increasingly of the view that the 2nd Army's offensive against the Messines Ridge must be coming soon. For one thing, tests showed that many of the older mines were deteriorating so fast that they must be used soon or not at all. For another, the Allies' fantastically costly victory at the Somme had been duly won, and the question automatically followed of where now? Messines seemed the likeliest answer.

Attention was briefly diverted by three events in April (1917). On the 6th, the United States declared war on Germany; on the 9th, the British Battle of Arras began and was quickly reported a success; and on the 16th, the French launched a huge offensive further south, across the River Aisne. But this attack, though expressly designed to "end the war"—failed; now bitterness gripped the weary French soldiers, many of whom were soon to come out in open mutiny.

At the same time, Britain's other big ally, Russia, was writhing in the first stages of her Bolshevik revolution. The British C.-in-C., Sir Douglas Haig, was faced with an alarming situation: until American troops could arrive (which would take months), his men would have to fight alone. He remained calm. On May 7th, he asked Plumer, of the 2nd Army, when he could be ready to attack at Messines.

The white haired, precise and imperturbable Plumer was ready for the question. "A month from today," he said, and meant exactly that. So the date was fixed at last: June 7th, 1917. For the tunnelling companies involved, it meant a final frantic effort.

Excluding the lost mine at Petit Douve, the scheme was developing as a 21 charge barrage, laid from twelve main shafts and tunnels. But Plumer decided that the two southernmost mines (30,000 lbs. of ammonal each) were too far to the right of his attack front to be of immediate use. Orders went out that they were to be readied in all respects, but held in reserve. As many as possible of the remainder were to be prepared for simultaneous firing at zero hour, in one stupendous storm of destruction spanning 10 miles of the ridge.*

Exactly how many mines would be wholly complete by the 7th was even now in doubt. Three were still being dug or loaded, and one, Spanbroekmolen, was not yet repaired. But with luck, it seemed 19 could be hoped for.

The northernmost mine was a 53,500-lb. mixture of ammonal and guncotton beneath Hill 60. Next came 70,000 lbs. of ammonal less than 200 yards south-east—at the Caterpillar spoil heap. Both charges had been laid from the famous Berlin Tunnel, the deep drive started amid such difficulties and hardship by Cowan's 175 Company nearly two years before.

The two charges had actually been placed by the 3rd Canadian Company in the autumn of 1916. But soon after, in November, the Canadians had moved out (to the other end of the ridge) and the 1st Australian Company had taken over. Now, in May, 1917, they were still there. And, as an Australian officer once said of that time, "It was getting on all of our nerves."

Füsslein's miners knew there was something big near by, and

* The British intended digging up the charges after the war and assured the Belgians that this would be done. But after the German advance of 1918, the precise position of the charges was lost and they were eventually abandoned.

One blew up dramatically on July 17th, 1955, apparently set off by an electrical storm; it did slight damage to distant property but caused no casualties. The other is, presumably, still in place.

they never let up with their probing. The Hill 60 system was by now an amazingly intricate, 50-listening post, four-decker warren with well-developed galleries at 15, 45 and 90 feet, and a rudimentary one 100 feet down. The 45-foot level, known as the "intermediate section", was by far the most hectic and exciting. Four of its listening posts were located a mere six to ten feet clear of a main German gallery; Oliver Woodward, M.C., a Captain since October and officer in command of the Hill since November, never forgot the tensions that went with duty in those posts. Absolute quiet was required—and obtained. "I have listened," Woodward has recalled, "as immovable as a piece of statuary and as cold, from fear."

Water was slopping through the galleries the way it always had at Hill 60, when the Australians took over. The Caterpillar mine was known to be totally immersed, although 60 men were kept constantly at work on the handpumps. Eventually, after months of labour and the use of circular steel caissons, a deep vertical shaft was successfully sunk through the running sands to replace Cowan's long incline, a major source of leaks. Electric pumping was also installed. So conditions, which had been having their own effect on the men's nerves, were somewhat improved.

But other sources of strain had to be endured. A shift hardly passed without reports of German activity coming in from some of the listening posts, and numerous camouflets were blown by both sides. One had to be hurriedly fired by Woodward so close to the big mine under the Hill that there was a general fear the shock might set it off. Nothing so dramatic happened, but damage was done to the wiring.

On April 4th (1917), the Germans blew a minor camouflet and followed with another the next day. In the late evening of the 9th (Easter Monday), a raiding party attacked overland, entered the British front line and threw portable charges into several mine-shafts causing casualties and damage. A costly and exhausting action followed as the Australians, with hand grenades and rifles, helped the infantry to fight the raiders off. Then, just a few hours later, on the morning of Tuesday the 10th, another German camouflet went off, doing further damage to the galleries. Amazingly, the two great mines still appeared to be intact. But by now the Australians were openly questioning their chances of protecting them much longer.

A few days later, on the 25th, a calamitous accident shocked the company. Two officers, Captain Wilfred Avery and Lieutenant Arthur Tandy, were preparing a guncotton priming charge that was to be used to fire an ammonal camouflet. They passed a feeble test current through the detonators *after* inserting them in the explosive (it should have been done before) and the charge, 50 lbs. of it, promptly fired. Avery and Tandy were blown to pieces and the entire dug-out they were in was wrecked; the blast flashed on through a corridor and into the Proto storeroom to take more casualties there.

The total loss came to three officers and seven men dead, four officers and twelve men gassed, many seriously. Captain William McBride, a large, cheery, temperamentally extrovert mining engineer from Adelaide, took charge of the cleaning-up operation. He found sand almost filling the dug-out and sieved as much of it as possible, extracting the remains of the two disintegrated officers which he wrapped in blankets and sent down for burial with the other bodies. McBride was awarded the M.C. for completing this terrible work.

Then, early in May, German miners caused a new wave of anxiety by working up close to the main Hill 60 charge. Lieutenant Royle heard the tut, tut, tut of a windlass revolving, and later confessed that "by this time we felt we were at breaking-point. It was doubtful how much longer we could have held out."

They were not to have to try for long. On May 15th, Major Henry, the O.C., sent for Woodward and told him he was putting him in charge of the firing party. He was to be assisted by two officers, Royle and Lieutenant James Bowry, an N.C.O., and 40 sappers. A profound relief spread through the company at the hint of action soon to come. On June 3rd, tamping, which had been partly removed from the Hill 60 charge to allow of wiring repairs and better listening, was replaced. The Germans were still at work close by and there was chilling, recent evidence that they were again advancing towards the charge. An estimate of their speed and distance to go showed that with luck the mine would be fired shortly before they reached it. But Woodward was uneasy as the endless bags went into place; there was no denying that the mine was being left to chance.

That day British artillery, which had been unusually active for days, began a monstrous bombardment that crashed and roared in the background, adding greatly to the eve-of-battle feeling now gripping all men in the salient.

On June 5th, Woodward reported to the infantry commander, Brigadier-General T. S. Lambert, commanding the 69th Brigade. Lambert announced formally that zero hour had been fixed for three-ten in the morning of the 7th. He planned to be present in the firing dug-out himself to give the signal.

Woodward suffered considerably next day, the 6th, from pre-battle tension. The electric wires had still to be run back from the shaft top to a light-proof, firing dug-out located about 400 yards back from the mines. This delicate and important work was done that day. There were three separate circuits passing through the two charges in series. Each circuit had its own throw-over type switch but, if all went well, only one—Woodward's—would be used. When Woodward threw the blade across, current from the 500 volt d.c. lighting generator should flow to the charges to set them off. But if the current failed, then Royle and Bowry would close the two other switches and fire the mines by exploder boxes already hooked up and at their feet.

By one-fifteen in the morning of the 7th, with less than two hours to go, the wires were in the dug-out and ready, only the last minute connexions to the switches waiting to be made. Woodward was standing by, tense and responsible, haunted by irrational doubts about whether the circuits had been correctly linked. With a Wheatstone Bridge, he tested and re-tested, tested and re-tested again and again. As each reading showed correctly, he promptly took another. A summer storm broke, and the rain drummed heavily on the dug-out roof. Royle and Bowry were inside with him. Somebody mentioned the question haunting them all: what were the Germans doing? Had they heard that this was the night and quietly withdrawn?

Haig had had a similar anxiety some days before and discussed it with Plumer. He wondered whether the mines should be fired ahead of the attack. But after some discussion, the decision was made to go ahead as planned. It was obvious that the Germans must know an attack was coming; the bombardments and massing of troops would tell them that. It was just to be hoped that security arrangements had at least kept the vital news about the date and time of the attack secret.

In fact, this information was soon spreading dangerously fast. Milicien (conscripted private) Victor Maes, a 24-year-old Belgian, was on short leave in Bailleul on June 5th. That evening he was frolicking with some girls in an *estaminet*, when one of them told him there was to be a great attack by mines at Messines. Maes asked when, and the girls said (correctly), "Thursday morning." Maes asked what time. "Three o'clock," they replied. Maes' interest grew. Who had given them the information? he asked next. Laughing and giggling, the girls said they had been told by some young British officers.

Maes wondered at first whether to believe them or not. He was soon to find out.

The next deep mine to the Hill 60 pair was a vast single charge lying two miles to the south (and somewhat west) at St. Eloi, that other long-standing mining hotspot. Here, Major Cy North's 1st Canadian Company had developed a 1,650 foot tunnel, picking up and re-using part of the drive left by 172 Company after their great eruption at this same place of more than a year before. The Canadians, under the immediate control of Section Officer Captain Stuart Thorne, had laid the biggest charge of the war, a breathtaking 95,600 lbs. of ammonal. It was also at the greatest depth—125 feet. The job, which had started late—in August, 1916—was only just completed in time. Charging finished on May 28th, 1917, nine days before the start of the battle.

Twin circuits were run out, ready for hooking up to simple exploder boxes. There were no refinements, no special precautions to the firing of this, the greatest of the Messines mines. The firing party was to stand in a convenient standard dug-out or, more probably, in an open trench to the rear. One plunger was to be pressed by a young electrical engineer from Winnipeg, Lieutenant Richard O'Reilly; the other (it is thought), by Thorne himself.

South of St. Eloi came the mines laid by Cropper's 250 Company, an astounding *tour de force* of 7 major charges. Cropper himself was not present to see the finishing touches put to them. The long strain of commanding an overworked company through its most difficult times had been pulling him down. Then, shortly before Christmas 1916, he had caught German measles and Controller of Mines Stevenson had been firm that he must go for treatment and probably leave. To Cropper this had meant only one thing: that he would miss the firing of the mines. "I don't want to go," he had said with feeling, but unavailingly. Stevenson and the Medical Officer sent him off still protesting, and he never returned to Messines.

The first of the 250 Company mines was a cluster of three at Hollandscheschuur: 34,200, 15,900 and 17,500 lbs., completed at the rate of one a month between June and August, 1916, and all to be fired by exploders.

A 1,000 yards or so to the right lay twin ammonal-with-blastine mines: 30,000 lbs. each, more than 1,800 feet down the second longest tunnel of them all—Petit Bois, the tunnel in which the rock of a man, Sapper Bedson, and the eleven others had been trapped, and where the now forgotten boring machine still lay, quietly rusting.

Next to Petit Bois came the second biggest charge of the series: Maedelstede Farm. Here 94,000 lbs. of (mostly) ammonal was still being laid on June 2nd, a slender four days ahead of zero; but the job was done in time. This, and the two Petit Bois charges, were all elaborately wired for firing by lighting set electricity.

South of Maedelstede was Peckham, the last of the 250 Company mines, and one that had been so beset by constructional difficulties that only miners of heart could have carried on. Such a man was Captain Haydn Rees, the stocky little Welshman from the collieries and section officer in charge. At least three serious landslips had damaged the 1,150-foot main tunnel—a tunnel which even in good times was full of water, sand and slime. Then, in January, 1917, when it seemed that most of the troubles had been overcome, the main gallery suddenly collapsed. Resolutely, Rees had re-driven it, using steel in place of wood props, by-passing the ruined part, and re-wiring the 87,000-lb. charge for firing by an exploder that he planned to use himself.

The situation at 171 Company's mighty Spanbroekmolen mine (next in line running south) was uncertain to the end. A new tunnel had been driven painfully past the section crushed by German camouflets,¹ through a tract of gas-drenched ground (which took the lives of three of Hudspeth's men) to reach the 91,000-lb. charge of ammonal no more than hours ahead of zero. For speed, Hudspeth decided to place a dynamite priming charge hard up against the ammonal, and to wire this for firing by the lighting set, instead of attempting a hurried repair of the badly tangled original circuits. It was a rough and ready method, but he reckoned it *ought* to work. During the evening of June 6th, he sent a quickly pencilled note to the 36th Divisional H.Q. saying it was "almost certain" the mine would go up on time. The Division, responsible for the surface assault in that sector, had to know. Hudspeth devoutly hoped he would not be letting them down. He and Captain Francis Thornton, whose duty it would be to throw the switch, stood by in tense anticipation through the last hours of the battle eve.

Beyond Spanbroekmolen came another 171 Company site, Kruisstraat, a three-mine cluster of one 49,000 and two 30,000-lb. charges, again almost wholly the powerful ammonal. This Kruisstraat Tunnel, at 2,160 feet the longest of them all, reached as far as the German third line of defence, where one of the mines was placed. Hudspeth had put up a proposal that this advanced mine should be fused to go off some seconds later than the others, to catch German soldiers running back. But Major-General C. H. Harington, Chief of the 2nd Army General Staff, after anxious consideration, said No; the infantry commanders feared an accident that might somehow blow up their own men, he explained, and were against taking the risk. Hudspeth argued for a while and then gave up. The mines were prepared for simultaneous firing by lighting-set electricity.

Next in line, and the last of the 171 Company mines, was a heavy single charge known as Ontario Farm, 60,000 lbs. of ammonal laid 103 feet below the surface—the second deepest of the Messines mines. Here, too, there had been a desperate rush to complete in time, due to almost continuous trouble from fast running sand, met deep underground. No more than hours before zero, duplicated firing wires were run out ready for connecting to two exploders. Breathlessly, Lieutenants Percy Ellis and Henry Daniell, the firing party, took their places beside them, and waited.

Four more mines, to the south of Ontario Farm, completed the great Messines scheme. These, arranged as two pairs and all heavily charged with ammonal, were in the hands of the 3rd Canadian Company, still under the command of the able Major Davis. Most of the unit's 26 officers seemed eager to be in on the firing. At about the end of May, Davis announced the names he had chosen: Lieutenant Garner and another (now unknown) to fire the northern pair, a 36,000 and a 50,000-lb. mine—prosaically named simply "Trench 127"; and Lieutenants Cecil Hall and George Dickson to fire the other two at Factory Farm (or Trench 122), 20,000 and 40,000 lbs., the tail end of the long line of mines.

On about June 4th, to Hall's consternation, a marauding six-inch shell landed directly over a minor, upward-sloping escape tunnel that ran from near the foot of the main entry shaft at Factory Farm. He hurried forward and peered down the 70-foot deep shaft towards the firing wires lying neatly coiled at its foot. A torrent of sand was spurting out from the damaged escape tunnel and the wires would soon be deeply buried. Hall and an N.C.O., Sergeant Beer, scrambled down the rough wooden ladder to check the flow, eventually damming it with timber. Together they also cleared up the mess.

Hall understood that Dickson and he were supposed to fire their mines from the bottom of the shaft. It occurred to him now that their chances of ever getting out again were slim; more likely the shock of the mines blowing up would open the timber lining to the shaft and let the sand pour in on top of them.

At four in the afternoon of June 6th, Captain Urie, the section officer, walked over with sealed orders and a service watch. Hall opened the orders to learn for the first time that zero was three-ten in the morning, plus, in his case, 13 seconds to allow for a slight in-accuracy in the service watch; also that he was *not* to operate from the base of the shaft but should extend the firing leads up the 70 feet and into an adjoining trench. The mine had been equipped with the astonishing number of six separate circuits (twelve wires) and Hall calculated he would need every minute he had to be ready in time.

Dickson had been affected by gas shells that had been coming over in reply to the mounting British pre-battle barrage, and had had to retire to a dug-out. So Hall was forced to work alone. He handed the watch to Beer, told him to keep an eye on the time but warned him not to nag; then, sweating profusely beneath his gas mask, he began long hours of clambering up and down the shaft, splicing the wires together, nailing them to the woodwork and leading them set by set into the trench. At two-fifty, very tired, he was ready and relatively calm. There was much to be said for having been busy. He had been spared the anxiety of his opposite number, Woodward, standing tensely beside his switch more than nine miles north at the other end of the ridge.

At about this same time in the morning, the British artillery abruptly stopped its shelling. By now 100,000 men were lying in position, ready to assault. The storm clouds of an hour or two before had gone and the moon shone brightly. Silence fell upon the battlefield, a mysterious, uneasy quiet that all observers noticed. Little sounds began to carry—the cough, the whisper, the movement of a safety catch; and then, most incredible of all, nightingales were heard in song.

The Germans became alarmed; brilliant illuminating fireworks arced through space in growing numbers from their lines as the minutes slowly passed. They strained their eyes towards the British lines in search of explanation.

At Hill 60, General Lambert, Woodward, Royle and Bowry stood side by side in their light-proof, brightly lit dug-out. Lambert, watch in hand, was calling out each individual minute. Woodward was standing by his switch, his hand resting lightly on the handle. The others waited, patient, watchful, the emergency exploders at their feet. There were no dramatics; no one looked in to wish the party luck; there was no conversation—or almost none; just Lambert's voice calling out the minutes and, at last, right at the end, the seconds.

At all eleven firing points the same tense silence had settled in. Hudspeth was in the Spanbroekmolen post, waiting and wondering, thankful that soon he would know the worst or best about the great charge they had lost and recovered just in time.

Hall, at the tail end, passed the last few minutes standing quietly in the open trench with Beer. Dickson was still sick, and the gallant Beer had begged to help with the firing. Hall had fixed him up with a battery powered exploder which he hoped was too weak to work. They stood side by side now, still in their gas masks, Hall peering through rapidly misting eyeholes at the watch.

As the second hand swept round to zero, he murmured a warning, paused, then yelled the signal: DOWN! Both men rammed their plungers home and the mines roared out, some freak back pressure blasting them off their feet and tossing them yards along the trench.

The first of the Messines mines had gone off. It was seven seconds early. Woodward heard the distant rumble and had time for a moment's envy—one lucky firing party's job was safely over.

Then Lambert was counting the seconds and shouting, FIRE! Woodward threw the switch; threw it so fast, in fact, that the touched the live pole and was hurled on to his back by a violent electric shock. He struggled to his feet, confused and uncertain what had happened. But he soon knew. Even here, 400 yards back from the mines, the ground was heaving beneath him and it was all the proof he needed. Both charges had fired, *must* have fired at full destructive power.

Spanbroekmolen was also in monstrous, majestic eruption at exactly this moment. Huge clods of clay the size of farm carts were whirling through space to leave the greatest clay crater of them all, 430 feet across the rims. Hudspeth stood watching with only one emotion in his heart: Profound, profound relief. The great mine, the mine that had been lost and so lately recovered, *had* gone off after all.

And at Ontario Farm, Ellis and Daniell were lurching about on their feet as the shock wave from their heavy mine whipped through the ground with a force that amazed them. Strangely, this charge left no crater; just a vast circular, pulpy-looking patch that bubbled slowly for days like porridge coming gently to the boil.

Each of the eleven firing teams had its own ecstatic story of success to tell, as 933,200 lbs. of the strongest known explosive erupted in the heart of Messines Ridge. All nineteen mines had fired in a drawn-out tumult of sound that carried hundreds of miles. Prime Minister Lloyd George heard it at home. So did Norton Griffiths, the man who had started the whole "big idea" (with a thumbnail sketch that had angered the Engineer-in-Chief, twenty-five months before). And so did a student, Ormsby-Scott, lying awake in Dublin, 500 miles from the scene.

Closely after the mines, the artillery opened fire with every gun that could be used and nine divisions of infantry, their heads surely singing with the noise, advanced through billowing smoke. The Battle of Messines had begun.

War correspondents were studying the spectacle with awe. "The most diabolical splendour I have ever seen," wrote Philip

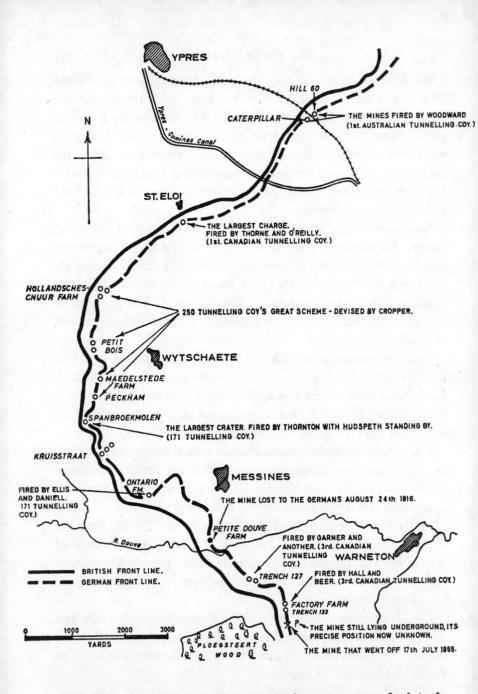

Of the 21 mines ready for action on June 7th, 1917, 19 were fired, in the positions shown here. Two (at the southern end) were not fired. Another (black circle) was earlier lost to the Germans

Gibbs later that day. "Out of the dark ridges of Messines and Wytschaete and that ill-famed Hill 60, there gushed out and up enormous volumes of scarlet flame from the exploding mines and of earth and smoke all lighted by the flame spilling over into fountains of fierce colour, so that all the countryside was illuminated by red light. Where some of us stood watching, aghast and spellbound by this burning horror, the ground trembled and surged violently to and fro. Truly the earth quaked . . ."

W. Beach Thomas was equally amazed. "An hour before dawn," he wrote, "as we stood over the dim valley where the black tree tops looked like rocks in a calm sea, we saw what might have been the doors thrown open in front of a number of colossal blast furnaces.

"They appeared in pairs, in threes, and in successive singles. With each blast the earth shook and shivered beneath our feet. 'It is worse than an earthquake,' said someone who had known one of the worst.

"Thunderclouds of smoke rose in solid form to immense heights from Hill 60, from Wytschaete Wood and other places . . .

"Hill 60, the scene of the cruellest fights of 1915, went up in fine dust, and a million and more pounds of ammonal, of which a pound would be enough to destroy the Mansion House, went off in many mines."

Harvey sat with Stevenson, David and others on a primitive seat placed near the top of Kemmel Hill to watch. He left his own prosaic description of what happened: "A violent earth tremor, then a gorgeous sheet of flame from Spanbroekmolen, and at the same time every gun opened fire. At short intervals of seconds the mines continued to explode . . . I found it difficult to concentrate on looking . . . there was so much going on and the scene, which baffles description, developed so quickly . . . The earth shake was remarkable and was felt as far as Cassel."

No official guess was ever made at the extent of the loss suffered by the Germans from the blasting mines. But by the end of the battle, 10,000 of their men were missing (besides known dead) and

7,354 had been taken prisoner—many so dazed that they hardly knew who or where they were.

The demoralization of their surviving front-line troops had been extraordinary. Hardened German soldiers were seen staggering blindly about the ridge, many weeping, some on their hands and knees, groping in numb confusion for any kind of help.

The British and Commonwealth troops had expected a bitter fight. Instead, much of the advance went almost unopposed. With delight the men strode past countless silent and drunken-looking concrete posts, the typical German machine-gun nests that, but for the mines, would now be fighting back with brutal vigour. By seven in the morning, the villages of Messines and Wytschaete were both in British hands. Two hours later, the whole of the ridge-top had fallen. So many more soldiers arrived there intact than had been expected that serious overcrowding soon developed. They made an easy target—and paid for it. But it was only at this late stage that serious casualties struck the British.

Yet, comment was not entirely on the tunnellers' side. A number of infantry commanders had strongly opposed the use of the mines before the battle, and still held to their opinions now. They reported that some forward assault troops had been startled by these monstrous explosions, and in places, due to the curve of the salient, had actually thought the mines were erupting behind them. It was argued also, that as the men approached the giant craters, they had been forced to divide in dangerous confusion to pass around them.

Harvey, of course, showed great pleasure with results and sent his enthusiastic congratulations to all the units concerned. But he, too, had had growing doubts about the wisdom of a major mining effort—which, after Messines, was virtually discontinued by both sides, and has never been tried again. Lecturing to trainee Royal Engineers in 1929, he said he had some "paradoxical advice" to give: "If you are in a position of responsibility in the next big war, do everything you can to prevent mining being done . . ."

So spoke the former Inspector of Mines, Brigadier-General Robert Napier Harvey.

But after the war, Sir John Norton Griffiths, Bart. (as he became) still liked to remind a forgetful public of the military miner's "stupendous importance". In an after-dinner speech in 1927, he looked back upon Messines with these words:

"All we said had come true. There was not the slightest doubt that the frontal attack without the mines would have been absolute failure and would have cost . . . 50,000 men . . . This stupendous artificial earthquake shook the ridge from end to end . . . and enabled the army—as we had promised—to walk to the top of the ridge in comparative safety."

Indeed, this was not much wrong. It had certainly been the tunnellers' finest hour.

THE END

BIBLIOGRAPHY
(Principal books consulted)

Brice, Beatrix. *Battle Books of Ypres.* John Murray, 1927.

Churchill, Winston. S. *The World Crisis, 1911–1918.* Odhams, 1925.

Cruttwell, C. R. M. F. *A History of the Great War, 1914–1918.* Oxford, 1934.

David, Margaret E. *Professor David.* Arnold, 1937.

Edmonds, Brigadier-General Sir James. *Official History of the War.* Macmillan.

Esher, Reginald Viscount. *The Tragedy of Lord Kitchener.* John Murray, 1921.

Falls, Cyril. *The First World War.* Longmans, 1960.

Graham, Captain H. W. *The Life of a Tunnelling Company.* (Private printing.) 1927.

Grieve, Captain W. Grant and Bernard Newman. *Tunnellers.* Herbert Jenkins, 1936

Hart, Liddell. *A History of the World War, 1914–1918.* Faber and Faber, 1930.

Military Engineering (Demolitions and Mining). H.M. Stationery Office, 1923.

Murray, Major Hon. A. C. (Viscount Elibank.) *European War, Reports, Sketches.* (Private Circulation.)

Murray, Lt.-Col. Hon. Arthur C. (Lord Elibank.) *Master and Brother.* John Murray, 1945.

Smart, Rex C. *Recent Practice in Self-contained Breathing Apparatus.* Griffin, 1921.

Stokes, Brigadier R. S. G. *Register of Tunnelling Company Officers.* (Private printing.)

Tunnellers Old Comrades Association Bulletins. (Private printing.)

Wolff, Leon. *In Flanders Fields.* Longmans, 1959.

Woodward, O. H. *My Story of the Great War.* (Private circulation.)

Work of the R.E. in the European War, 1914–1919. Published by the Institution of Royal Engineers, 1922.

German books (and papers)

Betrachtungen (Considerations). *German General Staff Report.*

Füsslein, Lt.-Col. *Report to the Staff, 4th (German) Army.*

Lange, Ludwig. *Sprengung bei La Basse, from Ehrenbuch der deutchen Pioniere.*

Michael, Wilhelm. *Infantrist Perhobstler.* Rembrandt-Verlag.

Ritter, Major Albrecht. *Regimentsgeschichte des Bay. Infanterie Regiment 18.*

Name of Mine	Date of Completion of Charging	Depth of Charge in feet	Charge in Lbs.	Crater Dimensions in Feet			Length of Gallery in Feet	Diagram of Mines
				Diameter at Ground Level	Width of Rim	Diameter of Complete Obliteration		
HILL 60								
A LEFT	1.8.16	90	{45,700 Am. 7,800 Gc. 53,500	191	47	285	Branch 240	
B CATERPILLAR	18.10.16	100	Ammonal 70,000	260	77	380	1,380	
ST. ELOI	28.5.17	125	Ammonal 95,600	176	77	330	1,340 300	
HOLLANDSCHESCHOUR								
No. 1	20.6.16	60	{30,000 Am. 4,200 Blas. 34,200	183	80	343	825	
No. 2	11.7.16	55	{12,500 Am. 2,400 Bla. 14,900	105	55	215	Branch 45	
No. 3	20.8.16	55	{15,000 Am. 2,500 Bla. 17,500	141	30	201	Branch 395	
PETIT BOIS								
No. 2 LEFT	15.8.16	57	{21,000 Am. 3,000 Bla. 30,000	217	100	417	Branch 210	
No. 1 RIGHT	30.7.16	70.	{21,000 Am. 9,000 Bla. 30,000	175	100	375	2,070	
			90,000 Am.					

Mine	Date	Depth	Charge (lb.)				Charge distance
PECKHAM	19.7.16	70	1,000 Gc, Dyn. 87,000	240	45	330	1,145
SPANBROEKMOLEN	28.6.16 (Recovered 6.6.17)	88	Ammonal 91,000	250	90	430	1,710
KRUISSTRAAT							
Nos. 1 AND 4	5.7.16	57	Ammonal 30,000	235	80	395	—
	11.4.17	57	18,500 Am. 1,000 Gc. 19,500				
No. 2	12.7.16	62	Ammonal 30,000	217	75	367	Branch 170
No. 3	23.8.16	50	Ammonal 30,000	202	65	332	2,160
ONTARIO FM.	6.6.17	104	Ammonal 60,000	200	10	220	1,290
TRENCH 127							
No. 7 LEFT	20.4.16	75	Ammonal 36,000	182	25	232	Branch 250
No. 8 RIGHT	9.5.16	76	Ammonal 50,000	210	65	342	1,355
TRENCH 122							
No. 5 LEFT	14.5.16	60	Ammonal 20,000	195	64	323	Branch 440
No. 6 RIGHT	11.6.16	75	Ammonal 40,000	228	64	356	970

The Messines mines—particulars in brief.

INDEX

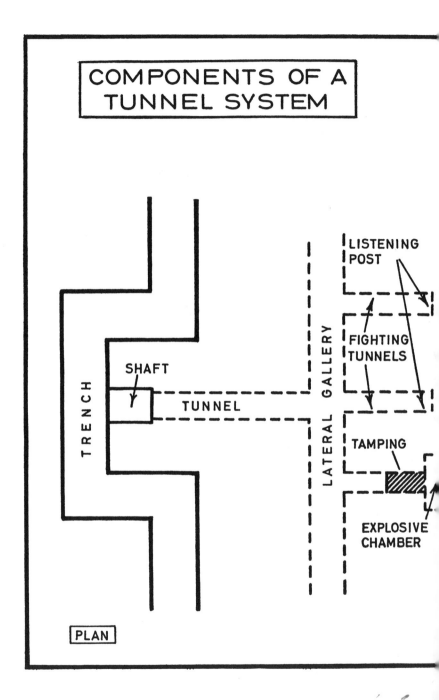

COMPONENTS OF A TUNNEL SYSTEM

LISTENING POST

FIGHTING TUNNELS

LATERAL GALLERY

TRENCH

SHAFT

TUNNEL

TAMPING

EXPLOSIVE CHAMBER

PLAN